Jacob Jacoby is Merchants Council Professor of Marketing and Director of New York University's Institute of Retail Management. He is a past president of both the Association for Consumer Research and the Division of Consumer Psychology of the American Psychological Association.

Jerry C. Olson is a professor of marketing and Binder Faculty Fellow at The Pennsylvania State University. A past president of the Association for Consumer Research, he has published a number of papers on advertising effectiveness, attitude theory, and belief formation.

W9-AQG-176

Perceived Quality

The Advances in Retailing Series

The Institute of Retail Management (IRM) was established to advance the understanding and practice of retailing by serving as a bridge between the academic community and industry. Two of the principal avenues the IRM uses to achieve this goal are conferences focusing on the latest ideas and research, and publications, including the *Journal of Retailing* and conference proceedings. Thus, the IRM's two most important audiences are academic scholars and practitioners in retailing-related fields.

The Advances in Retailing Series brings together the IRM's conference and publication programs. Initiated with valuable input from both retailers and academics, the series presents an enduring collection of up-to-date studies of problems and issues in retailing theory and practice. It is intended to respond to a variety of pervasive needs by: presenting timely assessments of new developments in the field, bringing fresh perspectives from other industries to critical issues in retailing, stimulating further research on challenging issues raised at conferences, and fostering productive communication and cooperation between retailing executives and academic researchers.

We believe that, as a whole, this series effectively addresses these and other needs. We invite comments and suggestions from our readers on how it can best fulfill its purpose.

The books in the Advances in Retailing Series are:

Personal Selling: Theory, Research, and Practice
Edited by Jacob Jacoby and C. Samuel Craig

Managing Human Resources in Retail Organizations
Edited by Arthur P. Brief

Perceived Quality: How Consumers View Stores and Merchandise
Edited by Jacob Jacoby and Jerry C. Olson

The Service Encounter
Edited by John A. Czepiel, Michael R. Solomon, and Carol Suprenant

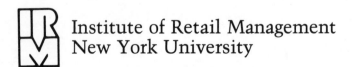 Institute of Retail Management
New York University

Perceived Quality

How Consumers View Stores and Merchandise

Edited by
Jacob Jacoby
New York University

Jerry C. Olson
Pennsylvania State University

88-1548

Lexington Books
D.C. Heath and Company/Lexington, Massachusetts/Toronto

Library of Congress Cataloging in Publication Data

Main entry under title:

   Perceived quality.

   Includes index.
   1. Consumers' preferences—Addresses, essays, lectures.
2. Quality of products—Addresses, essays, lectures.
3. Selectivity (Psychology)—Addresses, essays, lectures.
I. Jacoby, Jacob. II. Olson, Jerry Chipman, 1917–
HF5415.2P455   1984   658.8'343   83–49531
ISBN 0–669–08272–4 (alk. paper)

Third printing, February 1986

Published simultaneously in Canada
Printed in the United States of America on acid-free paper
International Standard Book Number: 0–669–08272–4
Library of Congress Catalog Card Number: 83–49531

To Fran, Robin and Jon Jacoby and Becky, Matt and Seth Olson for enhancing the quality of our lives.

Contents

Preface and Acknowledgments

This book contains most of the papers that were presented at a conference on "Consumer Perception of Merchandise and Store Quality" which was cosponsored by the New York University Institute of Retail Management and the Association for Consumer Research.

The Institute of Retail Management (IRM) is a division within the Schools of Business at New York University. IRM's mission is to advance the understanding and practice of retailing. Conferences and publications are two programs used to achieve these objectives. To ensure that the issues addressed are viewed as being relevant and important by the retailing community, IRM periodically conducts informal interviews and round-table discussions with knowledgeable industry representatives, as well as mail surveys of its council members. Through such procedures, *perceived quality* was identified as a topic of growing interest to retailing executives. Given this expressed interest, and because the editors had been active researchers in the perceived-quality domain, it was decided that a conference devoted to the subject of perceived quality might provide useful information for practitioners and scholars alike.

Our broad purpose was to bring together academicians (from various disciplines) and practitioners (from various retailing and industrial firms) to discuss the latest research and thinking on perceived quality and to explore its relevance for retailing practice. We also had several more-specific objectives. These were to (1) provide executives with ideas and insights that they could use in their work, (2) expose academic researchers to the ideas of knowledgeable executives so that their subsequent research might be more relevant to real-world problems, (3) highlight perceived-quality problems currently facing the retailing industry and identify the kinds of research needed to address those problems, and (4) identify opportunities for joint research between retailers and scholars.

So that all readers of this book begin with a common framework, we should emphasize that the focus of the conference was on *perceived* quality, not *objective* quality. Consider figure 1. Many will recognize it as a variant of the basic stimulus-organism-response (S-O-R) model of the social sciences. Our purpose in presenting this model is to emphasize that the consumer's various responses—including store patronage, product purchase, and related word-of-mouth communications to others regarding stores and products—are a function of how that consumer perceives and interprets the elements of the objective, external (or stimulus) environment. This environment consists, among other things, of manufacturers who produce the products (brands) that are then sold through retailers to consumers. The basic point is that there may be a large difference between product or store quality as these actually exist and can be objectively determined, and the level of product or store quality that is subjectively perceived by the consumer. Since it is not objective reality but subjective reality that determines most of human behavior, the principal concern of the conference was on perceived quality.

Our agenda also included a broader and longer-term perspective. Through both the conference and this book, we hope to rekindle scholarly interest in the challenging research questions posed by the subject of perceived quality. Research on perceived quality has not been strong of late. Robert Peterson and William Wilson (chapter 15) present a graph depicting how the amount of scholarly research on perceived quality peaked in the 1970s and has tapered off since then. Although seemingly of declining interest among academics, quality is currently a popular topic in marketing and retailing management and quality-related issues are key elements in retailing and advertising strategies.

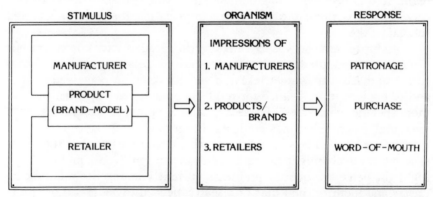

Figure 1. Relating Objective Quality (the Stimulus) to Perceived Quality (a Consumer Impression) and Overt Response (e.g., Patronage).

How consumers perceive the quality of products and services, and how those perceptions affect consumers' shopping behavior and purchase decisions, have become critically important issues to many marketing executives. Competition between manufacturers and retailers increasingly involves the quality of products and services. Clearly, then, product and service quality are topics of major interest to practitioners.

In sum, we hope that this book will stimulate academic researchers to become sufficiently interested in the many fascinating issues regarding perceived quality, that they will develop research programs for exploring these issues. Moreover, we hope that marketing and retailing executives will become interested enough to join with academics in studying perceived-quality issues of mutual interest and perhaps even contribute funding for such research. We believe that this kind of synergistic cooperation between industry and academia has the potential to greatly advance our knowledge of how consumers perceive quality.

Once the rationale and objectives for the conference were decided, the Association for Consumer Research (ACR) was invited to collaborate as a conference cosponsor. ACR is an international organization of more than nine hundred consumer researchers from academia, industry, and government. Consistent with its interdisciplinary focus, ACR's academic members come from a variety of disciplines, including marketing, psychology, economics, sociology, communications, law, and home economics. ACR agreed to cosponsor the conference and provided valuable assistance in reaching a broad group of potential contributors.

There are many whose contributions to this conference deserve special mention. They include Sid Stein, director of marketing research at JC Penney, for his early emphasis on the importance of perceived quality for the retailer. Len Morgan, manager, corporate manufacturing and engineering, and his staff at General Electric (especially Neil Love), are to be thanked for preparing a videotape which opened the conference. Also deserving mention are the contributions made by the following retailing executives to a panel discussion on needed research: Jane Wikstrom, director of consumer and public relations, Target Stores; Donald A. Hughes, manager of merchandising research, Sears, Roebuck & Co.; Ike Lagnado, director of research, Associated Merchandising Corporation; Barry Miller, director of consumer research, Federated Department Stores; Steven Rawley, vice-president of marketing research, General Mills; and Charles Turlinski, vice-president and director of corporate research and planning, Saks Fifth Avenue. The staff at IRM, particularly George Agudow, Tim Cicak, and Linda Nagel, also deserve mention for their efforts in making the conference flow smoothly. We also thank the authors for their efforts in preparing the chapters of this book.

Finally, we hope that the reader will find this book interesting, informative, intriguing, and provocative, but most of all useful in some important way.

Jacob Jacoby
New York, New York

Jerry Olson
State College, Pennsylvania

Part I
The Concept of Quality

1
Perceived Quality in Consumer Decision Making: An Integrated Theoretical Perspective

Richard W. Olshavsky

ractitioners and academicians have long assumed that a consumer's perception of the quality of a brand or store is related in an important way to the purchase of that brand or to the patronage of that store. Accordingly, manufacturers and retailers are frequently concerned with achieving a high-quality image for their brand or store. Unfortunately, considerable confusion exists today concerning the meaning of perceived quality, the determinants of perceived quality, and the actual relationship between perception of quality and purchase or patronage behavior. The purpose of this chapter is to attempt to reduce this confusion by presenting a new theoretical perspective on the role of perceived quality in purchase or patronage behaviors.

The theoretical perspective attempts to accommodate four different issues that are judged to be crucial in any attempt to theoretically relate consumers' perceptions of quality to their behavior.

The first issue concerns the need to integrate two separate streams of research on perceived quality. The first of these two streams of research is that in which a consumer's preference for an alternative is assumed to be based upon the perception of quality, which in turn is assumed to be based upon one or more *extrinsic cues* such as price. Olson (1977) provides a review of this first type of research. The second stream of research is that in which a consumer's preference for an alternative is assumed to be based upon some type of evaluation process or decision-making process involving one or more *intrinsic cues* of the alternatives involved. Research that is illustrative of this stream is presented in Bettman (1979), Engel and Blackwell (1982), and Howard and Sheth (1969). In this second stream of research, preferences may or may not be based upon perceived quality; if not, preferences may be based on some other overall evaluation (such as attitude) or preferences may be formed without the development of an overall evaluation on any basis (see Bettman 1979, chap. 7). The theoretical perspective presented in this chapter integrates these two streams of research by treating preference formation as a basic process that encompasses several different strategies by which preferences are formed and several different bases for overall evaluations, besides perceived quality. It is postulated that the specific preference-formation strategy adopted by a consumer on any particular occasion is contingent upon the state of certain consumer and certain environmental variables.

The next issue concerns the validity of the long-standing assumption that perception of quality is always related to purchase/patronage. Presently, little if any direct evidence exists to support this assumption; conversely, considerable indirect evidence exists that the alternative with the highest perceived quality is frequently *not* the purchased or patronized alternative (for example, generic brands). In this chapter this issue is divided into two separate issues: (1) the relationship between perceived quality (or preferences in general) and intentions, and (2) the relationship between intentions and purchase/patronage behavior. The integrated theoretical perspective presented here handles the perceived-quality-intentions issue by postulating a separate intentions-formation process, while the intentions-behavior issue is addressed by postulating a separate acquisition process.

The fourth and final issue concerns the need to move beyond merely descriptive models of consumer behavior to a true theory of consumer behavior, in the sense that a true theory possesses explanatory power (Hunt 1983). I attempt to achieve this goal by adopting the view toward theory construction originally advocated by Newell and Simon (1972). Specifically, the theoretical perspective presented here includes a flow diagram that is intended as a generalized strategy or schema that (when sufficiently detailed) can be formalized in a computer language and executed on a digital computer. Hence, the flow diagram is not merely another descriptive model. In the form of a simulation model, the theory possesses predictive capability and satisfies several other criteria for theory discussed by Hunt (1983).

This chapter begins with a brief description of the types of consumer behavior that are and are not of interest here, a brief description of the basic theory to be used, and an overview of how the behavior of interest is explained by the theory. Then the three types of behavior that are of greatest relevance—preference formation, intentions formation, and acquisition—are each described and explained in separate sections. Finally the implications of this integrative theory for future research and managerial strategy concerning perceived quality are discussed.

Consumer Behaviors of Interest

Because of the diversity of definitions that still exists concerning consumer behavior it is necessary to begin with the definition that is adopted here. *Consumer behavior* is defined as those behaviors of a household involved in the formation of goals and in the acquisition, consumption, and disposition of economic goods.[1]

Goal formation, as defined here, refers to all those behaviors of a household that are involved in the establishment and change of that household's overall goal in life (that is, life goal). Goal formation consists of four types of behavior: exposure, attention, perception, and integration. Each of these behavior types consist of other types or subtypes of behavior. Perception is particularly complex and involves behaviors relating to pattern recognition and comprehension. Integration refers to those behaviors involved in the addition of information to or changes in one or more structures contained in long-term memory. Integration involves several basic types of cognitive processes: learning, concept identification, judgment, decision making, problem solving, and reasoning. Integration also includes certain types of behavior that are compounded out of two or more of these basic cognitive processes. Changes in attitudes or in beliefs are examples of the outcome of certain integrative behaviors. Two types of integrative behaviors that are of central importance are preference formation and intentions formation.

Preference formation refers to those behaviors directly involved in the establishment or change of a life goal in terms of its composition (number and type of goals), the relative importance of goals within the life goal, and the degree of specificity of each goal. As such, preference formation subsumes several different types of behavior studied in the literature: direct learning, decision making, judgment, perception of quality based on extrinsic cues, and other types of behavior such as following a recommendation and conforming to group norms.

Intentions formation refers to all those behaviors of a household by which specific goals to be sought within a particular (short) time period are identified. Goals that are intended to be pursued may or may not be those that are most preferred. Intentions formation includes a variety of behaviors traditionally studied under the name of "planning," "budgeting," and certain other aspects of family decision making (for example, "conflict resolution").

Acquisition refers to all those behaviors of the household involved in the achieving of intended goals. It includes behaviors such as locating a particular store, transporting oneself to that store, exchanging money or some other financial consideration for possession of the product, and transporting the product to one's place of residence. Acquisition also involves certain types of selection behaviors when intentions are expressed in a vague fashion. Acquisition behaviors will be addressed in a separate section.

Consumption refers to all those behaviors of the household involved in the application of a particular acquired good to achieve a particular goal or to serve as a means to the achievement of a goal. Consumption includes behaviors such as storing, preparing, serving, and eating food products to reduce the hunger and thirst need. Driving an automobile to shop for food products is an example of using one good (an automobile) as a means to the achievement of another goal (that is, reducing hunger and thirst needs). Consumption behaviors are only of tangential interest in this chapter.

Disposition refers to all those behaviors of the household involved in the disassociation of the good from the household. Disposition includes behaviors such as discarding the good in the trash, selling it, giving it away, and trading it in on another good (see Jacoby, Berning, and Dietvorst 1977). Disposition behaviors are not of interest in this chapter.

Information-Processing Theory

The theoretical framework that is adopted here is the information-processing theory (IPT) originally proposed by Newell and Simon (1972). However, the specific manner in which their theory will be extended and applied to consumer behavior differs significantly from existing information-processing theories of consumer behavior (for example, Bettman 1979).[2]

Newell and Simon's theory of human problem solving is characterized by several important concepts and perspectives, but two that are especially important are the information-processing system (IPS) concept and the adaptive system concept.

According to the IPS concept, "cognitive" man is but one instance of a class of general purpose, information-processing systems; a digital computer is another familiar instance and it serves as an important analogy here. An IPS is hypothesized to consist of five basic components: receptors, central processing unit, short-term memory, long-term memory, and effectors. The central processing unit is capable of interpreting and executing a small number of *elementary information processes* (such as compare, retrieve, and store). When these elementary information processes are assembled in particular sequences they form a *program*. The program guides the behavior of the IPS, but it does not completely determine the behavior of the IPS; that is where the adaptive system concept becomes important.

According to the adaptive system concept, the behavior of any organism is determined by the interaction that occurs, over time, between the characteristics of the organism and the characteristics of the environment in which the organism is seeking its goals. Representative characteristics of the organism that are important determinants of behavior include its goal, its program, and its information-processing capabilities and constraints. Another important characteristic of the organism is its internal representation of the external task environment (that is, the *problem space*). Characteristics of the task environment that are important determinants of behavior are factors like its size and the amount and quality of information available in the environment.

Applying IPT to Consumer Behavior

The integrative framework to be presented here begins with the assumption that human behavior, in general, and consumer behavior, in particular, is guided by a hierarchical series of programs or schemas (Abelson 1981) at different levels of generality. At a high level of generality is a schema called the *episode*. The episode guides behavior through the four types of behavior described in the definition of consumer behavior presented earlier. Specifically, when evoked by certain events (for example, an advertisement) the episode directs behavior to occur in the following sequence: goal formation → acquisition → consumption → disposition.[3]

Each stage of the episode involves a separate goal or subgoal and a separate generalized schema for the identification of a particular strategy for achieving that goal. It is further assumed that the specific strategy that is identified at each stage of the episode is determined by the states of one or more of four types of variables. These variables relate to characteristics of the consumer and to the characteristics of three types of environments—the marketplace, the social environment, and the physical environment.

Once a particular strategy has been identified, that strategy directs the subsequent behavior of the consumer just as a program directs the "behavior" of a digital computer. The detailed behavior that occurs however, at both the outcome and process levels, depends upon the interaction that occurs, over time, between the consumer and the task environment as prescribed by the adaptive systems concept. Thus, the particular good that is most *preferred*, the particular good that the consumer *intends* to acquire, and the particular good that is actually *acquired* are all determined by a contingent series of information-processing behaviors. Each of the three types of behavior will be described and explained in the next three sections.

Preference Formation

Description of Preference-Formation Behaviors

The focus of this chapter will be restricted to only those preference-formation (PF) behaviors involved in the establishment or change of household goals directly involving economic goods. Further, the focus will be restricted to only those behaviors involved in the establishment or change in preferences for goods at the *selective* level—that is, at the level of brands and stores. Space limitations permit only a very brief description of the major types of PF behaviors that have actually been observed either in laboratory studies or in field studies.

Direct Learning. Direct learning is possibly the most basic type of PF behavior. The two basic types of learning that are principally involved in direct learning are verbal learning and observational learning. Other types of learning that may be involved, particularly with very young consumers, are classical and instrumental conditioning (Greeno 1980; McNeal 1969; Ward 1974).

Decision Making. Decision making (DM) is the second major type of PF behavior. DM refers to those PF behaviors in which a consumer personally establishes or changes a preference for an alternative from among two or more alternatives on the basis of one or more evaluative criteria. DM, as defined here, involves (mainly) the intrinsic properties of the alternatives. DM behaviors can be classified, on the basis of the type of choice rules used, into two major types—compensatory and noncompensatory.

Compensatory DM refers to those DM behaviors in which an overall evaluation of each alternative is formed and in which preferences are established or changed on the basis of these overall evaluations. Overall evaluations can occur on a variety of dimensions but the two that have been most frequently investigated are perceived quality and liking (attitude) (Fishbein and Ajzen 1975; Green and Wind 1973). The alternative judged to have the highest overall evaluation is the preferred alternative.[4] Most theories of consumer choice incorporate the compensatory rule as the basis for DM (for example, Engel and Blackwell 1982; Hansen 1972; Howard and Sheth 1969).

The noncompensatory rule involves the testing of each alternative on the basis of one or more evaluative criteria in a discrete rather than overall fashion. A distinguishing aspect of the noncompensatory rule is that trade-offs cannot occur across intrinsic cues within an alternative. Several different types of noncompensatory rules have been observed. (See Bettman 1979 for a more detailed description of noncompensatory rules.)

Several studies have reported that subjects utilize two or more types of DM rules in a combined or phased fashion. Typically, a noncompensatory rule is used to screen a large number of alternatives and then a compensatory rule is applied to evaluate the few remaining alternatives (for example, Lussier and Olshavsky 1974, 1979; Olshavsky 1979; Payne 1976; Wright and Barbour 1977).

Judgment. Decision making (at the selective level) is meaningfully defined only in those situations in which two or more alternatives exist. Yet situations arise in which a consumer either is aware of only one alternative or only one alternative exists. In this condition a preference may be established by a third type of PF behavior here referred to as *judgment* (Anderson 1965).

Surrogate-Based PF. A fourth major type of PF behavior is that in which the consumer forms an overall evaluation (usually perceived quality) of each alternative on the basis of one or more extrinsic cues. These cues serve as an index or surrogate of the overall evaluation and presumably are based upon a belief, held by the consumer, that a reliable association exists between the cue and the overall evaluation.

The most frequently researched surrogate or index of perceived quality is price. But other cues that have been identified are: country of origin, brand name, manufacturer's reputation, brand familiarity, popularity of brand, and certain intrinsic product cues such as package design, size (for example, of hi-fi speakers), length of warranty, materials used (for example, wood versus plastic), style (for example, of car), odor (for example, of bleach or stockings), and design (exterior or interior) of a retail structure. Also store image may serve as a cue to quality of a brand and vice versa.

Early laboratory studies investigated the impact of a single cue on perceived quality. Later studies of surrogate-based PF typically involved two or more extrinsic cues. (See Olson, 1977, for a comprehensive review.) Some of these multiple-cue studies of surrogate-based PF have involved both extrinsic and intrinsic cues, as these terms are defined by Olson and Jacoby (1972).

Other-Based PF Behaviors. All of the PF behaviors described so far are predicated on the assumption that the consumer forms preferences on the basis of his or her own evaluation of alternatives. Clearly this assumption is invalid in view of the many studies that have demonstrated that consumers frequently "subcontract" the PF task to others (Olshavsky and Granbois 1979). The fifth type of PF behavior therefore is referred to here as *other-based.*

The many different forms of other-based PF behaviors are classified here into four distinct types: (1) following a recommendation (Feldman and Spencer 1965; Formisano, Olshavsky, and Tapp 1982; Kohn Berning and Jacoby 1974; Myers and Robertson 1972; Olshavsky and Rosen 1983), (2) conforming to group norms (Burnkrant and Cousineau 1975; Moschis 1976; Venkatesan 1966), (3) imitating others (Bandura 1969), and (4) complying with a specific request. Relevant research here are those studies concerned with opinion leadership, reference groups, and other studies concerned with interpersonal influence, such as customer-salesperson dyadic interactions.

Consumers can combine two or more of these other-based behaviors. For example, if the brand recommended by one source is also the brand adopted by the reference group (for example, conformity) then that alternative is more likely to be preferred. Or, if several individuals recommend the same alternative then that alternative is more likely to be preferred.

Hybrid PF Behaviors. Consumers may utilize more than one of these five types of PF behaviors. Two or more can be combined to form a hybrid PF behavior. A familiar example of a hybrid choice strategy is contained in the extended Fishbein and Ajzen attitude model. In this model attitude to the act (that is, Aact) is combined with conformity (that is, SN) in a linear, additive equation (1965, p. 301). Also, multiple PF behaviors can occur. In this type of PF behavior the household establishes preferences using more than one PF strategy. The final preference represents some combination of the outcomes of these strategies or only the outcome from the strategy that is judged to be the best. As an example of the latter, a consumer may prefer Brand X on the basis of his or her own DM, but a friend recommends Brand Y. If the friend is judged to be more competent in the product domain, Brand Y is preferred.

Explaining Preference Formation

A viable theory of the relationship between perceived quality and behavior must be able to account for all of the types of PF behaviors described. IPT, as described here, can provide such an explanation with the postulation of a generalized preference-formation schema (GPFS) that guides the selection or identification of a particular PF strategy or combination of strategies on any particular occasion in which preferences may have to be established.

The GPFS. The GPFS is presented in flow diagram form in figure 1–1. This schema guides the selection of a specific PF strategy and the selected strategy, in turn, guides PF behavior of the consumer. (Here it is emphasized that the GPFS is not intended as another descriptive model of consumer behavior.)

Determinants of the Specific PF Strategy. It is further postulated that the specific PF strategy that will be selected is contingent upon the state of four types of variables.[5] These four types of variables relate to the characteristics of the consumer, the marketplace, the social environment, and the physical environment. The specific variables within each type and the nature of the relationship between these variables and specific PF strategies will be briefly described in this section. This description is not meant to be exhaustive or highly specific, only representative. (Hence, this attempt to build theory is referred to here as a theoretical perspective or framework rather than a theory, at this stage of development.)

The characteristics of the consumer that are assumed to determine the selection of the PF strategy on any particular occasion, either alone or in combination with other variables, can be classified as "hardware" or "software" characteristics, using the digital computer as an analogy.

The hardware category includes variables such as the basic physiological needs, the affective or emotional system, the information-processing system components (that is, sensory, central processing unit, short-term memory, long-term memory, and motor), and the general morphology of the consumer. This category also includes age as a general indicator of stage in the biological life cycle. Characteristics of devices specifically designed to facilitate consumer characteristics in a man-machine system fashion are also referred to as consumer characteristics. For example, a microscope extends sensory capacity and a personal computer expands information processing capabilities (Olshavsky 1983).

Several hardware characteristics can influence the selection of a PF strategy. For example, the limited capacity of short-term memory can influence the selection of a particular DM rule, (Payne 1976). Or, the "importance" of the need (for example, hunger) can influence the type of DM strategy (Einhorn, Kleinmuntz, and Kleinmuntz 1979). Or the limitations of the sensory modalities (that is, the absolute threshold or the difference threshold) can influence the selection of an own-based or surrogate-based PF strategy (Allison and Uhl 1964).

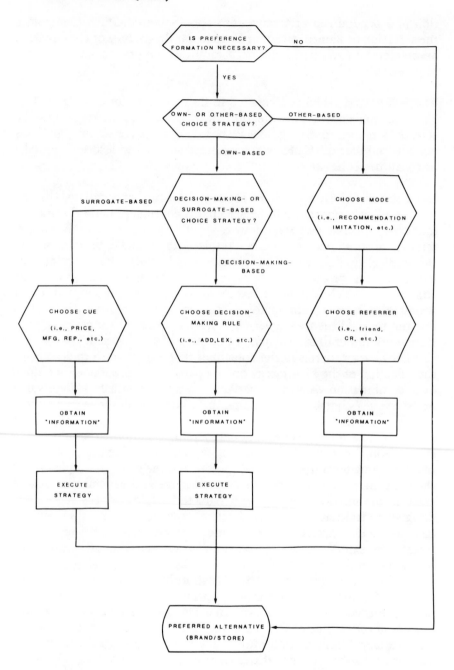

Figure 1–1. The Generalized Preference-Formation Schema

The software category includes variables such as acquired needs, affect, attitudes, beliefs, skills, life goal, and intentions. The software level also includes the financial (disposable income) and temporal (disposable time) characteristics of the consumer.

Several of the software characteristics can determine the selection of the PF strategy. One consumer characteristic that deserves special attention here is the life goal. If preferences for goods already exist, then PF will be judged to be unnecessary. Wright (1975) refers to this type of behavior as "affect referral." Olson (1977) appears to be addressing the same relationship in his "chunking" explanation of the influences of brand name on perceived quality. "Routinized" choice behavior (Howard 1977) may be explained in this fashion.

Other software characteristics that can influence PF strategy are beliefs that a consumer has concerning the relationship between some cue (for example, price) and some overall evaluation of an alternative (for example, quality) (Cox 1962), knowledge of the product category (Bettman and Park 1980), time limitations (Wright 1974; Wright and Weitz 1977), and perceived importance of the good.[6]

As used here, the marketplace (MP) refers to the assemblage of goods existing within a particular nation or geographical locale within a nation. A good is defined as the basic product or service plus all associated services (including packaging, geographic proximity, warranties, and financing). Thus a specific brand sold in a specific retail outlet is a good.

The characteristics of an MP include features such as the number and type of alternatives, the similarity of alternatives, the sequence in which information is presented, the completeness of information, the quantity, quality, and type of information available (Nelson 1970), and the cost of that information in terms of money, time, and other considerations (for example, psychological costs).

It is assumed that several of the characteristics of the MP can determine the selection of the PF strategy. For example, the number of alternatives can influence the selection of the number of DM rules to be used (Lussier and Olshavsky 1979; Olshavsky 1979; Payne 1976). The format of information can influence the DM strategy used (Bettman and Kakkar 1977). The similarity of the alternatives available can influence a DM-based or surrogate-based PF strategy (Allison and Uhl 1964). Or the complexity of a good can influence the selection of an own-based or other-based PF strategy (Formisano, Olshavsky, and Tapp 1982).

The *social environment* (SE) as used here refers to the formal or informal groups that exist within a particular nation or within a particular geographic region within that nation. Formal groups include institutions such as the government, business firms, schools, religious groups, and social groups. Informal groups refer to both large and small "assemblages" of people (for example, people in a particular geographic region).

The characteristics of the SE include features such as the number and type of members of the group, its objectives or purpose for existence, the quantity, quality, cost, and type of information made available by these groups, and the type of strategies used to achieve its objective (for example, the amount and type of pressure exerted by a group).

Several of these SE characteristics can determine the type of PF strategy selected. For example, the availability of a recommendation from a product-testing agency can influence the selection of an own-based or other-based PF strategy (Olshavsky and Rosen 1983). The type of information presented in an advertisement can influence the type of DM rule used (Bettman 1982; Wright 1976). Or the amount of pressure present can influence the mode of other-based PF strategy used (Olshavsky and Granbois 1979).

The *physical environment* (PE), as defined here, refers to the structural, climatic, and certain other aspects of a particular nation or a particular geographic region within a nation. The structural aspects refer to man-made or natural features of an environment such as highways, bridges, and mountains. The climatic aspects refer to features such as amount and type of precipitation and temperature range. Other PE aspects include factors such as amount and type of other organisms, plants, and so on, that are present.

Several PE characteristics are hypothesized to influence the selection of a PF strategy. For example, the state of repair or availability of a highway may influence the type of DM strategy. Or, inclement weather may influence the selection of an own-based or other-based PF strategy. Or, the presence of a large number of consumers within a store (that is, crowding) may influence the own-based or other-based choice strategy. Because of the "obvious" nature of the relationships involved here few studies have been performed.

Obtain Information. Once a particular PF strategy has been selected, the next step in the GPFS is to obtain the information appropriate to that particular strategy.[7] The term *information* takes on a different meaning within each strategy. For instance, when a DM strategy is involved, then information refers (mainly) to those intrinsic properties that are salient to a consumer. For a DM strategy information also pertains to the specific alternatives available and possibly to the underlying beliefs regarding the evaluative criteria to be used. In contrast, when a surrogate-based PF strategy is used, then information refers (typically) to those extrinsic cues that are perceived to have predictive value for that product.

Execution of Selected PF Strategy. Once a particular PF strategy has been selected and information appropriate to that strategy has been obtained, the consumer next attempts to execute that strategy. If that strategy is successfully executed then the particular brand or store that is preferred and the information-processing steps that lead to this outcome will be determined by the interaction that occurs between the consumer and the environment as that environment is represented internally, as prescribed by the adaptive system concept.

For the purposes of illustration suppose that a consumer's goal is to acquire and use a hand-held calculator with several particular features (for example, memory, square root, and solar powered). And suppose that to identify one particular preferred brand this consumer selects a DM-based strategy using a conjunctive rule. Now, if this consumer confines his or her information collection to the alternative brands known to this consumer (that is, stored in long-term memory) then the behavior of this consumer will be determined in the following way. Alternatives will be generated (that is, retrieved from memory) and evaluated sequentially until one is found that meets all three evaluation criteria. The particular brand preferred and the detailed steps by which that alternative is decided are determined by the particular alternatives included in the choice space and the order in which they are retrieved from memory as well as by the particular evaluative criteria and PF strategy used.

Types of Outcomes. If PF is judged to be unnecessary, then the nature of the outcome will depend upon the particular reason for that judgment. Typically PF will not occur because the consumer already has a preference established for a particular brand or store. In this case, the outcome will be that preferred alternative (that is, affect referral). But if the reason is that the consumer regards the product class as unimportant or if the alternatives are perceived to be highly similar (for example, commodities), then the outcome may be no preference at all. Here the good is specified only at the generic level (for example, drugstore, discount store, salt, detergent). A similar outcome could occur if a consumer judges PF to be necessary but impossible to engage in for some reason (for example, limited time). (This latter outcome of no preference is not represented in figure 1–1.)

If PF is judged to be necessary and possible and if the execution attempt succeeds, several different types of outcomes are possible. First, a single brand or store may be designated as the most preferred alternative. Second, the alternative brands or stores may be rank ordered in terms of preference from most preferred to least preferred. (This rank need not be complete.) Third, two or more alternatives may be tied for the most preferred position; that is, the consumer is indifferent between these alternatives. Fourth, no preference of any type emerges. This could happen, for instance, if the alternatives are (eventually) perceived to be so similar that none emerge as better than the others or if the consumer has very vaguely defined evaluative criteria. (This letter outcome is not represented in figure 1–1.)

If the execution fails for some reason, then a different PF strategy may be selected or the PF behavior may be postponed until the selected strategy can be executed. It is important to distinguish merely postponed PF from that in which no preference is ever established. In the latter case, the identification of a specific good occurs either at the intentions-formation stage or at the acquisition stage, without a preference even having been established.

Clarifications. It is perhaps necessary to point out, even if PF is judged to be necessary, that the seemingly complex process of selecting a particular PF strategy need not occur on every occasion. Over time, consumers may develop a preference for one particular strategy and thus use that strategy in nearly all situations. For example, a consumer might automatically engage in own-based DM using a noncompensatory rule.

Second, certain states of the determinant variables or combinations of these states may lead to the selection of more than one PF strategy. These strategies may then be used in a phased manner, in some hybrid manner, or in a multiple fashion, as these behaviors were previously described. Whenever two or more PF strategies are evoked, however, then the behavior generated by these strategies is more difficult to predict. This complex type of behavior may be occurring in recent studies of perceived quality where several cues are presented (see Olson 1977).

Third, when attempts to execute a selected PF strategy fail, a different strategy may be selected until one is found that can be executed. Or, the execution of the same strategy may be postponed until conditions change (for example, until more information becomes available by means of a visit to the store). But, the postponing of the execution of a PF strategy until the consumer is in transit or in the store should not be confused with those circumstances in which PF is never engaged in and a preference is never established.

Fourth, even though several types of information may be available to a consumer the specific types that are acquired by the consumer will be determined by the specific PF strategy selected. This means a consumer in an information-rich environment who selects a surrogate-based PF strategy utilizing price as a cue to quality may ignore all other types of information available except price.

Fifth, certain extrinsic cues may be utilized as an intrinsic cue. For example, price can be treated as an intrinsic cue in the determination of an overall evaluation of perceived quality using a compensatory rule (that is, snob appeal) or value using a compensatory rule (where value equals overall evaluation divided by price). Conversely, certain intrinsic cues can be used as surrogates of perceived quality. For example, the odor of a bleach can be used as an index of quality (or cleaning ability).

Sixth, direct learning, judgment, and affect formation (Zajonc 1980) can all result in an overall evaluation of goods, yet they are not included in the GPFS. That is because they are special cases of PF. Each process is a basic type of behavior that occurs, actively or passively, as an ongoing cognitive process within the goal-formation stage. But, the mere presence of a learned preference, affect, attitude, or judgment on some other basis (for example, quality) does not necessarily mean use in a PF strategy.

Seventh, if an other-based PF strategy is selected, this corresponds to one of the behaviors that Olshavsky and Granbois (1979) call "nondecision making." In effect, the consumer decides not to make his or her own decision regarding the brands or stores involved.

Intentions Formation

Intentions formation (IF) is the second type of goal-formation behavior that is of importance in this chapter. A brand or store established as the preferred alternative is not necessarily the alternative that will actually be sought by the consumer. Intentions-formation behavior is assumed to be a separate set of behaviors designed to identify which of the many different competing goals of the consumer will actually be pursued during a particular time period, given the financial and temporal constraints of that consumer. Intentions-formation behavior takes as one of its information inputs the preferences (or lack of preferences) established by the PF behaviors for all of the competing goods (relating to each of several separate episodes).

Description of Intentions-Formation Behaviors

As with PF, the focus of this chapter will be restricted to only those IF behaviors that involve the establishment and change of goals directly involving economic goods. Further, only intentions concerning goods at the selective level will be considered.

Unlike PF, IF at this level has not received much attention from either researchers or theorists. This is probably due to the frequent practice of equating (effectively) the preferred alternative to the intended alternative (for example, Howard and Sheth 1969; Engel and Blackwell 1982; Howard 1977; Fishbein and Ajzen 1975). However, a limited amount of research on IF has occurred under the rubric of "planning," "budgeting," certain types of "family decision making," and certain studies concerned with the ability of intentions to predict acquisitions (Ferber 1973; Hill 1963; Olander and Seipel 1970).

Nearly all of these studies have involved IF only at the generic level (for example, expenditures across categories, types of products or services, spending versus savings). If inferences to the selective level are made on the basis of the results of these studies at the generic level then it appears that IF behaviors occur in a variety of ways. These variations occur not only across products within a household but also across households with similar products and over time within the same household and product.

Since little is actually known about planning and budgeting behaviors, here it will simply be stated that these behaviors can range between two extremes. At one extreme the consumer engages in extended and deliberative planning and budgeting. A total money cost is developed for all goods relevant to a particular time period (for example, at the end of a month planning purchases for the next month). This total cost is arrived at by a consideration of the price of each good, the amount to be purchased, and so forth. The total cost is then compared to the total amount of money available for that time period. If the total cost exceeds the available funds, then the list of goods to be purchased is adjusted by dropping the least important goods or by moving to a less preferred alternative within one or more retained product categories. For instance a consumer may sacrifice a preferred national or private brand for a generic brand. This adjustment and comparison process continues until the total cost approximately equals the money available. This type of behavior is referred to here as *iterative* budgeting. At the other extreme, the consumer does not engage in any type of planning or budgeting. Here, the consumer forms intentions in a sequential fashion. Preferred alternatives are sought in order of occurrence until funds no longer remain. This type of IF behavior is referred to here as the *residual* method. Over time IF behavior may become *habitual*—that is, no IF behavior of any kind occurs. Intentions from prior periods are the same in subsequent periods.

Certain studies of household time expenditure suggest that the IF process also includes attention to the time cost of use of various products and services (for example, eighteen holes of golf typically require more time to play than three sets of tennis) (Jacoby, Szybillo, and Berning 1976). Time cost is especially important in the identification of retail outlets when multiple items are on the shopping list (Crask and Olshavsky 1983). Although the data are not explicit on this, it will be assumed that a similar range in planning and budgeting behaviors occurs with respect to time. That is, time-related IF behavior can range from iterative budgeting to residual budgeting.

Behaviors intimately related to IF are information acquisition and strategy selection. Unfortunately, little is known about these behaviors.

Explaining Intentions Formation

As with PF, a viable theory of the relationship between perceived quality and behavior should be able to explain all of the various types of IF behaviors that occur. The IPT being presented here could provide such explanatory capability with the postulation of a generalized intentions-formation schema (GIFS). The GIFS guides the selection of a particular IF strategy on any particular intentions-formation occasion. However, because of the paucity of descriptive data on IF and because of space limitations, the GIFS is not described here. Were it presented it would be similar to the GPFS in that it would be intended as a schema and not a descriptive model. One example of an IF strategy would be iterative budgeting. The GIFS would also allow for the likely possibility that some consumers would have a set of intentions already formulated, due to direct learning or prior IF, that satisfies the money and time constraints (that is, routinized IF behavior).

Determinants of IF Strategy. It is further postulated that the four types of variables previously described will determine which IF will be used on any particular occasion. For example, consumer characteristics such as attitude toward performing planning and budgeting will determine which planning/budgeting strategy is selected. Again because of the lack of data no further attempt to elaborate these contingencies will be made here.

Obtain Information; Execute Strategy. Once a particular IF strategy is selected, the consumer attempts to execute that strategy. Typically this will be preceded by the acquisition of relevant information. Information in this context takes on yet a different meaning. Here it refers to factors such as the disposable income and disposable time, cost of goods in terms of money and time, and the number and type of competing goods. If the attempt to execute the selected strategy succeeds, then the behavior of the consumer will be determined by the interaction between the consumer and the environment.

If the attempt to execute the selected IF strategy fails then a different strategy may be selected, the attempt to execute may be postponed (for example, until in the store), or the attempt may be abandoned altogether.

Types of Outcomes. The outcome of the intentions-formation process can vary considerably in terms of the degree of correspondence between preferences and intentions. The simplest and most straightforward outcome is the type that specifies the most preferred alternative within all product types. This might occur, for instance, when relatively important goods are involved or when disposable income is high. Another type of outcome represents a specific good that is not the most preferred good (for example, the second or third choice) within one or more product categories. This would occur, for instance, when one or more very expensive products are involved. Yet another type of outcome occurs when preferences are never stated and intentions are consequently expressed only at the generic level. A fourth type of outcome represents the failure to execute successfully the selected IF strategy. In this instance no intentions of any kind are formed for that period or intentions for only selected goods are formed.

Clarifications. It must be emphasized that the postulation of an intentions-formation stage implies that price plays yet another role in the determination of the purchase of a good. This role is quite different than that played at the PF stage and represents, in those cases where price entered into PF in some fashion, a multiple role of price in the determination of consumer purchase or patronage behavior.

Acquisition

As previously described, acquisition refers to those behaviors involved in locating, transporting, exchanging, and, under those conditions where intentions are specified only at the generic level, selecting a specific brand and store. Because of the specific behaviors that occur at this stage, goods that are intended are not necessarily the goods that are acquired. Further, intentions that are specified only at the generic level can still result in the purchase of a specific brand or patronage of a specific store.

Description of Acquisition Behaviors

While acquisition behavior has received a considerable amount of research attention at the outcome level (that is, market share, unit sales, dollar sales), at the process level very little research has been done. Little is known about the way consumers locate stores within a city (MacKay and Olshavsky 1975) or brands within a store, transport themselves to a retail store, transport goods to their home, exchange some type of financial consideration for the good, and select alternatives in transit or in the store when so specific intentions are ever formed.

One possible reason for the dearth of research on these behaviors is the assumption that they are too trivial and too obvious to warrant investigation. Still, in the interest of having a comprehensive understanding of the relationship between perceived quality and behavior, and especially in terms of being able to explain the "slippage" that occurs between intentions and acquisitions, such behaviors must be investigated.

Studies that appear to provide some insight concerning acquisition behaviors are those involving unplanned purchases (Bellenger, Robertson, and Hirschman 1973). In actuality these studies are largely concerned with PF or IF that is postponed until the consumer is in the store. But, there have been some studies that actually investigate acquisition behaviors. These studies suggest that certain superficial cues such as shelf height, location on shelf, and chance (for example, flipping a coin) influence brand purchase (Frank and Massy 1970).

Related behaviors involving the acquisition of information or the selection of particular strategies for each type of acquisition behavior have received little research attention.

Explaining Acquisition

Since so little is known about any of the various types of behaviors involved in acquisition it is premature to attempt to provide a theoretical explanation of these behaviors. However, such an explanation would most likely be similar to that provided for PF and IF—that is, a generalized acquisition scheme would be postulated and the specific acquisition strategy that would be used for each of the basic types of behavior involved (that is, locating, exchanging, and so on) would be contingent upon the state of certain consumer, marketplace, social environment, and physical environment characteristics. The specific brand purchased and specific store patronized would then be determined by the interaction that occurs over time between the consumer, using the evoked strategy, and the task environment.

Again, as with PF and IF, allowance would be made for the occurrence of combination strategies, failure to execute certain strategies, and for the possibility that a certain acquisition strategy is automatically evoked under most circumstances.

The outcome of the acquisition behaviors can vary considerably in terms of degree of correspondence to intentions established at the IF stage. The simplest outcome is when all of the intended goods are acquired. A second type of outcome is when some but not all of the intended goods are acquired. A third type is when none of the intended goods are acquired. In the latter two cases, intended goods that are not acquired may result in one of several behaviors. PF and/or IF may be evoked again such that a new intention is formed and that intention is acquired. Or, the consumer may postpone the acquisition behavior until a later date. Or the consumer may abandon the acquisition effort altogether (or, the intention may remain but the time period for its execution is left unspecified, not merely postponed). Finally, it is perhaps useful to point out here that acquisitions can occur without intentions as when free goods (samples) are provided or goods are received as gifts.

So-called impulse purchases are not regarded here as unplanned purchases. Rather, such purchases are regarded as instances of PF and/or IF that occur in the store or out of the context of the typical PF–IF process. Certain types of impulse purchases may simply represent instances wherein acquisitions that had been postponed or abandoned at an earlier period are executed in some later period. The presence of a particular good in-store, for example, could trigger the retrieval of this intention.

Implications of the Integrative Perspective

To summarize, preferences for a specific good may or may not be based upon perceived quality. Further, even if preferences are based on perceived quality, preferences for a particular good may or may not be reflected in intentions to buy that good. And, even if the intended good is the one with the highest perceived quality, the intended good may or may not be the good that is actually acquired. This complex, contingent view of the relationship between perceived quality and purchase and patronage behaviors has several implications for future research and managerial strategy.

Directions for Future Research

Possibly the most important implication of this new theoretical perspective is that studies of perceived quality based on one or more extrinsic cues are investigating only one of several methods by which consumers form or change preferences. This suggests that the trend in studies in this area, from single cue to multiple cue, will lead to studies that investigate the conditions under which one or several types of PF strategies are used. In this chapter the types of variables that determine the specific PF strategy have been proposed. With further development, this theoretical perspective should provide a single systematic explanation of the seemingly conflicting results on perceived quality (Olson 1977) and could generate specific hypotheses that are empirically testable. Further, viewed from this new perspective, it becomes clear that inquiries about the validity of the price–perceived-quality relationship should be abandoned in favor of inquiries concerning the specific conditions when price is used as a cue to quality. Also it becomes clear that the complexities of the multiple-cue studies may be explained in terms of the use of combined or hybrid PF strategies.

This new perspective also implies that more research is required of an observational nature to determine the bases actually used in an overall evaluation of alternatives. Undoubtedly perceived quality is an important basis, but other bases that may prove to be as important for some consumers with some goods are: attitude (or liking), value, worth, and affect (Zajonc 1980), as well as other bases that may underlie perceptions of quality that are not the same as perceived quality (for example, the "cleaning ability" of a detergent or the emotional "impact" of a musical performance).

More research is required to identify the conditions under which two or more PF strategies are likely to be evoked. And little is presently known concerning the manner in which preferences established by two or more separate PF strategies are combined. For instance, how are preferences formed by an own-based, DM rule integrated with preferences established by a recommendation from a trustworthy and expert source like *Consumer Reports*? Or how are preferences formed by each member of a household combined if they are in conflict? Or, how are expectations, established by advertising and other promotional efforts, combined with judgments based on trial or consumption of the brand or store (Olshavsky and Miller 1972).

Future research should also focus on IF. Presently very little is known about the way preferences are translated into intentions. Much descriptive research is required simply to identify the alternative IF behaviors. Investigation of this type of behavior should provide valuable information concerning the role of price, time cost, income, and time availability in the formation of intentions. Also, as Crask and Olshavsky (1983) have suggested, the exact composition of a multi-item shopping list may affect the set of retail outlets intended to be patronized.

Future research should also focus on acquisition behaviors, but with a new set of objectives. Whereas past studies of in-store behavior have largely investigated PF that has been postponed or is evoked by in-store stimuli (for example, point-of-purchase displays) the new perspective being presented here suggests that there are several important behaviors that occur at this stage that warrant separate inquiry. In particular, little is presently known concerning postponed IF or the determinants of acquisition when intentions are never formulated beyond a vague, generic level.

Finally, there is a need to formalize this theoretical perspective or aspects of it such that predictions can be generated and tested for accuracy. The one approach that appears to be best suited for the type of schema-driven theory presented here is computer simulation, as originally advocated by Newell and Simon (1972). Attempts to formalize this theoretical perspective would lead not only to tests of its validity but also to a more detailed and more precise statement of all of the contingencies and strategies that were briefly described here.

Marketing Management Implications

For the manufacturer or retailer this new theoretical perspective implies that the task of identifying the appropriate marketing mix for a particular brand or store is more difficult than previously thought. This is because the appropriate mix depends upon the specific PF strategy being used. For example, decisions concerning pricing greatly depend upon whether price is used as a surrogate of quality or whether price is treated as an intrinsic aspect of alternatives and is combined as one of several other intrinsic cues in a particular DM rule. To make matters even more complex, different consumers may use different PF strategies even for the same product category, and multiple PF strategies may be used. Clearly, managers should make an effort, through marketing research, to identify the specific PF strategies involved in their particular goods. Obviously, it is potentially misleading to assume, as is true in most marketing research, that all consumers use a DM-based, PF strategy. Complexity would be reduced somewhat if it were learned that certain demographic or socioeconomic segments tended to use similar PF strategies. For example, "upscale" consumers may tend to use own-based, DM strategies more frequently for certain goods.

On the positive side, the theory suggests that a manager is able to influence the type of PF strategy used. For example, the provision of intrinsic information in a convenient, usable form may encourage consumers to engage in certain types of own-based DM. (See Wright, 1976 for a more detailed description of this possibility.) This could be done in a variety of ways but one obvious method is to present such information in comparative ads. Alternatively, the manager could encourage the use of an other-based strategy by the provision of endorsements by recognized and trustworthy experts in the product category both in ads and on packages or on the product itself. The fact that much PF behavior appears to be postponed until the consumer is in the store suggests that greater attention should be paid to package design, sales promotion, personal selling, and point-of-purchase materials.

Another important implication of this theory concerns the importance of perceived quality as a determinant of purchase or patronage. It makes little sense for a manager to exert great effort and money to create an image of "highest quality" if consumers either do not use quality as the basis for an overall evaluation or if the highest quality brands are screened (due to perceived high price) during the intentions-formation stage. Again, it behooves the manager not only to identify the particular PF strategy used but also to identify the specific basis used for an overall evaluation, if that type of strategy is involved. The recent shift in consumer purchasing from national and private labels to generic brands and the longer-term shift toward discount stores are important examples of how perceived quality may not be important to certain segments or to any segment in certain product categories under certain economic conditions (such as high inflation and recession). Studies that have consistently demonstrated a weak relationship between attitudes and behavior signal that similar results between perceived quality and behavior (acquisition) will be observed.

Finally the theory suggests that certain acquisition behaviors are occurring in transit to a store or in the store that are not related to either PF or IF, yet these behaviors have an important impact on brand purchase and store patronage. It is well known that stock outages, failure to stock, or failure to locate a particular brand can result in either brand switching or loss of a sale. And it is well known that certain services that facilitate the exchange (for example, check cashing, credit cards, financing) or that facilitate the transport of goods or consumers can influence purchase. But, certain other behaviors are hypothesized here to be occurring that have not received much attention from either practitioners or academics. Studies should be undertaken that investigate which in-transit or in-store variables influence purchase and patronage when intentions are vague. Such research could shed new light on old issues concerning the effect on purchase/patronage behaviors of variables such as the location of a store within a city, location of a good within a store, location of a brand on a shelf, shelf height, amount of crowding or traffic that occurs in certain product areas, store atmosphere, and store size.

Notes

1. See Jacoby (1976) for a similarly comprehensive but not identical definition of consumer behavior.

2. For a more detailed description of Newell and Simon's theory as it is being adapted and extended here see Olshavsky (1975).

3. Significant departures from the episode can and do occur. For instance, the disposition stage will not occur if consumption implies complete exhaustion of the good or if the good is stolen. Departures such as these are ignored to simplify the exposition and to keep within space limitations.

4. As defined here, *attitude* refers to the degree of liking toward some object, activity, attribute, and so forth. Preferences may be based on attitude, but preferences are not the same as attitudes. It is possible that a consumer can strongly like a brand yet have a low preference for it because preference is established by some other PF strategy or by some other measure of overall evaluation (for example, perceived quality). *Perceived quality* refers to an overall measure of goodness or excellence of a brand or store.

5. See Bettman (1982), Lussier and Olshavsky (1974; 1979), Payne (1976), and Wright (1976) for further discussion of the determinants of the specific rule to be used in DM. See Olshavsky and Granbois (1979) for further discussion of a contingent model of consumer choice that includes all types of PF strategies.

6. The term *involvement* is purposely avoided here since it is viewed as a characteristic of behavior and therefore it is a dependent variable. Moreover, whether a PF task is judged high or low in importance may or may not imply the use of surrogates or other-based PF strategies. For example, choice of a physician is likely to be judged important yet unavailability of information about physicians may lead the consumer to use of recommendation.

7. To simplify the exposition, the types and sources of information pertaining to each of the four types of factors that determine strategy selection are not addressed in this chapter.

References

Abelson, Robert P. (1981), "Psychological Status of the Script Concept," *American Psychologist* 36:715–29.

Allison, R.I. and K.P. Uhl (1964), "Influence of Beer Brand Identification on Taste Perception," *Journal of Marketing Research* 1:36–39.

Anderson, N. (1965), "Averaging versus Adding as a Stimulus-Combination Rule in Impression Formation," *Journal of Experimental Psychology* 70:394–400.

Bandura, A. (1969), *Principles of Behavior Modification*, New York: Holt, Rinehart, and Winston.

Bellenger, Danny N., Dan H. Robertson, and Elizabeth Hirschman (1973), "Impulse Buying Varies by Product," *Journal of Advertising Research* 18:15–18.

Bettman, James R. (1979), *An Information-Processing Theory of Consumer Choice*, Reading, Mass.: Addison–Wesley Publishing Co.

———. (1982), "A Functional Analysis of the Role of Overall Evaluation of Alternatives in Choice Processes," in *Advances in Consumer Research*, ed., Andrew Mitchell, vol. 9, 87–93.

——— and Pradeep Kakkar (1977), "Effects of Information Presentation Format on Consumer Information Acquisition Strategies," *Journal of Consumer Research* 3:233–40.

_____ and C. Whan Park (1980), "Effects of Prior Knowledge and Experience and Phase of the Choice Process on Consumer Decision Process: A Protocol Analysis," *Journal of Consumer Research* 7:234–48.

Burnkrant, Robert and Alain Cousineau (1975), "Informational and Normative Social Influence in Buyer Behavior," *Journal of Consumer Research* 2:206–15.

Cox, D.F. (1962), "The Measurement of Information Value: A Study in Consumer Decision Making," in *Emerging Concepts in Marketing,* ed., W.S. Decker, Chicago: American Marketing Association, 413–21.

Crask, Melvin and Richard W. Olshavsky (1983), "The Multiitem, Multistop Store Choice Process: An Exploratory Study," *Advances in Consumer Research* 10:351–5.

Einhorn, Hillel J., Don N. Kleinmuntz, and Benjamin Kleinmuntz (1979), "Linear Regression and Process Tracing Models of Judgment," *Psychological Review* 86:465–85.

Engel, James F. and Roger D. Blackwell (1982), *Consumer Behavior,* Chicago: The Dryden Press.

Feldman, Sidney P. and Merlin C. Spencer (1965), "The Effect of Personal Influence in the Selection of Consumer Services," in *Marketing and Economic Development,* ed., Peter Bennett, Chicago: American Marketing Association, 440–52.

Ferber, Robert (1973), "Family Decision Making and Economic Behavior: A Review," in *Family Economic Behavior: Problems and Prospects,* ed., Eleanor B. Sheldon, Philadelphia: Lippincott, 29–61.

Fishbein, M. and I. Ajzen (1975), *Belief, Attitude, Intentions and Behavior,* Reading, Mass.: Addison–Wesley Publishing Co.

Formisano, Roger A., Richard W. Olshavsky, and Shelley Tapp (1982), "Purchase Strategy in a Very Difficult Task Environment," *Journal of Consumer Research* 8:474–9.

Frank, Ronald E. and William F. Massy (1970), "Shelf Position and Space Effects," *Journal of Marketing Research* 7:59–66.

Green, Paul E. and Yoram Wind (1973), *Multiattribute Decisions in Marketing,* Hinsdale, Ill.: The Dryden Press.

Greeno, James G. (1980), "Psychology of Learning, 1960–1980," *American Psychologist* 35:713–28.

Hansen, Flemming (1972), *Consumer Choice Behavior: A Cognitive Theory,* New York: Free Press.

Hill, Reuben (1963), "Judgment and Consumership in the Management of Family Resources," *Sociology and Social Research* 47:460–6.

Howard, John A. (1977), *Consumer Behavior: Application of Theory,* New York: McGraw-Hill.

_____ and Sheth, Jagdish N. (1969), *The Theory of Consumer Behavior,* New York: Wiley and Sons.

Hunt, S.D. (1983), *Marketing Theory—The Philosophy of Marketing Science,* Homewood, Ill.: Richard D. Irwin.

Jacoby, Jacob (1976), "Consumer Psychology: An Octenium," in *Annual Review of Psychology,* eds., Paul Mussen and Mark Rosenzweig, vol. 27, 331–53.

_____ , Carol A. Berning, and Thomas Dietvorst (1977), "What About Disposition?" *Journal of Marketing* 41:22–28.

_____ , G.J. Szybillo, and C.A. Kohn Berning (1976), "Time and Consumer Behavior: An Interdisciplinary Overview," *Journal of Consumer Research* 2:320–39.

Kohn Berning, Carol A. and Jacob Jacoby (1974), "Patterns of Information Acquisition in New Product Purchases," *Journal of Consumer Research* 1:18–22.

Lussier, Denis and Richard W. Olshavsky (1974), "An Information-Processing Approach to Individual Brand Choice Behavior," annual conference of the Operations Research Society of America, The Institute of Management Sciences, San Juan, DePuerto Rico.

_____ and _____ (1979), "Task Complexity and Contingent Processing in Brand Choice," *Journal of Consumer Research* 6:154–65.

MacKay, David B. and Richard W. Olshavsky (1975), "Cognitive Maps of Retail Location: An Investigation of Some Basic Issues," *Journal of Consumer Research* 2:197–205.

McNeal, James U. (1969), "An Exploratory Study of the Consumer Behavior of Children," in *Dimensions of Consumer Behavior*, ed., James U. McNeal, New York: Appleton-Century-Crofts, 255–75.

Moschis, George P. (1976), "Social Comparison and Informal Group Influence," *Journal of Marketing Research* 13:237–44.

Myers, John H. and Thomas S. Robertson (1972), "Dimensions of Opinion Leadership," *Journal of Marketing Research* 9:41–6.

Nelson, Phillip (1970), "Information and Consumer Behavior," *Journal of Political Economy* 78:311–29.

Newell, Allen and Herbert A. Simon (1972), *Human Problem Solving*, Englewood Cliffs, N.J.: Prentice-Hall, Inc.

Olander, Folke and Carl-Magnus Seipel (1970), *Psychological Approaches to the Study of Saving*, Urbana, Ill.: Bureau of Economics and Business Research, University of Illinois.

Olshavsky, Richard W. (1975), "Implications of an Information-Processing Theory of Consumer Behavior," in 1975 Combined Proceedings, *Marketing In Turbulent Times and Marketing: The Challenge and the Opportunities*, ed., Edward M. Mazze, 151–5.

_____ (1979), "Task Complexity and Contingent Processing in Decision Making: A Replication and Extension," *Organizational Behavior and Human Performance* 24:300–16.

_____ (1983), "A Theoretical Perspective for Predicting the Impact of Personal Computers on Consumer Behavior," forthcoming in *Proceedings*, Joint Conference of American Marketing Association, Central Indiana Chapter of the AMA, and the Marketing Department of Ball State, eds., Don Mulvihill and Jim Lowry.

_____ and Donald H. Granbois (1979), "Consumer Decision Making—Fact or Fiction?" *Journal of Consumer Research* 6:93–100.

_____ and John A. Miller (1972), "Consumer Expectations, Product Performance, and Perceived Product Quality," *Journal of Marketing Research* 9:19–21.

_____ and Dennis L. Rosen (1983), "A Reexamination of the Manner in which *Consumer Reports* Is Used by Its Subscribers," Discussion Paper no. 233, Graduate School of Business, Indiana University, Bloomington, Ind.

Olson, Jerry G. (1977), "Price as an Informational Cue: Effects in Product Evaluations," in *Consumer and Industrial Buying Behavior*, eds., Arch G. Woodside, Jagdish N. Sheth, and Peter D. Bennett, New York: North Holland, 267–86.

_____ and J. Jacoby (1972), "Cue Utilization in the Quality Perception Process," in *Proceedings of the Third Annual Conference of the Association for Consumer Research*, ed., M. Venkatesan, Iowa City: Association for Consumer Research, 167–79.

Payne, John W. (1976), "Task Complexity and Contingent Processing in Decision Making: An Information Search and Protocol Analysis," *Organizational Behavior and Human Performance* 16:366–87.

Venkatesan, M. (1966), "Experimental Study of Consumer Behavior Conformity and Independence," *Journal of Marketing Research* 3:384–7.

Ward, Scott (1974), "Consumer Socialization," *Journal of Consumer Research* 1:1–14.

Wright, Peter L. (1974), "The Harrassed Decision Maker: Time Pressures, Distractions, and the Use of Evidence," *Journal of Applied Psychology* 59: 555–61.

_____ (1975), "Consumer Choice Strategies: Simplifying versus Optimizing," *Journal of Marketing Research* 11:60–67.

_____ (1976), "An Adaptive Consumer's View of Attitudes and Choice Mechanisms, as Viewed by an Equally Adaptive Advertiser," in *Attitude Research at Bay*, ed., William D. Wells, Chicago: American Marketing Association, 113–31.

_____ and Frederic Barbour (1977), "Phased Decision Strategies: Sequels to an Initial Screening," in *North Holland–TIMS Studies in Management Sciences*, vol. 6, *Multiple Criteria Decision Making*, eds., Martin K. Starr and Milan Zeleny, Amsterdam: North Holland, 91–109.

_____ and Barton Weitz (1977), "Time Horizon Effects on Product Evaluation Strategies," *Journal of Marketing Research* 14:429–43.

Zajonc, R.B. (1980), "Feeling and Thinking: Preferences Need No Inferences," *American Psychologist* 35:151–75.

2
Quality and Value in the Consumption Experience: Phaedrus Rides Again

Morris B. Holbrook and
Kim P. Corfman

I n *Zen and the Art of Motorcycle Maintenance*, Pirsig (1974) describes the odyssey of an autobiographical narrator who rides through the western countryside while engaging in philosophical ruminations on such subjects as the difference between romanticism and classicism and the nature of value. This narrator recounts the intellectual adventures of an alter-ego named Phaedrus who once searched in vain for an answer to the question "What is quality?" Unfortunately, the metaphysical complexities of this issue drove Phaedrus mad before he ever discovered the meaning of quality. It is, therefore, with some trepidation that we address essentially the same question in the context of marketing and consumer behavior.

The chapter begins by examining the sparse literature on quality and formulating a classification of its definitions in various disciplines. The disparity and confusion among these definitions suggest inadequate conceptualization and reflect a failure to distinguish quality from other types of value. We therefore turn to the theory of value or axiology and attempt to specify how quality differs from such types of value as beauty, convenience, and fun. This investigation provides a model of linguistic competence in the use of normative language. Of more immediate concern to consumer researchers, however, are questions about psycholinguistic performance in the actual usage of value terms to describe consumption experiences. Accordingly, we discuss an experimental study that obtained such value judgments. The results show some anticipated relationships and some interesting differences among subjects in their usage of value terms but suggest that, contrary to our expectations,

The authors gratefully acknowledge the support of the Faculty Research Fund, Graduate School of Business, Columbia University. More complete conceptual development, numerous references, and full methodological details pertaining to this chapter may be obtained by writing to Morris Holbrook.

perceived quality acts as a relatively global value judgment that mediates the effects of perceived beauty, convenience, and fun on overall preference.

Definitions of Quality

One finds almost as many definitions of quality as writers on the subject. Perhaps fortunately, then, the latter have been remarkably few in number considering the obvious importance of the concept and the frequent appearance of the term *quality* in everyday language.

In the vernacular, *quality* often seems simply to express general approval—as in "That ice cream is made with quality ingredients" or "Bernstein's performance of the *Eroica* was of the highest quality." Preeminent among such approbative uses of the term are the self-congratulatory applications found in advertising and other promotional materials. For example, among automotive manufacturers alone, one finds insistent quality claims made by Ford ("Quality is Job 1"), Lincoln-Mercury ("the highest quality cars of any major American car company . . . a commitment to quality"), Chrysler ("Quality engineered to be the best"), Corvette ("This is a car with . . . impressive quality"), GMC trucks ("Quality-built yet economical"), American Motors ("When it comes to building quality cars, we mean business"), Oldsmobile ("Fulfilling the . . . quality needs . . . of . . . American drivers"), Cadillac ("Quality that endures"), Renault ("A firm commitment to building quality automobiles"), Audi ("Quality Backed by Our Outstanding New Warranty"), and Datsun ("the world-wide company whose name stands for quality").

It appears that in everyday marketing language "quality" or "high in quality" means "good." However, these promotional uses of the term convey approval in an extremely imprecise way. We shall not progress conceptually until we probe beneath this pleasant patina to examine some more serious attempts to deal with the subject of quality in various disciplines. At the risk of oversimplification, we shall develop a classification of such quality definitions based on three dimensions.

Dimension 1: Implicit/Explicit Quality

The first dimension distinguishes between definitions that regard quality as something present *implicitly* in an object as opposed to some *explicit* aspect or function thereof. The first view tends to regard quality as an embodied essence or as a characteristic left over after one deals with what one really cares about. The second focuses on quality directly as a key aspect of interest.

Dimension 2: Mechanistic/Humanistic Quality

A second dimension contrasts more *mechanistic* definitions of quality with those more *humanistic* in nature. The first genre tends to view quality as an objective aspect or feature of a thing or event—something that is present whether or not anyone happens to notice it. The second sees quality as a subjective response of people to objects and therefore as a highly relativistic phenomenon that differs between judges.

Four Broad Types of Quality Definition

Combining Dimensions 1 and 2 generates four broad types of quality definition. *Production-based definitions* regard quality as an implicit characteristic that depends mechanistically on the inputs and processes used to create a thing or event. *Reliability-based* definitions remain mechanistic, but focus on such explicit aspects of an object as its durability or freedom from defects. *Qualitative* definitions generally recognize that quality depends on human responses but tend to treat such phenomena as implicit aspects not covered by the theory or technique of primary interest (often contrasting such "qualitative" phenomena with the "quantitative" phenomena of greater concern to the investigator). Finally, *features-based* definitions typically regard quality as a subjective response to various explicitly recognized properties or characteristics of an object.

Dimension 3: Conceptual/Operational Quality

A third dimension distinguishes *conceptual* definitions of quality from those relatively more *operational* in nature. The former tend to emerge from purely theoretical discussions and to embody rules for the systematic use of language. The latter generally arise in the context of making measurements intended to guide practical action and embody rules for repeatable, interpersonally valid observations via various instruments or procedures.

A Classification of Quality Definitions

Combining all three dimensions generates the classification of quality definitions found in table 2–1. This table distinguishes among eight different perspectives on quality and suggests an example of each. We shall discuss each briefly before advancing our own integrative approach.

Table 2–1
Classification of Definitions of Quality

		Implicit	Explicit
Mechanistic		Production based	Reliability based
	Conceptual	Classical economics	Ordinary consumer language
	Operational	Value analysis	Quality control
Humanistic		Qualitative	Features based
	Conceptual	Microeconomics	Philosophy
	Operational	Macroeconomics quality of life	Multiattribute and multicue models

Classical Economics

In business, the production-based view of quality prevails when product design is guided primarily by considerations of technological innovativeness and engineering sophistication. Though Levitt (1960) attacked this production orientation, others have embraced it. For example, Tuchman (1980) defines quality as synonymous with skillful effort, sound materials, and painstaking method. This production-based view is congenial to the engineering mentality, which recognizes the effect of product quality on cost of production (Peters and Oliva 1981). However, it requires a dangerous reversal in logic to conclude that increasing costs improve product quality (Clawson 1970).

The production-based conception of quality parallels the classical economic theory of value espoused by Smith, Ricardo, Marx, and (more recently) Sraffa. According to Young (1978), classical economic views value as stemming from the factors and techniques of production. Often, this perspective focuses on the labor theory of value (Steedman et al. 1981). However, production-based (or other cost-based) theories of value need not be preoccupied solely with embodied labor inputs, but may emphasize any input factor (Boulding 1967). Indeed, Hodgson (1981) shows that one could equally well construct a value theory based on embodied lubricating oil.

The problem with all such mechanistic views is that they ignore the human values underlying market phenomena (Alexander 1967; Young 1978). Thus, as Levitt (1960) argued, the production-based view cannot provide an adequate account of value. Similarly, Lamont (1955) insists on the irrelevance of production cost to our valuations. In Fallon's (1971) illustration, breaking a pencil adds to its embodied labor but reduces its value.

Value Analysis

Value analysis, value engineering, or value management involves a set of procedures developed by Miles (1961) for identifying the function of a product and providing that function at the lowest possible cost (Heller 1971; Mudge 1971). In this definition, as in the perspective typical of classical economics, one notes an emphasis on production cost. However, value analysis views costs as inversely related to value so that the two perspectives are diametrically opposed (Fallon 1971).

Perhaps because their major focus is on cost reduction, writers on value engineering devote little attention to the problem of defining quality. Implicitly, however, they treat "quality" as synonymous with performance of a product's essential function (Clawson 1970; Mudge 1971). Thus, their central objective becomes the minimization of cost subject to a constraint on "quality" (Heller 1971; Mudge 1971). This specification of their satisficing problem permits value engineers to get on with their practical business by dealing with quality operationally without defining it conceptually.

Ordinary Consumer Language

We have already alluded to the vague manner in which the word *quality* is bandied about in the ordinary language of promotional messages. More relevantly to the purpose at hand, one might ask consumers for the explicit definitions that inform their usage of the word in everyday discourse. When this project began, Holbrook adopted the practice of noting usage of the word *quality* and stopping people in midsentence to inquire "What do you mean by that?" This interruption technique suggested that quality is often used as a rough synonym for reliability. In short, when our friends speak of quality, they generally mean that a product is durable and will remain free of defects after continued usage. This view seems to conform to the standards adopted by *Consumer Reports* and other aids to consumerism.

The reliability-based perspective seems also to have won acceptance by business dignitaries. For example, in a recent public-relations piece, Chrysler chairman Lee Iacocca treated quality as synonymous with durability and reliability while Ford chairman Philip Caldwell equated increased quality with a 59 percent better showing in a survey of things gone wrong. Similarly, Holusha (1983) describes Buick's push toward quality in terms of reduced complaints from buyers. This focus on reliability is rendered operational by the techniques of quality control.

Quality Control

Quality control may be regarded as a set of procedures for defining, measuring, and improving reliability so as to reduce defects and lower rejection rates (Crosby 1972; Heller 1971; National Academy of Engineering 1972). When operationalized as synonymous with reliability, the assessment of quality involves the design of appropriate sampling techniques, the specification of control limits, the counting of defective rejects, and the calculation of probabilities for errors of Types I and II (Cowan 1964; Gedye 1968).

Quality control reaches its apotheosis in the so-called quality circle. This management technique relies on a participative involvement of workers in the control of quality in all aspects of the business. Often, however, its success continues to be measured in terms of the familiar criterion of reliability (Thompson 1982).

The focus of quality-control engineers on reliability has influenced the work of survey researchers concerned with variation and change in product quality throughout our economy. Thus, Katona (1972) suggests that quality at the societal level can be assessed by surveys intended to measure the extent of continuous performance or uninterrupted use, as compared with failure rates or costs and time needed for repairs. This reliability-based operationalization of quality has also permeated the work of survey researchers trying to establish numerical figures for the quality of a specific company's merchandise (Peach 1972).

All such reliability-based definitions of quality run afoul of a serious logical inconsistency. One is reminded of Woody Allen's story about a woman who criticizes the cuisine at a well-known resort by complaining that the food is terrible and they give you such small portions. If the food is so bad, why would she want more of it? Similarly, if an object performs poorly, why prolong the agony with greater longevity or durability? Clearly, reliability cannot logically be treated as synonymous with quality.

Microeconomics

In contrast to the explicit but mechanistic treatment given to quality by reliability-based definitions, microeconomics has tended to grant the concept stepchild status as part of a quantitative-versus-qualitative distinction pertaining to aspects covered versus not covered by the theories and techniques of central interest (Leontief 1959; Lerner 1959). From this perspective, qualitative analysis is what the microeconomist chooses to leave out as social rather than economic in nature (Sweezy 1981). Thus, conventional microeconomics excludes considerations of quality (Ladd 1967), ignores qualitative factors (Power 1980), and focuses instead on such quantitative issues as price determination (Abbott 1955). This implicit treatment of qualitative issues as aspects not covered makes it hard to ferret out exactly what they are supposed to be. Whatever their nature, however, we find some agreement that they concern human values lurking between the lines (Alexander 1967) as elements not accounted for (Boulding 1967).

Macroeconomics and Quality of Life

The typical treatment by microeconomists of quality as an implicit qualitative aspect not covered by their primary theory has also found its way into the work of those concerned with formulating operational measures of such macroeconomic entities as gross national product (GNP). Here, critics of the procedures embodied by national-income accounting lament difficulties arising from the index-number problem (Bell 1972) and conclude that GNP is a poor indicator (Singer 1972). This problem arises, for example, when one attempts to compare toasters manufactured in 1929 and 1983. If the former features the traditional two-slots-and-a-lever design while the latter employs complex servo-control mechanisms with microprocessor functions, digital readouts, and a synthesized voice that announces when the toast is ready, one might conclude that 1929 and 1983 toasters differ qualitatively in ways not captured by our conventional measures of GNP (Leontief 1959).

More seriously, even if one could allow for differences in physical quality, available measures would still omit important aspects of consumer happiness or well-being. Power (1980) notes, for example, that GNP and per capita income ignore such obvious components of welfare as leisure time. In the same humanistic vein, Scitovsky (1976) attacks the mechanistic shortsightedness of the national-income accounts, arguing that GNP provides only the most inappropriate index of human welfare.

While macroeconomists have mostly confined their efforts to lamenting the difficulties posed by these implicit humanistic issues, those concerned with gauging the quality of life have made systematic attempts to supplement our quantitative measures of economic welfare by collecting qualitative assessments. Briefly, we might characterize such research as recognizing the humanistic nature of well-being and trying to render it more explicit by means of data-based operational procedures (Power 1980). For example, Rokeach (1973) has interpreted his measures of values as indicants of the American quality of life. Similarly, Andrews and Withey (1976) focus on finding social indicators to construct an instrument for assessing perceptions of well-being.

Philosophy

Philosophers tend to use the word *quality* to refer to explicit features (that is, properties or characteristics) of an object as perceived by a subject (for example, Austin 1964, p. 44; Russell 1912, p. 94; Russell 1945, p. 745; Scruton 1981, p. 92). Hirst (1967) traces this notion to Locke, who supposed that the qualities of objects cause the representations in sensory awareness. This conception is enormously complicated by a host of attendant metaphysical issues concerning whether primary qualities can exist without their apperception by a conscious being (the "tree-in-the-forest" problem). Such ancient questions—as developed by Berkeley, elevated by Hume, and tentatively resolved by Kant—have entertained the philosophical community for centuries and cannot possibly be resolved here. Suffice it to say that, whatever the ontological status of Kant's *noumena*, we focus primarily on *phenomena* involving an explicit, humanistic account of subject–object interactions. This treatment appears broadly consistent with Kant's formulation, as well as with subsequent phenomenological and positivistic approaches to the problem (Russell 1945, pp. 712–13).

A focus on qualities in the sense of *features* raises questions about how these may be manipulated or arranged to provide maximum human satisfaction. Among artists and philosophers, this issue corresponds to the problem of design (Pile 1979; Read 1953). When operationalized according to explicit features-based models, it leads to various multiattribute and multicue approaches.

Multiattribute and Multicue Models

The operational features-based approach treats quality as a humanistic response to certain explicit properties or characteristics of an object. This features-based perspective has characterized a number of recent applications in psychology, economics, and consumer research. Since these areas of application overlap considerably, we shall not attempt a tight compartmentalization, but rather shall simply maintain a broad distinction between multiattribute and multicue models.

Multiattribute Models. In essence, multiattribute formulations use beliefs or perceptions to predict global evaluative judgments. Such models appear frequently in psychology (Fishbein and Ajzen 1975). In economics, Maynes (1976) has proposed a similar formulation. Consumer researchers have, of course, borrowed extensively from this general tradition of multiattribute model building. It is the authors' impression, however, that such marketing applications have tended to view product quality as a perceived attribute rather than as an overall evaluative judgment, thereby skirting the issue of what determines the quality perceptions themselves.

Multicue Models. A more forthright attack on the problem of quality emerges from studies that manipulate objective product cues so as to trace their effects on subjective quality judgments. Such multicue studies incorporate a view of perceptual judgment akin to Brunswik's (1956) lens model (Holbrook 1981) but typically employ the procedures developed for conjoint analysis or some ANOVA-based variation thereof (Wheatley, Chiu, and Goldman 1981). Laird's (1932) famous "smelly stockings" study provided the original work in this genre and showed that perceived quality varied significantly among samples with subliminal narcissus, fruity, sachet, and slightly rancid scents. This initial investigation has led to innumerable studies of consumers' quality perceptions. Helpful reviews by Gardner (1977), Monroe (1973), and Olson (1977) suggest that a key difference exists between the results found by single- and multiple-cue designs. The former have typically manipulated price and found positive price–quality associations. By contrast, where multiple-cue studies have manipulated more than one objective property, price effects have sometimes been strong, sometimes weak, and sometimes conditional on the level of other variables.

Most of these multicue studies of quality judgments have relied on relatively straightforward rating scales to assess perceived quality as the dependent variable, thereby sidestepping the need to define quality conceptually, even while measuring it operationally. Olson and Jacoby (1972) criticize such studies for their atheoretical nature, but do not themselves venture any conceptual definition of quality. This lack of theoretical grounding may cause confusion, as in a study by Rigaux-Bricmont (1982) that treats *quality, taste, attitude,* and *satisfaction* as synonyms. Such jumbling of concepts lends credence to repeated calls for theory development (Olson 1977; Wheatley and Chiu 1977).

Multicue studies of perceived quality in consumer research resemble a more general view of utility recently espoused by microeconomists. Abbott (1955) proposed that the traditional conception of choice among feasible product sets should be replaced by one based on the selection of preferred quality configurations. Similarly, Lancaster (1971, 1979) has developed models of choice in which consumers confront a consumption technology such that any set of consumption choices may be described by characteristics acquired from the goods purchased and consumers will select the feasible combinations associated with their highest attainable indifference curves. A conceptually less satisfactory, but more operational use of a multicue model by economists appears in the literature on hedonic prices (Rosen 1974). Here, if one makes certain highly questionable assumptions, one may decompose supplier's prices as functions of the implicit prices of objective product features.

Summary

It appears that available definitions fail to answer our basic question concerning the meaning of quality. The problem, in general, is that we find too many contrasting views—none of which is conceptually well enough grounded to provide definitive guidance. More specifically, we find that each attempts to treat quality in isolation without exploring its conceptual relationships to other types of value. This predicament suggests that we cannot adequately comprehend the meaning of quality without relating it to other terms within the broader sphere of normative discourse. We cannot understand quality unless we can specify how it compares with beauty, convenience, fun, and other types of value judgment. We turn, therefore, to a broader consideration of quality within the general theory of value.

A Definition of Value

Axiology

Our difficulties in defining quality have indicated a need to consider this concept within the broader context of the general *theory of value* or *axiology*. Rokeach (1973) suggests that value(s) might serve as a core concept in the social sciences. Yet, with rare exceptions (Boote 1975; Howard 1977), consumer researchers have neglected work in axiology. We shall therefore summarize some conclusions from Holbrook's (1984) review of the theory of value.

The Definition of Value as an Interactive Relativistic Preference Experience

Holbrook (1984) defines *value* as an interactive relativistic preference experience—or, more formally, as a relativistic (comparative, personal, situational) preference characterizing a subject's experience of interacting with some object. The object may be any thing or event.

This definition emphasizes four key points. First, value involves *preference*—broadly interpreted as favorable disposition, liking, positive affect, tendency to approach, pro attitude, and so on. Second, value is neither wholly subjective nor entirely objective, but rather entails a *subject–object interaction*. Third, value is *relativistic* in at least three senses: (1) it is *comparative* in that it depends on a rating or ranking of one object against another; (2) it is *personal* in that it differs among individuals; and (3) it is *situational* in that it hinges on the context within which an evaluative judgment occurs. Fourth, value is an *experience* and resides not in acquisition of the object but rather in its consumption (its usage or appreciation).

Types of Value and a Definition of Quality

The foregoing definition of value as an interactive relativistic preference experience advances us only part way toward understanding the nature of quality. It remains to distinguish quality from other types of value. Toward this end, Holbrook (1984) has constructed a typology of value in the consumption experience. This typology embodies three underlying taxonomic dimensions that we shall now describe briefly.

Dimension 1: Extrinsic/Intrinsic Value

The first dimension employs a distinction commonly drawn in axiology between *extrinsic* and *intrinsic* value. Extrinsic value characterizes those judgments that regard some thing or event as a means useful in bringing about some further end or purpose. Extrinsic value is therefore instrumental, utilitarian, and practical. By contrast, intrinsic value characterizes the appreciation of some experience for its own sake, apart from any other consequences that may result therefrom. Intrinsic value is therefore autotelic, nonutilitarian, and ludic.

Dimension 2: Self-Oriented/Other-Oriented Value

The second dimension distinguishes between value based on a *self-oriented* perspective and that based on an *orientation toward others*, where "others" may include relevant members of society or any other pertinent aspects of the environment. The self-oriented perspective covers those self-interested values sometimes referred to as "prudential" while other-orientation covers all values that look beyond the self toward one's place in the social or cosmic order.

Dimension 3: Active/Passive Value

The third dimension distinguishes *active* from *passive* value. The former occurs when valuing results from an active manipulation of the object by the subject. By contrast, the latter occurs when the subject simply apprehends and appreciates an object, responding to it without necessarily acting upon it in any other way.

A Definition of Quality as a Type of Value in the Consumption Experience

Combining the three dimensions generates a typology of value in the consumption experience. This typology appears in table 2–2 and moves

Table 2-2
A Typology of Value in the Consumption Experience

		Extrinsic	Intrinsic
Self-oriented	Active	Efficiency (convenience)	Play (fun)
	Passive	Excellence (quality)	Esthetics (beauty)
Other-oriented	Active	Politics (success)	Morality (virtue)
	Passive	Esteem (reputation)	Religion (faith)

Source: Holbrook (1984)

us considerably closer to specifying a definition of quality by distinguishing this type of value from other kinds of evaluative phenomena. Specifically, based on the typology, we may define *quality* as extrinsic self-oriented passive value.

We may further summarize by considering the manner in which quality differs from other closely related kinds of value. First, quality differs from convenience in that the latter involves a more active pursuit of self-oriented extrinsic value. Second, quality differs from beauty in that the latter, while self-oriented and passive, involves an experience appreciated intrinsically for its own sake. Third, quality differs from reputation in that the latter extrinsic passive value is oriented more toward others than the self.

Each contrast of quality with convenience, beauty, and reputation involves a difference on only one underlying dimension of value. One feels intuitively that these are the three values most likely to be confused with quality in everyday discourse. One would expect to find quality confused far less frequently with values differing on two dimensions (fun, success, faith) or three dimensions (virtue).

These intuitive considerations add some face validity to our typology. However, they also raise another issue that we have avoided thus far—namely, the difference between competence in linguistic use (as in our formal typology) and performance in psycholinguistic usage (among real people engaged in everyday discourse). Recognition of this distinction dictates a shift in methodological perspective to which we now turn.

Competence in Linguistic Use versus Performance in Psycholinguistic Usage

Our progress thus far toward understanding such value terms as quality recalls Wittgenstein's (1953) dictum that a word's meaning lies in its linguistic use as part of a game played according to certain rules of ordinary discourse (Fann 1969; Gier 1981). This focus on the rules for linguistic use has become a credo of the ordinary-language philosophers (Chappell 1964; Kenny 1973).

Thus far, we have dealt primarily with a formal conceptual model of linguistic use in value terminology. This approach has helped to define quality as extrinsic self-oriented passive value and to distinguish it clearly from other related value terms. Certainly, we need not apologize for this attempt to clarify the use of language concerning value concepts. Indeed, Hartman (1967) argues that such refinement of language under-lies all scientific progress. However, we must now acknowledge that consumers may or may not use value terms according to the rules by which we have defined them conceptually.

This distinction between the idealized and realistic use of language has often been recognized in such constraints as those between langue and parole, use and usage, semantics and pragmatics, or competence and performance. For example, Ryle (1964) notes a difference between the or-dinary use of language (its standard use) and the use of ordinary language (how it functions colloquially). He equates the first with use, the second with usage. Similarly, Morris (1946) distinguishes between semantics (the signification of signs) and pragmatics (the use of signs in behavior). The former appears to encompass much of Ryle's "use," the latter much of his "usage." Further, Chomsky (1965) emphasizes the distinction be-tween competence (knowledge of a language) and performance (actual use of that language). He ties this contrast to Saussure's distinction be-tween langue and parole. In the case of each split, the first member is the proper subject of linguistics while the second raises concerns of interest to psycholinguistics. We may therefore summarize this contrast by the phrases "competence in linguistic use" and "performance in psycholin-guistic usage."

The aforementioned thinkers have clearly recognized that knowl-edge of use or competence may tell us relatively little about usage or per-formance (Chomsky 1965; Ryle 1964). This discrepancy has been ac-knowledged by the linguistic philosophers though much of linguistic analysis rests on the introspective verbal habits of the philosophers themselves (Gendlin 1973). Linguistic philosophers therein encounter something of a quandary since they are committed to understanding the empirical regularities of utterance (Scruton 1981), yet retain the medita-tive habits of their profession (Morris 1964). Accordingly, one might question the verifiability of conclusions drawn by ordinary-language philosophers (Mates 1964).

Such questions have led some philosophers to call for the empirical investigation of speech (Carnap 1966). Morris (1956; 1964) moved strongly in that direction, turning increasingly to laboratory techniques for investigating the usage of words in psycholinguistic performance as a basis for understanding their meaning. In short, Morris adopted a strategy of empiricism and strove to assess the signification of a term by studying the conditions that govern its usage. Like Morris, we are primarily concerned with the signification of value terms such as quality. Accordingly, we shall follow his methodological prescription by investigating how words like *quality, beauty, convenience,* and *fun* are applied in the context of consuming behavior. These terms correspond to the four types of value found in the top half of our typology. Hence, the typology provides a theoretical basis for the generation of hypotheses about how value judgments should behave (competence) while the data from actual consumption experiences will indicate how they do behave (performance).

Method

Experimental Tasks

The experiment was designed to lead subjects through a series of thirty-two complex consumption experiences. These experiences differed on the following systematically manipulated task variables.

Instruction Card. Subjects began each task by selecting an instruction card from a shuffled deck. Half of the cards indicated the right hand, the other half the left. Subjects performed the rest of the task using only the indicated hand. They registered this hand by circling "right" or "left" on an answer sheet. This variable (Hand) was coded $+1$ (-1) if the instruction card did (did not) match a subject's preferred handedness.

Information Card. Next, subjects selected an information card from another randomly ordered pack. Half contained straightforward factual messages and half contained *New Yorker* cartoons selected for their humor by a pretest using twelve comparable respondents. Subjects read the message on the information card and then wrote its number in the appropriate blank on the answer sheet. The resulting variable (Info) was coded $+1$ for cartoons and -1 for facts.

Reward Card. Subjects then selected a reward card from a randomized pack. Half representd 50-cent wins and half 50-cent losses (added to or subtracted from a $5.00 participation fee). Subjects recorded each outcome in an appropriate blank on the answer sheet. This variable (Reward) was coded $+1$ for a win and -1 for a loss.

Music Tapes. Finally, subjects listened to one of thirty-two randomly numbered and ordered music tapes. Each tape contained a different performance of "I Found Love" (the theme song from NBC's *Bare Essence*). The music tapes were constructed to vary systematically according to a $2 \times 2 \times 2 \times 2 \times 2$ factorial design based on four esthetic features and one fidelity manipulation. The esthetic features were manipulated by programming the basic melody and chords on a Casio CT-701 keyboard and then using the controls of that instrument to create systematic variations on four stylistic dimensions. The fifth feature, fidelity, was manipulated by recording half the tapes directly from the Casio keyboard into the appropriate "line" input of the tape deck (low distortion) and the other half into its inappropriate "microphone" input (high distortion due to impedence mismatch). The resulting five features may be summarized as follows.

1. *Timbre* (-1 = organ sound, $+1$ = piano sound).
2. *Comping* (-1 = sustained background chords, $+1$ = 16th-note arpeggios)
3. *Rhythm* (-1 = an even 8th-note rock pattern, $+1$ = a syncopated 16th-note disco pattern)
4. *Speed* (-1 = 72, $+1$ = 96 beats per minute)
5. *Fidelity* (-1 = high distortion, $+1$ = low distortion)

Rating Scales

Immediately after listening to each music tape, subjects rated the overall task experience on 16 seven-position bipolar scales to provide three-item indices of perceived Convenience (alpha = .96), Fun (.92), Beauty (.92), and Quality (.96) and one four-item index of Preference (alpha = .94).

Romanticism/Classicism

Besides its treatment of quality, another important theme in Pirsig's (1974) book involves the different world views characteristic of romanticism versus classicism. This split is a familiar topic in the study of philosophy in general and esthetics in particular (Brinton 1967; Jenkins 1962; Nozick 1981; Osborne 1970), but has not drawn attention from consumer researchers. True, the classical–romantic contrast appears to reflect issues related to arousal-, sensation-, and variety-seeking. Yet the romanticism–classicism dimension seems more general in nature and better grounded in the history of esthetics and art criticism. It may therefore be more relevant to the musical experience under study in the present experiment.

Briefly, the classical–romantic contrast may be depicted by bipolarities such as logical/emotional, controlled/impulsive, rational/intuitive, orderly/disorderly, normal/eccentric, organized/chaotic, timid/heroic, analytic/holistic, conventional/individualistic, familiar/exotic, drab/colorful, formal/natural, restricted/spontaneous, and cultivated/passionate. These contrasts served as the basis for developing a Romanticism/ Classicism index (*RC*). In a pretest, twelve subjects indicated their agreement on six-position check-mark scales from "strongly disagree" to "strongly agree" with 100 statements intended to represent the classical and romantic viewpoints. After normalizing these responses within respondents and reversing scale directions for the classical items, the item intercorrelations and face validities were examined to select a reduced set of twenty-eight items with reasonably satisfactory internal consistency (alpha = .67). In the main study, principal-components analysis was used to reduce these twenty-eight items to the following set of fourteen *RC* statements:

I am a practical person (*C*);

In art, color excites me more than form (*R*);

I enjoy art that expresses the artist's emotions (*R*);

I am organized (*C*);

I think of myself as eccentric (*R*);

Every decision deserves to be carefully thought out (*C*);

I like to touch sculpture (*R*);

I am impulsive (*R*);

I like to keep my home neat and orderly (*C*);

I prefer to live in a certain amount of chaos (*R*);

I think of myself as a precise person (*C*);

I am precise about where I keep my possessions (*C*);

I am easily distracted (*R*);

I am a controlled person (*C*).

Again, agreement ratings were normalized, reversed, and summed to create an overall *RC* index (alpha = .83). Subjects were split at the *RC* median into Romanticist and Classicist groups, as indicated by a dummy variable coded *R* = +1 and *C* = −1.

Subjects

Twenty-one M.B.A. students served as subjects and received a participation fee of $5.00 plus or minus the amount won or lost in the Reward manipulation.

Hypotheses

Our working hypotheses appear schematically in figure 2–1.

Hypothesis H1. We expected, first, that Beauty would depend upon Timbre, Comping, Rhythm, and Speed (though the directions of these effects could not be predicted, as indicated by question marks in the diagram). Similarly, Quality should depend on Fidelity (+), Convenience on Hand (+), Fun on Info (+), and Preference on Reward (+).

H2. Preference should depend on Beauty (+), Quality (+), Convenience (+), and Fun (+).

H3. Due to the uncorrelated nature of the eight experimental manipulations, Beauty, Quality, Convenience, and Fun should vary independently. Note that this is a strong assumption in view of the possible role of halo effects (Holbrook 1983).

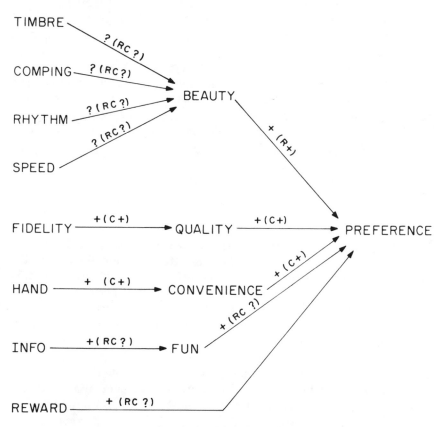

Figure 2–1. Schematic Diagram of Key Hypotheses

H4. Romanticism/Classicism should moderate the aforementioned relationships (as indicated in the diagram by *RC* interactions shown parenthetically). Specifically, the effects of esthetic features on Beauty, Info on Fun, and Fun on Preference should differ between Romanticists and Classicists though one cannot predict a priori in what directions such differences should occur (*RC?*). The effects of Fidelity on Quality, Hand on Convenience, and Quality and Convenience on Preference should be more positive for Classicists (*C* +). Conversely, in determining Preference, Beauty should exert a more positive effect for Romanticists (*R* +).

Analysis

These hypotheses were tested by means of ordinary least-squares (OLS) regressions using indices scored and dummy variables coded in the manners described previously. All *RC* interaction effects were coded as multiplicative terms, as were the interaction effects of Sex examined later.

We began at the individual level of analysis, but this approach proved unworkable due to the relatively weak nature of the relationships involved. However, the individual-level results showed a moderately high degree of homogeneity. Specifically, of the significant relationships found, only about 11 percent (16 of 150) were in mutually contradictory directions (as opposed to the 50 percent expected by chance). Conversely, among the potentially contradictory effects, only about 4 percent (15 of 329) were significant (as opposed to the 10 percent expected by chance). We therefore conducted all analyses at the aggregate level on data combined across subjects.

Results

Findings

The hypotheses represented by figure 2–1 received mixed support, leading to a systematic search for better-fitting models. Results of the final set of OLS regressions appear in table 2–3. This table includes only those beta coefficients significant at the .10 level or better.

The findings in table 2–3 are clarified by the diagram in figure 2–2, which provides a schematic representation of the regression results. Those links hypothesized but not found are indicated by dotted lines. Other relationships significant at the .10 level or better (two-tailed tests) are indicated by solid lines with a + or − sign to show the direction of the effect. Moderating effects of Romanticism/Classicism and Sex are indicated by parenthetical expressions showing the group for which a

Table 2–3
Results of OLS Regressions

Dependent Variable (Multiple R)	Independent Variables	Beta	t value	p level
Beauty	Timbre	.128	3.12	.002
R = .33,	Rhythm	.115	2.79	.005
p < .001	Speed	.265	6.43	.0001
	RC × Speed	−.077	−2.04	.04
	RC × Fidelity	.074	1.95	.05
	Sex × Speed	.075	1.80	.07
Quality	Beauty	.476	12.75	.0001
R = .71	Fun	.369	11.36	.0001
p < .0001				
Convenience	Hand	.709	25.08	.0001
R = .76	RC × Hand	−.074	−2.89	.004
p < .0001	Sex × Hand	−.088	−3.07	.002
Fun	Info	.242	6.68	.0001
R = .57	Reward	.061	1.70	.09
p < .0001	Beauty	.417	10.26	.0001
	Convenience	.126	2.91	.004
	RC × Info	−.062	−1.88	.06
	Sex × Info	.077	2.12	.03
	Sex × Beauty	−.064	−1.80	.07
Preference	Beauty	.297	9.95	.0001
R = .88	Quality	.460	13.96	.0001
p < .0001	Fun	.312	12.08	.0001
	RC × Beauty	.087	3.09	.002
	RC × Fun	−.044	−1.79	.07
	Sex × Beauty	−.081	−3.03	.003
	Sex × Quality	.119	3.60	.0003

Note: Probability values are based on a sample size of 672 observations (32 recordings × 21 subjects). Nonsignificant coefficients are omitted from this table, but are available from Holbrook.

relationship becomes significantly more positive or negative. For example, (R +) and (F +) indicate that an effect is significantly more positive for Romantics and females, respectively.

Interpretation

H1. Hypothesis H1 was supported by significant positive effects on Beauty of Timbre, Rhythm, and Speed. Contrary to our expectations, however, Comping exerted no significant effect on Beauty. Moreover, the overall relationship of Beauty to its determinants, though significant, was rather weak. The results did support the anticipated positive

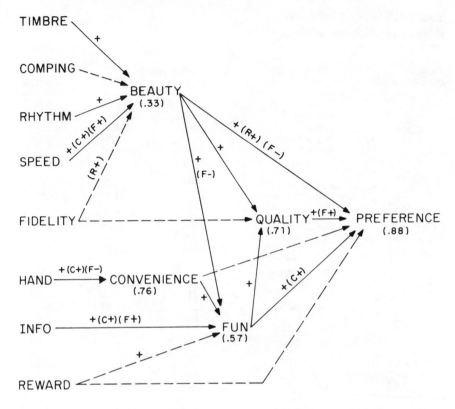

Note: Parenthetical expressions above arrows indicate the direction of moderating effects for C (Classicism), R (Romanticism), F (Female), and M (Male). In general, (C+) = (R−), (F+) = (M−), and vice versa.

Figure 2–2. Schematic Representation of OLS Regression Results

effects of Hand on Convenience and Info on Fun. However, Fun also depended on Reward (as well as on Convenience and Beauty). This result, though unexpected, makes sense intuitively. By contrast, for reasons inaccessible to intuition, the predicted effects of Fidelity on Quality and Reward on Preference failed to appear.

H2. As expected, Beauty, Quality, and Fun made strong positive contributions to the prediction of Preference. However, contrary to our hypothesis, perceived Convenience and Reward failed to contribute significantly to the Preference prediction.

H3. The anticipated independence among Beauty, Quality, Convenience, and Fun failed to appear. Thus, Fun depended significantly on

Beauty and Convenience while Quality was significantly related to Beauty and Fun. This finding suggests that, even when objective determinants are uncorrelated by design, the four kinds of value judgment cannot be viewed as independent mediators of overall preference. Rather, they appear to embody a complex causal structure in which perceived quality mediates the effects of perceived beauty, convenience, and fun on overall preference. The exact nature of this causal structure requires further study. The present results do suggest, however, that perceived quality acts as a relatively more global value judgment, capturing some (but not all) of the content of perceived beauty, convenience, and fun so as to intervene between these value judgments and overall preference.

H4. With respect to the moderating effects of Romanticism/Classicism and Sex, our hypotheses again received moderately encouraging support. Though directions had not been predicted, the effects of Speed on Beauty and Info on Fun were significantly more positive for Classicists, as was the effect of Fidelity on Beauty for Romanticists. As expected, the effect of Hand on Convenience was more positive for Classicists. Classicism also exerted a positive moderating effect on the link between Fun and Preference. Most importantly, as anticipated, Romanticists showed a more positive contribution of Beauty to Preference.

Several of the moderating effects of sex, though not predicted, are quite interesting in their own right. In particular, our female subjects appear to be significantly more sensitive than males to Speed, Info, and Quality and less sensitive to Handedness and Beauty. This suggests that, with respect to convenience and fun, they adopted a more playful orientation whereas, with respect to beauty and quality, they were more practical.

Discussion

Limitations

Before drawing conclusions from this study, one should note its major limitations. First, the study employed a small sample of M.B.A. students clearly atypical of the general consuming population.

Second, our procedures for data analysis may have introduced some search bias. Though many of our findings represent true hypothesis testing, results concerning the relationships among value judgments and the moderating effects of sex must be regarded as tentative until validated on new sets of data.

Third, the failure to find an effect of Fidelity on Quality seems disturbing. It suggests either (1) that our subjects were insensitive listeners or (2) that they were so distracted by other aspects of the task experience that they paid insufficient attention to the music tapes. The second interpretation is reinforced by the relatively weak explanation of variance in Beauty. Some subjects may simply have been so fascinated with the instruction, information, and reward cards that they de-emphasized the musical part of the task.

Fourth, value judgments concerning Beauty, Quality, Convenience, and Fun should be examined for halo-effect biases using a method such as that proposed by Holbrook (1983). However, because exogenous variables like Reward and order-of-presentation showed no significant effects on Preference, the structural model of halo remained unidentified so that we could not assess the possible role of affective feedback in biasing judgments of Beauty, Quality, Convenience, and Fun. Though serious, this limitation is typical of almost all consumer research using multiattribute models.

Conclusions

Within the circumspection dictated by these limitations, the results do offer some support for three of our four hypotheses. H1 is supported by positive effects of Timbre, Rhythm, and Speed on Beauty; Hand on Convenience; and Info on Fun. H2 is supported by significant positive contributions of Beauty, Quality, and Fun to the prediction of Preference. H4 is supported directly by the moderating effects of Romanticism/Classicism on the Speed–Beauty, Hand–Convenience, Info–Fun, Fun–Preference, and Beauty–Preference relationships (especially the latter) and indirectly by the nonhypothesized moderating effects of Sex.

However, H3 concerning the anticipated independence of Beauty, Quality, Convenience, and Fun is disconfirmed by our data. Specifically, Quality judgments are strongly related to judgments of Beauty and Fun. This shows that the linguistic-competence model embodied by our typology of value fails to correspond to the performance model demonstrated by our subjects' actual usage of value terms such as *quality, beauty, convenience,* and *fun.* Rather, to some extent, quality appears to serve as a global assessment and therefore to mediate the effects of perceived beauty, convenience, and fun on preference. Thus, our typology goes only part way toward elucidating the meaning of quality. It suggests how the term should be used for conceptual clarity, but fails to represent its usage in actual verbal behavior describing this particular type of consumption experience.

Summary

We began by asking the question "What is quality?" We attacked this issue by examining a broad range of definitions in various disciplines. These suggested a prevailing confusion about the concept of quality. We therefore attempted to reduce this confusion by proposing a typology of value in the consumption experience. This typology defined quality as extrinsic self-oriented passive value and distinguished it on these dimensions from such types of value as beauty, convenience, and fun. This conceptualization provided a linguistic-competence model of how value terms should be used for semantic clarity, but showed nothing about the essentially empirical issue of their actual usage in psycholinguistic performance. Accordingly, we undertook an experimental study to investigate how various aspects of a consumption experience affect the usage of the value terms just mentioned. This experiment supported three of our key hypotheses but, contrary to the fourth, suggested that quality was treated by our subjects as lying somewhere between a specific and a global concept of value. This result indicates that a gap exists between our logical typology and the colloquial usage of language to describe a consumption experience. We seem, therefore, to have provided at best a partial answer to our motivating question concerning the meaning of quality. It appears that the spirit of Phaedrus still roams the hills. Far from running out of gas, Phaedrus still has a long way to ride.

References

Abbott, Lawrence (1955), *Quality and Competition*, New York: Columbia University Press.

Alexander, Sidney S. (1967), "Human Values and Economists' Values," in *Human Values and Economic Policy*, ed., Sidney Hook, New York: New York University, 101–16.

Andrews, Frank M. and Stephen B. Withey (1976), *Social Indicators of Well-Being: Americans' Perceptions of Life Quality*, New York: Plenum Press.

Austin, J.L. (1964), "A Plea for Excuses," in *Ordinary Language*, ed., V.C. Chappell, New York: Dover Publications, 41–63.

Bell Carolyn S. (1972), "Discussion," in *Product Quality, Performance, and Cost*, ed. National Academy of Engineering, Washington, D.C.: National Academy of Engineering, 38–41.

Boote, Alfred S. (1975), "An Exploratory Investigation of the Roles of Needs and Personal Values in the Theory of Buyer Behavior," doctoral dissertation, Columbia University, Graduate School of Business.

Boulding, Kenneth E. (1967), "The Basis of Value Judgments in Economics," in *Human Values and Economic Policy*, ed., Sidney Hook, New York: New York University Press, 55–72.

Brinton, Crane (1967), "Romanticism," in *The Encyclopedia of Philosophy*, ed., Paul Edwards, New York: The Macmillan Company, 206–9.

Brunswik, Egon (1956), *Perception and the Representative Design of Psychological Experiments*, Berkeley: University of California Press.

Carnap, Rudolf (1966), *An Introduction to the Philosophy of Science*, New York: Basic Books.

Chappell, V.C. (1964), "Introduction," in *Ordinary Language*, ed., V.C. Chappel, New York: Dover Publications, 1–4.

Chomsky, Noam (1965), *Aspects of the Theory of Syntax*, Cambridge, Mass.: The Massachusetts Institute of Technology Press.

Clawson, Robert H. (1970), *Value Engineering for Management*, Princeton: Auerbach.

Cowan, Alan (1964), *Quality Control for the Manager*, Oxford: Pergamon Press.

Crosby, Philip B. (1972), "Consumer Preference: Good, Better, Best," in *Product Quality, Performance, and Cost*, ed. National Academy of Engineering, Washington, D.C.: National Academy of Engineering, 37–38.

Fallon, Carlos (1971), *Value Analysis to Improve Productivity*, New York: Wiley.

Fann, K.T. (1969), *Wittgenstein's Conception of Philosophy*, Berkeley: University of California Press.

Fishbein, Martin and Icek Ajzen (1975), *Belief, Attitude, Intention and Behavior*, Reading, Mass.: Addison–Wesley Publishing Company.

Gardner, David M. (1977), "The Role of Price in Consumer Choice," in *Selected Aspects of Consumer Behavior*, ed., Robert Ferber, Washington, D.C.: National Science Foundation, 415–33.

Gedye, Rupert (1968), *A Manager's Guide to Quality and Reliability*, New York: Wiley.

Gendlin, Eugene T. (1973), "Experimental Phenomenology," in *Phenomenology and the Social Sciences*, vol. 1, ed., Maurice Natanson, Evanston: Northwestern University Press, 281–322.

Gier, Nocholas F. (1981), *Wittgenstein and Phenomenology*, Albany: State University of New York Press.

Hartman, Robert S. (1967), *The Structure of Value: Foundations of Scientific Axiology*, Carbondale, Ill.: Southern Illinois University Press.

Heller, Edward D. (1971), *Value Management: Value Engineering and Cost Reduction*, Reading, Mass.: Addison–Wesley Publishing Company.

Hirst, R.J. (1967), "Primary and Secondary Qualities," in *The Encyclopedia of Philosophy*, vol. 6, ed., Paul Edwards, New York: The Macmillan Company, 455–57.

Hodgson, Geoff (1981), "Critique of Wright: 1. Labour and Profits," in *The Value Controversy*, ed., Ian Steedman et al., London: Verso, 75–99.

Holbrook, Morris B. (1981), "Integrating Compositional and Decompositional Analyses to Represent the Intervening Role of Perceptions in Evaluative Judgments," *Journal of Marketing Research* 18 (February):13–28.

_____ (1983), "Using a Structural Model of Halo Effect to Assess Perceptual Distortion Due to Affective Overtones," *Journal of Consumer Research* 10 (September):247–52.

_____ (1984), "Axiology in Consumer Research," in preparation.

Holusha, John (1983), "Detroit's New Push to Upgrade Quality," *New York Times*, 12 May, D1, D6.

Howard, John A. (1977), *Consumer Behavior: Application of Theory*, New York: McGraw-Hill.

Jenkins, Iredell (1962), "Romanticism," in *Dictionary of Philosophy*, ed. Dagobert D. Runes, Totowa, N.J.: Littlefield, Adams & Co., 272–73.

Katona, George (1972), "Product Quality: Economic and Psychological Considerations," in *Product Quality, Performance, and Cost*, ed., National Academy of Engineering, Washington, D.C.: National Academy of Engineering, 44–48.

Kenny, Anthony (1973), *Wittgenstein*, Cambridge, Mass.: Harvard University Press.

Ladd, John (1967), "The Use of Mechanical Models for the Solution of Ethical Problems," in *Human Values and Economic Policy*, ed., Sidney Hook, New York: New York University Press, 157–69.

Laird, Donald A. (1932), "How the Consumer Estimates Quality by Subconscious Sensory Impressions," *Journal of Applied Psychology* 16(2):241–46.

Lamont, W.D. (1955), *The Value Judgment*, Westport, Conn.: Greenwood Press.

Lancaster, Kelvin (1971), *Consumer Demand: A New Approach*, New York: Columbia University Press.

_____ (1979), *Variety, Equity, and Efficiency*, New York: Columbia University Press.

Leontief, Wassily (1959), "The Problem of Quality and Quantity in Economics," in *Quantity and Quality*, ed., Daniel Lerner, New York: The Free Press of Glencoe, 117–28.

Lerner, Daniel (1959), "On Quantity and Quality," in *Quantity and Quality*, ed., Daniel Lerner, New York: The Free Press of Glencoe, 11–34.

Levitt, Theodore (1960), "Marketing Myopia," *Harvard Business Review* 38 (July– August):24–47.

Mates, Benson (1964), "On the Verification of Statements about Ordinary Language, in *Ordinary Language*, ed. V.C. Chappell, New York: Dover Publications, 64–74.

Maynes, E. Scott (1976), "The Concept and Measurement of Product Quality," in *Household Production and Consumption*, ed. Nestor E. Terleckyj, New York: National Bureau of Economic Research, 529–60.

Miles, Lawrence D. (1961), *Techniques of Value Analysis and Engineering*, New York: McGraw-Hill.

Monroe, Kent (1973), "Buyers' Subjective Perceptions of Price," *Journal of Marketing Research* 10 (February):70–80.

Morris, Charles (1946), *Signs, Language, and Behavior*, New York: George Braziller.

_____ (1956), *Varieties of Human Value*, Chicago: The University of Chicago Press.

_____ (1964), *Signification and Significance*, Cambridge, Mass.: The Massachusetts Institute of Technology Press.

Mudge, Arthur E. (1971), *Value Engineering*, New York: McGraw-Hill.

National Academy of Engineering (1972), *Product Quality, Performance, and Cost*, Washington, D.C.: National Academy of Engineering.

Nozick, Robert (1981), *Philosophical Explanations*, Cambridge, Mass.: Harvard University Press.

Olson, Jerry C. (1977), "Price as an Information Cue: Effects on Product Evaluations," in Consumer and Industrial Buying Behavior, eds., Arch G. Woodside, Jagdish N. Sheth, and Peter D. Bennett, New York: North Holland, 267–86.

_____ and Jacob Jacoby (1972), "Cue Utilization in the Quality Perception Process," in Proceedings, Third Annual Conference, ed., M. Venkatesan, Ann Arbor: Association for Consumer Research, 167–79.

Osborne, Harold (1970), Aesthetics and Art Theory, New York: E.P. Dutton.

Peach, Robert W. (1972), "Discussion," in Product Quality, Performance, and Cost, ed., National Academy of Engineering, Washington, D.C.: National Academy of Engineering, 58–61.

Peters, Michael and Terence Oliva (1981), Operations and Production Management, Boston: Prindle, Weber & Schmidt.

Pile, John F. (1979), Purpose, Form and Meaning, New York: W.W. Norton and Company.

Pirsig, Robert M. (1974), Zen and the Art of Motorcycle Maintenance: An Inquiry Into Values, New York: Bantam Books.

Power, Thomas M. (1980), The Economic Value of the Quality of Life, Boulder, Colo.: Westview Press.

Read, Herbert (1953), Art and Industry, Bloomington, Ind.: Indiana University Press.

Rigaux-Bricmont, Benny (1982), "Influences of Brand Name and Packaging on Perceived Quality," in Advances in Consumer Research, vol. 9, ed., Andrew A. Mitchell, Ann Arbor: Association for Consumer Research, 472–77.

Rokeach, Milton (1973), The Nature of Human Values, New York: The Free Press.

Rosen, Sherwin (1974), "Hedonic Prices and Implicit Markets," Journal of Political Economy 82(1):34–55.

Russell, Bertrand (1912), The Problems of Philosophy, London: Oxford University Press.

_____ (1945), A History of Western Philosophy, New York: Simon and Schuster.

Ryle, Gilbert (1954), "Ordinary Language," in Ordinary Language, ed., V.C. Chappell, New York: Dover Publications, 24–40.

Scitovsky, Tibor (1976), The Joyless Economy, Oxford: Oxford University Press.

Scruton, Roger (1981), From Descartes to Wittgenstein, New York: Harper Colophon Books.

Singer, S. Fred (1972), "Discussion," in Product Quality, Performance, and Cost, ed., National Academy of Engineering, Washington, D.C.: National Academy of Engineering, 33–36.

Steedman, Ian et al., eds., (1981), The Value Controversy, London: Verso.

Sweezy, Paul (1981), "Marxian Value Theory and Crises," in The Value Controversy, eds., Ian Steedman et al., London: Verso, 20–35.

Thompson, Philip C. (1982), Quality Circles, New York: Amacom.

Tuchman, Barbara W. (1980), "The Decline of Quality," The New York Times Magazine, 2 November, 38–41, 104.

Wheatley, John J. and John S.Y. Chiu (1977), "The Effects of Price, Store Image, and Product and Respondent Characteristics on Perceptions of Quality," Journal of Marketing Research 14 (May):181–86.

——— , ——— , and Arieh Goldman (1981), "Physical Quality, Price, and Perceptions of Product Quality: Implications for Retailers," *Journal of Retailing* 57 (Summer):100–116.

Wittgenstein, Ludwig (1953), *Philosophical Investigations*, New York: Macmillan Publishing Co.

Young, Jeffrey T. (1978), *Classical Theories of Value: From Smith to Sraffa*, Boulder, Colo.: Westview Press.

Part II
Manufacturer Perspectives on Perceived Quality

3

The Importance of Quality

Leonard A. Morgan

Quality is and has been a key company-wide effort at General Electric (GE). Many actions have been taken to aggressively move all GE businesses to a number one or two worldwide position and quality is a key part of every business's strategy. Our quality policy states that "Company-wide quality, as a corporate objective, means attaining a level of overall performance and attitude that makes General Electric the *natural* choice of our customers." This means we look at quality in the whole, like our customers do. We are not just concerned with the quality of the product, but with the quality of our advertising, service, product literature, delivery, after-sales support, and so on.

To support this quality thrust, GE's Corporate Engineering and Manufacturing arm has stepped up its consulting and training support of GE businesses around the world. One of its major efforts has been the development of a video-based curriculum of nine courses in quality techniques and strategies to be used on-site by GE businesses. This chapter describes the key points made in the videotapes used in the first two courses.

Quality and Changing Customer Demands

Customer demands are changing in all industries. The areas in which demands are changing for some of GE's key customers include energy efficiency, durability, and service. Similar quality demands surface in dissimilar industries.

Quality and Competition

Worldwide competition (especially from the Japanese) is a threat in all industries—not just consumer-good companies—and quality is a major

---

This chapter is a synopsis of a presentation at the conference on perceived quality that consisted of the presentations and discussion of portions of three videotapes on quality developed by GE for use in training general managers and their immediate subordinates.

competitive focal point. In our opinion, foreign competitors are more successful because they listen to customers, are more responsive to customer needs, and provide better value (performance versus price).

Quality and Demands on Suppliers

Changing demands of customers imply changing demands on suppliers, a kind of "reverse ripple effect." To serve these customers well, a company must demonstrate its commitment to quality. Life-cycle cost is now a key criterion for consumer purchase—not necessarily low price.

Quality in the Future

It is possible to produce the same quality at lower cost by increasing productivity and introducing more standardization. What customers seem to want most is more emphasis on efficiency and reliability (not necessarily increased technology). Management must be externally oriented and should not prejudge what is important for its customers. The companies who survive will be those who are the quality and productivity leaders.

There is a "quality-perception gap" between manufacturers and consumers. As one example, a *Fortune* survey of chief executive officers (CEOs) of the United States' largest companies showed that three out of five CEOs believed "quality is better today," and only 13 percent believed that quality was declining. Yet, a study of 7,000 consumers conducted during the same time period revealed that 49 percent believed quality was declining, and 59 percent believed it would continue to decline in the next five years. As a second example, a survey of appliance manufacturers and their consumers revealed that 50 percent of manufacturers said that reliability has improved, but only 20 percent of consumers agreed.

To illustrate how this quality-perception gap can arise, the Conference participants were shown a videotape, entitled "Quality: From Whose Perspective?" consisting of a series of excerpts from interviews in which GE employees, appliance dealers, and customers were asked to define quality. The excerpts were arranged to progress from product development, to manufacturing, to marketing and sales, to the shopper and finally the end user. A handout was provided prior to viewing the tape. It consisted of a matrix that listed the description of each interviewee (for instance, Program Manager, Dealer, Shopper) across the top and a list of attributes or characteristics of product quality that were

Figure 3–1. Attributes Cited by Each Person as the Key Elements of What is Perceived as Quality

	Program Mgr.	Mgr. Adv. Eng.	Mgr. Prod. Eng.	Mgr. QC. #1	Mgr. QC. #2	Fab. Foreman	Fab. Mach. Oper.	Methods Analyst	Quality Inspector	Assy For.	Assemb #1	Assemb #2	Mkt. Mgr.	Sales Mgr.	Dealer	Shopper	Owner
1. Appearance		X	X			X	X	X		X	X					X	X
2. Cleanability																X	X
3. Cost/Price		X													X		
4. Delivery															X		
5. Dependability					X		X										
6. Durability			X			X											
7. Ease of Use						X		X									
8. Features		X		X												X	X
9. Form/Fit		X		X						X							
10. Performance	X		X	X				X			X			X	X		
11. Product Information	X							X					X				
12. Reliability		X			X									X		X	
13. Safety																X	
14. Service													X	X			
15. Simplicity																	
16. Unit	X																
Consistency														X		X	
17. Workmanship									X	X							
18. Other																	

mentioned down the left side. Conference participants were asked to use this matrix as they watched the videotape and check the attributes each interviewee mentioned in defining quality. The program paused briefly after each excerpt to permit time for making notations.

Figure 3–1 presents a list of the correct responses. Note that appearance, reliability, and performance attributes were mentioned by most interviewees. Yet other attributes seemed to be mentioned more by one particular group of interviewees than by others. For example: only marketing mentioned serviceability; only consumers mentioned cleanability, simplicity, and safety.

What might be implied by these commonalities or differences between groups? How might the differences be managed? What market research is needed to qualitatively determine the key customer-based quality measurement? These are important questions we, as well as other providers of goods and services in today's marketplace, must concern ourselves with.

4
Product Attributes and Perceived Quality: Foods

P. Greg Bonner and
Richard Nelson

R ecent evidence from the Profit Impact of Market Strategies
(PIMS) project indicates high quality leads to both high return
on investment (ROI) and high market share.[1] It is little argued
that quality is an important component of competitive strategy. From the
parent who tests a cookie when baking cookies for the children to the
company that spends millions of dollars on quality-control programs, few
production processes exist in which a determination of the output quality
is not made by the producer, the consumer, or both. Quality-control programs on the production side of the dyad are generally based on some
type of measurement, versus a standard, of tangible, intrinsic characteristics of the product and product package or evaluation by a company-
employed "expert." The consumer's evaluation of quality may or may
not correspond with the producer's evaluation. This logically leads to
the question of how is quality measured by the consumer. Robert Buzzell
states:

> This [measuring quality] is hard enough within a single product
> category, because customers' needs and tastes vary. Is Budweiser 'better'
> than Schlitz? If one customer prefers brand A, another may prefer brand
> B precisely because its characteristics are different. The problem is com-
> pounded when we seek to measure and compare product quality across
> categories and industries.[2]

The method employed by PIMS for product quality assessment is
presented in the PIMS Data Manual and will not be detailed here.[3] Even
though the instructions for reporting relative product quality stress the
importance of taking the end-customer perspective, reported numbers
rest on the judgment of the corporate personnel. Lynn Phillips, Dae
Chang, and Robert Buzzell question the integrity of any demonstrated
relationships involving this product quality variable, and they utilize a
test-retest measurement framework to assess the reliability of the rela-

tive product quality measure employed by PIMS.[4] Results indicated a highly reliable quality measure (exceptions are noted on pages 41 and 42 of their article and, on balance, the causal modeling methodology employed by the authors generated results consistent with earlier PIMS findings.

The high reliability found by Phillips, Chang, and Buzzell for year-to-year relative product quality measurements indicates a consistency between successive executive informant reports.[5] It does not necessarily indicate any correspondence between the product quality measure employed and the end consumer's perception of quality. Bradley Gale shows how customer-perceived quality drives profitability and presents the three-step PIMS process for measuring product quality based on the customer's perspective:

1. Identify and assign weights to product and service attributes.
2. Rate your product and those of your three largest competitors on each attribute.
3. Calculate your overall quality position relative to your competitors.[6]

The crux of this measurement process is getting to the customers to validate management's perceptions of the customers' perceptions. Relative quality is viewed as a combination of specific, identified product attributes. This step appears to be an evolutionary improvement which further quantifies the process detailed in the PIMS Data Manual.[7]

The empirical work presented in this chapter is aimed at addressing the issue of which attributes determine a food product's quality. Specific questions addressed are:

1. Is quality a *global* or *product-specific* concept?
2. Which attributes contribute most to quality image?
3. How is brand equity (the differential advantage of a brand name) achieved?
4. How does packaging mediate the quality perception?

Theoretical Discussion

The fourth meaning given in the *American Heritage Dictionary* for *quality* is, "degree or grade of excellence: yard goods of low quality."[8] This is the meaning implied when one speaks of a high-quality good, a low-quality service, and so forth. The PIMS relative quality measure attempts to span all product categories by developing its quality measure relative to the served market of similar products. Therefore, a car may be of low relative quality and a box of cereal of high relative quality. The quality measure for the cereal is developed versus other cereals. In this sense quality is global, since indexing it to served markets allows analysis of strategic issues across various product categories.

A product serves a particular market through both its intrinsic and extrinsic product attributes, but it is the intrinsic product attributes that generally provide the sought utility. Quite clearly, the same intrinsic attributes that make a car of superior quality are not relevant to a box of cereal. Within a particular served market, quality should be determined by a similar set of attributes. For example, it makes sense to consider nutrition content as a possible quality-determining attribute among boxes of cereal, but nutrition content is meaningless relative to assessment of a car's quality level. In this sense, quality, to the extent it is determined from a product-specific set of attributes, is a product-specific concept.

The demarcation between attributes is quite clear in the example utilizing a box of cereal and a car. However, the distinction of product-specific quality becomes arbitrary when one considers a box of cereal and an egg, both of which often serve the same usage occasion. Does the same or similar set of attributes contribute to the assessment of an egg's quality versus the box of cereal's quality? In other words, does each product category within the broad product class of food have its own quality-determinant attribute set or is there a meaningful set of attributes across all food products? While the empirical analysis presented in this chapter will attempt to shed some light on this question, a priori reasoning suggests both sets of attributes may coexist.

The consumer, in what may be called a short-run decision mode, may decide in the supermarket between a box of corn flakes and a box of shredded wheat. A very specific set of attributes for evaluation of cold, boxed cereal quality may exist including price, nutrition, taste, convenience, and so forth. However, in the long-run decision mode of a consumer, assessment of food quality may be more general in scope as people make decisions on eating patterns and types of food to include in their diet. An example of this type of influence is provided by Food Marketing Institute (FMI) chairman D'Agostino when he reports, "in recent surveys, consumers responded that the produce department was the Number One department when choosing a supermarket. In the past, the meat department held this honor. Today with nutrition uppermost in the customer's mind, a new emphasis on fresh has emerged."[9]

The implications of across-category (within product class) quality comparisons are important to the business unit manager. A unit manager may have a superior quality product versus other products within his category, but the category itself may suffer relative to other categories.

That is, within a broad product class such as food, some type of generalized "absolute" quality may be thought of as existing which may drive trends in food usage, while direct "absolute" quality comparisons may be made for individual purchase decisions within a narrowly defined product category.

This chapter, rather than addressing the issue of how quality is measured, addresses the issue of how food quality is perceived.

Methodology

Subjects for this research were drawn from a nationally representative mail panel. Three thousand nine hundred eighty-three (3,983) usable questionnaires were returned from a total of five thousand (5,000) distributed; therefore, the response rate was 79.7 percent. The study scope included twenty-eight brands (see following list) and thirty-three product categories (see table 4–1).

Banquet frozen compartmented dinners

Minute Maid frozen orange juice

Prego spaghetti sauce

Sunkist oranges

Swanson frozen compartmented dinners

"V-8" cocktail vegetable juice

Swanson frozen fried chicken

Stouffer's frozen main-dish entrees

Chef Boy-Ar-Dee canned spaghetti or ravioli

Franco-American canned spaghetti or ravioli

Dannon yogurt

Campbell's canned condensed soup

Vlassic pickles

Lipton's regular dry soup

Pepperidge Farm bread

Totino's frozen pizza

Green Giant canned vegetables

Green Giant frozen vegetables

Kraft Velveeta cheese

Kraft bottled salad dressings

Ragu spaghetti sauce

Starkist chunk tuna

Swanson canned chunk white chicken

Perrier bottled sparkling water

Skippy peanut butter

Campbell's chunky soups

Campbell's pork & beans

Van Camp pork & beans

Table 4–1
Product Categories
(percentage answering)

	Top Box		Top 2 Box	
	User	Nonuser	User	Nonuser
Refrigerated orange juice	48	28	66	49
Soft drinks	17	16	28	23
Refrigerated package cheeses	45	36	70	64
Instant dry packaged soups	22	14	41	30
Frozen compartmented dinners	14	8	28	17
Frozen pizza	13	9	28	18
Boxed cake mix	39	24	63	48
Lettuce or tomatoes	53	49	75	72
Deli sliced cold cuts and cheeses	39	32	62	53
Jarred spaghetti sauce	24	10	44	23
Bread	39	39	63	57
Bag of oranges	56	52	78	73
Milk	59	56	79	72
Canned vegetables	16	9	36	18
Frozen vegetables	36	30	63	48
Cut-up fryer chicken	35	32	59	54
Refrigerated yogurt	44	24	69	40
Canned spaghetti	17	7	30	13
Cole slaw (deli)	28	11	50	27
Canned condensed soup	22	21	44	30
Frozen orange juice	47	31	73	52
Canned chunked boned chicken	32	16	54	31
Bottled/jarred pickles	35	29	59	50
Bottled salad dressing	25	13	50	34
Box of spaghetti or noodles	29	17	49	34
Bottled apple juice	48	28	71	54
Canned tuna fish	31	21	58	39
Homemade soup	74	60	88	73
Frozen single-serve main-dish entree	19	10	44	23
Eggs	55	64	78	74
Regular-grind coffee	47	31	66	48
Dry spices and seasonings	29	38	51	56
Ready-to-use cereals	25	15	44	24

Many brand/product categories were overlapped in order that an assessment of the difference in perceived quality between branded and nonbranded items could be established. In order to prevent fatigue in responding to sixty-one different brands/products, five versions of the questionnaire were employed. Each respondent rated twelve (thirteen on one version) products on nineteen attributes using a seven-point bipolar adjective (or phrase) scale. Table 4–2 lists the attributes for which data were gathered. Product/brand usage and demographic data were collected from the entire sample. The number of usable questionnaires, by subsample, ranged from a low of 774 (for version 4) to a high of 806 (for

Table 4–2
The Attribute Scale

Positive	Negative
Fresh	Not fresh
A good value for the money	Not a good value for the money
Looks appetizing	Does not look appetizing
Tastes fresh	Does not taste fresh
Healthy	Not healthy
Convenient	Not convenient
Can be used in many ways	Cannot be used in many ways
Low in calories	High in calories
Nutritious	Not nutritious
Modern	Old-fashioned
Low priced	High priced
Not salty	Salty
Fun to eat	Not fun to eat
Tastes natural	Tastes artificial
Low in fat/cholesterol	High in fat/cholesterol
High quality	Low quality
Rich/full flavored	Weak flavored
Good aroma	Poor aroma
Easy to digest	Hard to digest

version 2). Demographic comparison of the five subsamples showed no significant demographic differences among the samples. Products and brands were rotated within versions to avoid order bias. When one looks back at a study, obvious shortcomings emerge. Our collected data on attributes obviously suffers from our failure to include the attribute sweet–not sweet, and an attribute that distinguishes between items that contain additives or preservatives and those that do not.

Analysis and Results

The objectives of the analysis were to provide insights into the issue of food quality and how is it perceived by the consumer. Developmental hypotheses emerged along the way and provided direction for focusing the analysis and reporting results. The analysis will address the four questions presented earlier. All results reported here are on the total sample. Split sample runs on all data analysis were made and results were materially identical in all cases.

Is Quality a Global or Product-Specific Concept?

More directly, in terms of this analysis, this question should read: Is the concept of quality generalized across the entire product class of food or do specific categories of food command quality evaluations that are isolated from other categories? Table 4–1 presents "top box" and "top two box" ratings for users and nonusers across all products on the high quality–low quality scale. Both space considerations and the desire to maintain confidentiality prevent the listing of the results for brands. For users, top box ratings range from a low of 13 percent for frozen pizza to a high of 74 percent for homemade soup. Similarly, brands ranged from a low of 18 percent to a high of 71 percent. Various foods are perceived quite differently in terms of delivering quality. However, these raw quality scores tell us nothing as far as what constitutes a quality food item. Analysis of the second question is necessary.

Which Attributes Contribute Most to a Quality Image?

Correlation coefficients for the attributes were developed over all products and brands and by each individual product and brand. Table 4–3 presents the rank of orderings of the correlation coefficients. The consistency in the order in which a product's attributes correlate with its quality evaluations is quite high. This finding indicates that consumers employ a similar weighting scheme to the attributes to assess quality across food categories. Some notable exceptions appear in table 4–3 once you get below the top-ranked (sensate) attributes. For instance, for regular grind coffee, the correlation between quality and nutrition drops to last place suggesting consumers do some selective weighting of attributes relative to expectations. Large "weighting" shifts of this type occur primarily in the nonsensate attributes. However, the consistently high rank correlations (almost all above .80) between the attribute orderings support the hypothesis that quality is a global concept across differing food categories.

Since similar attribute weighting schemes are utilized to evaluate quality, the logical question is which attributes are given the most weight? The rank of the correlations in table 4–3 clearly shows high quality is most associated with rich/full flavor, tastes natural, tastes fresh, good aroma, and looks appetizing. Similarly, attributes were factor analyzed and factor scores were computed for each product evaluation and input to a stepwise regression with quality as the dependent variable. The first two factors entered into the regression were sensory factors named "Taste Appeal" and "Freshness," for which the factor loadings and regression results are as shown in tables 4–4 and 4–5. Clearly, the sensory attributes of food products drive the overall quality evaluation in the broad product class of food.

Table 4-3
Correlation Coefficient Ranks

	Quality with 18 Attributes (attributes ordered as in table 4-2)																	
	A1	A2	A3	A4	A5	A6	A7	A8	A9	A10	A11	A12	A13	A14	A15[a]	A17	A18	A19
Brands																		
Brand 01	7	10	6	4	3	12	14	17	8	13	18	16	11	2	15	1	5	9
Brand 02	7	8	5	4	9	13	12	15	6	14	16	17	10	2	18	1	3	11
Brand 03	7	11	6	2	5	14	12	15	8	13	18	16	10	3	17	1	4	9
Brand 04	8	9	4	6	5	13	12	15	7	14	18	16	10	3	17	1	2	11
Brand 05	10	11	8	4	5	12	14	16	6	13	18	15	9	3	17	1	2	7
Brand 06	8	11	7	2	5	10	16	18	6	13	17	18	12	3	14	1	4	7
Brand 07	8	9	4	5	10	6	13	17	14	12	15	16	7	2	16	1	3	9
Brand 08	7	12	9	2	5	10	13	17	6	14	15	16	11	3	15	1	4	11
Brand 09	5	9	6	3	8	14	13	16	7	12	18	17	11	3	17	1	4	8
Brand 10	10	11	5	4	6	14	12	15	7	13	16	15	9	5	17	1	2	10
Brand 11	9	10	2	6	4	13	12	18	7	14	18	15	11	1	16	2	3	8
Brand 12	7	11	4	3	5	12	14	17	8	14	18	16	9	4	18	1	6	10
Brand 13	6	8	3	5	7	10	13	16	11	13	16	15	10	4	15	1	2	9
Brand 14	3	11	6	2	7	13	12	18	12	14	18	16	9	2	16	1	5	8
Brand 15	7	11	6	3	5	11	14	15	9	14	18	15	8	3	16	1	4	10
Brand 16	8	12	5	6	4	13	12	16	7	13	18	17	10	3	18	1	6	9
Brand 17	10	11	4	4	8	12	13	18	7	14	16	15	9	4	18	1	2	9
Brand 18	5	7	6	2	8	14	13	15	10	14	17	17	9	3	18	1	2	5
Brand 19	6	9	7	3	5	9	12	16	8	14	17	12	10	3	16	1	3	11
Brand 20	7	12	8	8	5	12	13	18	6	14	16	16	10	4	18	1	4	11
Brand 21	11	10	6	5	7	12	13	17	4	14	17	14	9	3	15	1	2	7
Brand 22	8	10	2	2	5	13	15	17	4	14	15	18	11	3	18	1	9	6
Brand 23	4	11	9	4	10	12	14	16	8	13	16	14	7	3	15	1	11	6
Brand 24	5	10	6	5	6	13	13	18	7	12	17	18	8	3	17	1	2	9
Brand 25	7	7	5	4	6	12	14	18	9	14	18	15	11	2	17	1	4	11
Brand 26	9	7	8	5	6	13	13	15	3	12	16	15	10	4	17	1	11	10
Brand 27	2	14	5	1	3	7	12	18	15	9	13	16	10	4	17	8	11	6
Brand 28	9	6	4	5	8	11	13	15	10	14	16	18	7	3	17	1	2	12
Product Categories																		
Refrigerated orange juice	5	10	8	3	6	12	13	17	7	14	18	15	11	2	16	1	4	9
Soft drinks	4	6	7	2	8	12	13	18	11	14	15	16	10	3	17	1	5	9
Refrigerated packaged cheeses	8	9	6	3	7	11	13	15	5	14	17	18	10	2	16	1	4	12

	1	2	3	4	5	6	7	8	9	10	11	12	13	14	15	16	17	18
Instant dry packaged soups	10	8	9	5	3	14	12	16	6	13	17	15	7	2	18	1	4	11
Frozen compartmented dinners	5	11	7	4	8	14	12	15	6	13	18	17	10	2	16	1	3	9
Frozen pizza	3	5	6	2	8	13	12	18	9	15	14	16	11	1	17	2	7	10
Boxed cake mix	5	8	10	3	7	12	13	16	9	14	17	15	11	2	18	1	4	6
Lettuce or tomatoes	2	7	4	1	6	11	13	17	12	15	14	16	9	5	18	1	10	8
Deli sliced cold cuts and cheeses	5	11	7	2	6	13	12	16	8	15	18	15	10	3	17	1	4	9
Jarred spaghetti sauce	5	8	6	3	7	13	12	17	10	14	16	15	9	2	18	1	4	11
Bread	8	11	7	5	6	12	13	17	4	14	18	15	10	6	16	1	3	9
Bag of oranges	3	8	4	2	7	11	13	17	12	14	18	15	9	2	16	1	5	10
Milk	4	6	8	3	5	10	13	18	7	14	17	15	12	3	16	1	11	9
Canned vegetables	8	10	4	7	5	14	12	16	6	13	18	15	11	3	17	1	2	9
Frozen vegetables	8	11	5	3	6	12	13	18	7	14	17	15	10	2	16	1	4	9
Cut-up fryer chicken	4	7	7	2	6	13	12	18	10	15	14	16	9	3	17	1	5	8
Refrigerated yogurt	3	9	10	2	8	12	14	18	6	13	16	15	7	4	17	1	11	5
Canned spaghetti	8	11	7	6	4	13	12	17	5	14	18	16	9	2	15	1	3	10
Cole slaw	4	9	7	3	6	13	13	18	10	14	16	15	8	2	17	1	5	11
Canned condensed soup	9	11	6	5	5	12	13	18	7	14	16	15	10	2	17	1	4	8
Frozen orange juice	5	10	7	3	6	13	14	18	8	12	17	16	11	2	15	1	4	9
Canned chunk/boned chicken	10	11	8	7	5	13	12	18	9	14	16	15	4	3	17	1	2	5
Bottled/jarred pickles	6	7	10	3	5	9	14	16	12	13	18	17	8	2	15	1	4	11
Bottled salad dressing	3	8	5	4	4	12	14	17	9	13	18	16	11	2	15	1	6	10
Box of spaghetti or noodles	6	7	4	2	3	13	13	16	8	14	17	15	11	1	18	3	10	9
Bottled apple juice	6	7	8	4	5	12	14	17	10	13	18	15	11	2	16	1	3	9
Canned tuna fish	10	11	7	6	4	12	14	17	5	13	18	15	9	4	16	1	8	3
Homemade soup	7	9	8	3	6	15	15	18	5	13	12	14	11	2	17	1	2	10
Frozen single-service main-dish entrees	8	11	6	3	5	13	12	16	9	14	13	15	10	2	17	1	4	7
Eggs	4	8	7	1	6	8	10	17	5	14	16	15	11	2	18	3	9	7
Regular-grind coffee	5	9	6	3	12	7	16	17	18	11	13	14	8	2	15	1	4	10
Dry spices and seasonings	5	8	7	4	6	9	11	17	13	14	18	15	10	2	16	1	3	12
Ready-to-use cereals	7	10	8	5	4	13	12	18	3	14	17	15	11	2	16	1	9	6
Overall Rank	4	10	6	3	7	13	12	17	8	15	18	14	11	2	16	1	5	9
Overall Correlations	65	54	63	70	62	31	38	03	55	18	01	19	50	73	06	78	63	54

[a] A16 is the quality attribute, so it does not appear here.

Table 4–4
Factors That Drive Quality Evaluation—Factor Loadings

Attributes	Factor 1 (Freshness)	Factor 2 (Taste Appeal)
Tastes fresh	.78	—
Looks appetizing	.61	.45
Rich/full flavored	.45	.66
Fun to eat	—	.71
Fresh	.81	—
Good aroma	—	.76

How Is Brand Equity Achieved?

Brand equity is the goodwill adhering to a brand name. Table 4–6 presents examples of five brands that have successfully differentiated themselves from their category. Again, it appears the most effective positively differentiating attributes are those dealing with sensory appeals. A graphic example in figure 4–1 depicts a plot of brand and product positions (capital letters stand for brand; lower case letters for product category) on the two most important factors driving quality.

Brand *A* has successfully differentiated itself from category *a*, while brand *B* has not done so with respect to category *b*. It appears that those brands most successful in establishing a strong brand equity position have done so on the strength of their perceived sensory image. Brands that do not achieve an equity position with respect to their category are not necessarily ill positioned. Extremely dominant brands (those with high market share or exceptional recognition) "are" the category and, hence, are not perceived as providing differing sensory benefits from the category. Brand imagery for these brands should be measured against other brands in the category. For proprietary reasons brand-by-brand comparisons are not presented here but suffice it to say that per-

Table 4–5
Regression Results

	df	SS	MS	F	Sig. Level
Regression	2	47536	23768	16853.21	.0001
Error	45670	64409	1.41	—	—
Total	45672	111945	—	—	—

				t Value	Sig. Level
Factor 1 (Freshness)				127.96	.0001
Factor 2 (Taste Appeal)				131.98	.0001

R square = .43

Table 4–6
Brands with a More Positive Image Than Their Product Category

	Quality difference Brand to Category[a]	Positively Differentiating Attributes	Difference
Brand 1	15	Tastes fresh	20
Category 1		Looks appetizing	20
Brand 2	21	Looks appetizing	41
Category 2		Rich/full flavored	23
Brand 3	16	Fresh	20
Category 3		Looks appetizing	18
		Rich/full flavored	18
Brand 4	25	Tastes fresh	21
Category 4		Looks appetizing	19
Brand 5	21	Fresh	17
Category 5			

[a]Based on average difference of top box ratings on quality for product category and brand current users.

ceived sensory attributes provided the primary differentiation between brands.

How Does Packaging Mediate the Quality Perception?

The sixty-one brands and categories were grouped into six package categories: fresh, refrigerated, bottled, frozen, dry, and canned. While this analysis is dependent on the specific products/brands chosen within package categories, the generally broad scope of products included in the study is sufficient to generate at least a preliminary hypothesis about quality perception and packaging. Top box ratings for current users of the products by package form were calculated for the quality scale. These were as follows: fresh (52 percent), refrigerated (43 percent), bottled (40 percent), frozen (35 percent), canned (31 percent), and dry (29 percent). Clearly, how a product is packaged interacts with how a product's quality is perceived.

Discussion

Partial support is provided for the hypothesis that the concept of quality is generalized across the entire product class of food. The consistent rank of the attribute correlations in table 4–3 suggests consumers tend to weight attributes equally across the different food categories; and the

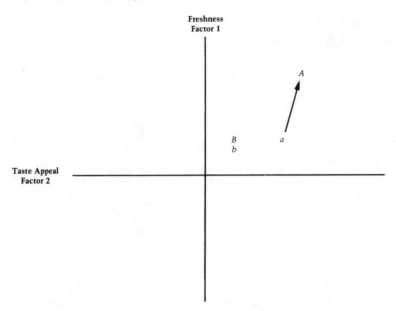

Figure 4–1. Brand Differentiation from Category

consistently high correlations of the sensory attributes suggest that it is the sensory qualities of food that lead to its quality perception. In this sense, quality is a generalized concept. However, many of the "low"-quality items in table 4–1 have very large sales volumes and, while other things in addition to quality drive sales, this suggests other categorizations of quality are also used.

Not all foods are acceptable in all usage situations and, when purchasing for a particular use situation (or set thereof), the perceived competitive framework for that use situation delineates the range of quality comparisons made. Therefore the quality of a frozen dinner is rarely operationally evaluated against boxed cereal. Even though there is empirical evidence that it is the sensory attributes that drive both evaluations of quality (frozen dinner and boxed cereal), and therefore make the quality concept a general one, the sales volume figures seem to indicate that decision-induced quality comparisons occur within a narrower framework and support the notion that operationally quality is a relative concept within food categories, with category admittance dependent on the use situation (or some other categorizing framework).

Some additional insight is possible by looking at the results of a regression of three-year sales trends of the products/brands studied versus their average quality image. This resulted in an R^2 of .06 and a regression significant at the .10 level. While this result is minor, albeit statistically significant, it provides some evidence that trends (changes in long-run consumer purchase allocations) are related to the overall generalized quality assessment within the food product class. At this juncture, it is fair to say the quality concept appears to be both "generalized" and "category specific" within the world of food. One hypothesis emerging from this work is that quality evaluations at point of purchase are relative to a particular competitive framework but that overall quality evaluations have long-run implications on how consumers change their purchase patterns between categories or alter their categorization schemes for foods.

Further examination of table 4–3 indicates attribute eleven—high priced–low priced—is among the least important attributes that affect quality perception. Some discussion of this finding is warranted due to the often extensive discussion in the literature of the price–quality relationship.[10] At least two hypotheses for our findings can be advanced. First, since individual food items are inexpensive relative to most purchases and products/brands employed in this study are widely distributed and used, respondent's evaluations of quality are based on product/ brand experience and not related to price.

Second, respondents, when forming an evaluation of high priced–low priced, were using a single item (product/brand) as a referent. If they applied the maxim, "you get what you pay for," one would expect no correlation between quality and price level. For example, if a perceived high-quality product had a high price, it would be given a middle evaluation since the perceived price level matched the perceived quality and, therefore, it was not "high priced." This result contrasts with the use of a multiple-referent data collection technique where the price level of an item is judged relative to other items in the same category.

Finally, quality and price evaluations were summed to the product level (that is, each product had its average perceived quality and perceived price levels computed) and a correlation analysis between the sixty-one quality and price levels resulted in no significant correlation. Price was not a factor in quality assessment in our study. However, it must be remembered our price cue was a respondent's assessment of the product's relative price. Since most brands were judged higher quality than the category and most brands have an actual price premium attached to them, we would have found a positive association between actual price and perceived quality if we had run such an analysis.

The facts that the sensory evaluations proved so important to quality evaluation and that current brand equity positions seem to be built primarily on sensory differentiation have important implications for brand positioning strategies. If a goal of a communication campaign is to improve the perceived quality of a food product, the presentation of that product must stress its superior sensate qualities. Advertisements that address caloric content, convenience, and the like, will not improve the perceived quality. Of course, quality evaluation is not merely a result of communication strategies and, especially with low-priced items such as food products, continual experiential evaluation is possible. The further implication is not only must the communication strategy stress the sensate qualities of the product, the product must deliver the promised benefits.

The results relating packaging form to quality ratings have a number of implications. Since the sensate attributes of food drive the quality image, products locked into the lower packaging forms suffer a differential disadvantage. The ascending order of the package types (dry, canned, and so on to fresh) can be viewed practically as a sensory maintenance scale for packaging. If overall quality (the generalized conception of quality) is impacting on food trends, two strategies are possible. One is to develop new products or make acquisitions that expand your packaging base into the package forms better able to convey the sensate qualities of the foods. A second option, not mutually exclusive with the first, is to attempt to reposition the package of your current products through a consumer education program of the package's benefits.

Package dynamics also impact when product quality is evaluated relative to the product's competitive framework. For example, suppose the usage situation is the categorization scheme employed by the consumer to define food needs. A frozen product may be rated superior in quality to other frozen, canned, or dry products applicable to a particular usage situation and enjoy superior positioning within the competitive framework. The introduction of a bottled, refrigerated, or fresh packaged product of the same item targeted for the same usage occasion may upset the status quo and quickly gain a differential advantage. The superior sensory maintenance abilities of the new packaging will quickly erode the former product's perceived quality superiority.

Summary

Quality, in the world of food, is strongly tied to a product's sensate attributes. Brand equity appears to be achieved by communicating and delivering on these attributes. The sensory maintenance ability of packaging differs by type and those packaging forms that can best deliver a rich/full flavor, natural and fresh taste, good aroma, and appetizing appearance are likely to gain market share as consumers continue to demand "quality" in what they eat.

Notes

1. Robert D. Buzzell, "Product Quality," *PIMSLETTER*, no. 4 (Strategic Planning Institute, 1978).

2. Ibid., p. 2.

3. Strategic Planning Institute, *The PIMS Data Manual* (Cambridge, Mass.: SPI, 1978), pp. 3.50–3.53.

4. Lynn W. Phillips, Dae R. Chang, and Robert D. Buzzell, "Product Quality, Cost Position and Business Performance: A Test of Some Key Hypothesis," *Journal of Marketing* 47 (Spring 1983):26–43.

5. Ibid.

6. Bradley T. Gale, "Study Product Quality/Profit Relationship So Firms Can Leapfrog Over Foreign Competition," *Marketing News*, 21 January 1983, Sect. 2, pp. 4–6.

7. Strategic Planning Institute, *Data Manual*.

8. *The American Heritage Dictionary of the English Language* (1981), 1068.

9. Steve D'Agostino, "News in a Nut Shell," *Check-Out Change*, (August–September 1982), vol. 3, issue 4.

10. See Robert B. Archibald, Clyde A. Haulman, and Carlisle E. Moody, Jr., "Quality, Price, Advertising and Published Quality Ratings," *Journal of Consumer Research* 9 (March 1983):347–56; I.R. Andrews and E.R. Valenzi, "Combining Price, Brand Name, and Store Cues to Form an Impression of Product Quality," *Proceedings of the 79th Annual Convention of the American Psychological Association* 6 (1971):649–50; J.D. McConnell, "Effect of Pricing on Perception of Product Quality," *Journal of Applied Psychology* 52 (1968):331–34; and Jacob Jacoby, Jerry C. Olson, and Rafael A. Haddock, "Price, Brand Name and Product Composition Characteristics as Determinants of Perceived Quality," *Journal of Applied Psychology* 55, no. 6 (December 1971), pp. 570–79.

5
Relating Product Features to Perceptions of Quality: Appliances

Sunil Mehrotra and
John Palmer

I n the Major Appliance Group at GE, an effort has been underway for
several years to understand how consumers perceive quality, how
their quality perceptions are formed, and how these perceptions affect brand preference and ultimately their choice of an appliance. This
effort started with the development of an overall model of the consumer
purchase process for major appliances.

The conceptual model of the purchase process for an appliance is
shown in figure 5–1. The stages in the purchase process outlined in this
figure are as follows:

1. The consumer begins the shopping process by entering a store with
   a commitment to different brands to varying degrees.
2. Typically, the consumer is soon intercepted by a salesman.
3. At this point, the salesman classifies the consumer based on what
   the consumer says she needs.
4. Then, the salesman tries to steer the consumer toward a brand and
   product which broadly fits the needs of the consumer, and which he
   is most interested in selling.[1]
5. The consumer evaluates the information provided by the salesman.
   At this point, the consumer has the opportunity to compare different products.
6. Out of this transaction the consumer decides either to buy one of
   the products at that store, or to shop for it elsewhere, or not to buy
   anything at all.

This shopping process has been more formally modeled. The model
shows that a brand's market share can be explained in terms of a number
of variables, as follows.

$MS_i \quad f(BC_i, RD_i, RS_i, RP_i)$

MS_i market share of brand i

BC_i commitment of consumers to brand i relative to other brands

RQ_i relative product quality of brand i as perceived by consumers

RD_i relative distribution strength of brand i

RS_i relative dealer or salesman effort devoted to selling brand i

RP_i price of brand i relative to other brands

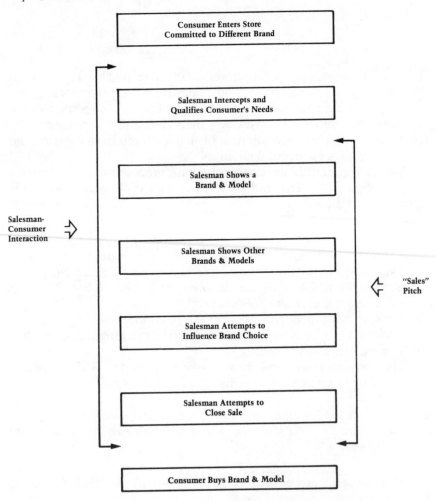

Figure 5–1. Appliance Purchase Decison Process

The model is set out in figure 5–2 and shows the marketing levers available to a manufacturer for impacting brand share. These levers are: brand reputation; product quality; distribution strength; merchandising effort; and price. Our interest in this chapter is with the lever of product quality.

Consumers perceive product quality at three stages in the buying process:

1. During a preliminary phase, when they are thinking about buying an appliance, gathering information, and giving consideration to specific brands and dealers.
2. At the point of purchase, before they buy the product.
3. While using the product.

Research efforts have been undertaken by GE in two areas to understand the product part of the market share equation: (1) to show how consumers perceive product quality at point of purchase; and (2) to show how consumers perceive product quality through using the product at home. The focus of this chapter is on the first of these, which at GE we refer to as the 'Product Cues Study.'

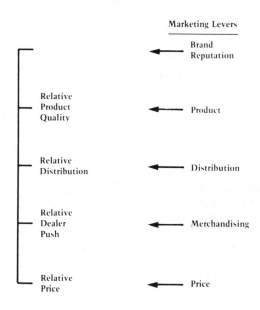

Figure 5–2. Model of the Major-Appliance Decision Process and Marketing Levers Available to Impact Commitment and Share

Theory

The term *product cues* is taken from consumer psychology and expresses the notion that a consumer's perceptions of product quality are influenced at point of purchase by specific things about the product—its price; its appearance; how it is made; its use of components and features; what the salesman says about it; and so forth. Product cues are stimuli to quality perceptions. The consumer uses perceptual cues to make judgments about the product's realities. We shall develop this idea further; but first we shall describe what goes on when a consumer about to buy a major appliance confronts alternative products at the point of purchase, say, a dealer showroom. The following excerpts from a protocol interview illustrate how Ms. Jones uses cues to evaluate different refrigerators.[2]

> "I want it to last . . . I'll spend the extra money if I think it will last a few more years."

> "They don't make them like they used to; it's all plastic; the one I have at home is made with porcelain."

> "This plastic material [pointing to door of butter compartment] is not good quality; it could easily crack."

> "I like the removable containers in the door, especially the one for eggs."

> "This refrigerator is really nice; I like the third door, it would mean the refrigerator wouldn't frost up so quickly."

> "I like the storage features in this refrigerator—the fact that it has only three shelves. (Ms. Jones said that the five shelves in another model she examined would make it difficult to store tall bottles and containers.) I also don't want shelves in the freezer compartment, and I like the hook they have put up here to hang bottles and the like."

> "I can never keep vegetables fresh for long periods so I don't want a large vegetable drawer—I want the meat drawer to be bigger."

> "These wire shelves would be difficult to clean. And this glass shelf at the bottom [above fresh food compartments] would collect dirt in this space [shelf is in two parts] and the surface is rough [stippled] so it would be difficult to rub clean."

> "The finish on these doors would collect fingermarks."

These excerpts give insights into what factors Ms. Jones is using to decide which product to buy. On the one hand, she employs tangible, concrete specifics of the product itself—for example, 'made with plastic,' 'number of shelves,' 'number of doors,' and 'removable containers.' On the other hand, she is making judgments using fairly abstract concepts which are in the nature of functional product benefits, such as:

Will it keep food fresh?

How long will it last?

How easy will it be to clean?

How attractive will it look in my kitchen?

Her decision-making protocol reflects an interplay between the tangible aspects of product features—what she sees—and the abstract notions of functional product benefits—what she wants.

For the consumer, in the showroom situation, many of these benefits are only promises. At point of purchase, the consumer has no way of determining the actual benefit delivery of an appliance product she has never used. She must rely on how she believes the product will perform once she gets it home and begins to use it. The problem for the consumer is to determine, before actually using the product at home, what the product's real benefits will be. To do this she relies on her prior experience, brand reputation, and the perceptual information she picks up in the showroom. The problem for the manufacturer is to understand how the consumer does this, and to make sure that the real benefits of the product are somehow communicated to the consumer in the showroom setting.

In the description of how Ms. Jones decided which refrigerator to buy, you will notice her recurring use of perceptual stimuli—what we call *product cues*—to signal expected benefit delivery. Product cues are the factual and perceptual things about the product with which no one can argue. One can have opinions about how many years a refrigerator is likely to last ('durability'—a benefit); but whether or not the refrigerator has a lining made of porcelain or plastic is a statement of fact. The kind of lining is a perceptual cue used by the consumer to evaluate the functional benefits of the product.

At point of purchase, the consumer's decision making reflects a kind of means-ends analysis whereby she links specific aspects of what she sees in the product to judgments of how the product will function when she gets it home. It is in this sense that we employ the term *product cue*. Product cues are specific, tangible aspects of the product that the consumer uses to signal one or more functional product benefits.

The term *quality cue* is sometimes used interchangeably with product cue and relates to the objective of finding out how to enhance the quality of a product by the judicious use of specific product attributes. In the field of consumer research, perceptions of quality are nothing more than how a consumer judges a product in terms of its functional benefits. Quality cues are what stimulate these perceptions—usually specific product cues.

In a recent paper, Jerry Olson and Thomas Reynolds review the literature and set out a more general view of how the consumer organizes different kinds of product knowledge.[3] They postulate a hierarchy of attributes, consequences, and values arrayed along a continuum of abstraction. Their view of consumer cognitive structure is entirely consistent with the one presented here.

In our working model of the appliance buying process, we have found it sufficient to deal with only two kinds of variables involving two levels of abstraction—product cues (not abstract) and functional product benefits (abstract).

To someone who is familiar with how refrigerators are made, it is clear from the Jones example that she is very selective in her use of possible product cues. Any refrigerator has several dozen possible cues. Ms. Jones is using very few of these to evaluate the alternative models.

What governs the consumer's selection of cues? Consumers use cues that they think signal specific functional benefits. This is the predictive aspect of cues which gives them their importance. Ms. Jones thinks that a porcelain lining will make the refrigerator easier to clean and last a long time. The porcelain lining signals these two important benefits—she uses it to predict eventual benefit delivery. The fact that a refrigerator has a porcelain lining is an important consideration for this consumer when choosing a refrigerator. Someone else may feel that plastic materials are superior to porcelain, in which case plastic would be more predictive than porcelain in signaling superior product quality. To find out which cues are important to consumers is the challenge for quality cues research.

In measuring cue importance, one must remember that cues are used to signal or to predict product benefits. They may have absolutely no functional value in their own right. They take on a value to the extent that they predict important benefits of the product. Glass refrigerator shelves are useless and without a functional benefit unless they are a part of a refrigerator. Any value a cue has for a consumer derives from the functional product benefits it is believed to predict. For example, glass shelves are important because glass is believed to be a good indicator of how easy the refrigerator will be to clean. 'Glass shelves' are not the value; 'easier to clean' is the value. Glass shelves have a predictive importance telling the consumer the refrigerator will be easy to clean. Therefore, in understanding which cues are important, we must determine how predictive they are of specific product benefits and how important these benefits are.

Some product cues might rightly be termed *features*. An ice-water dispenser is viewed by appliance manufacturers as a feature. Features fall between being products in their own right and being cues. To the extent that a feature delivers its own separate functional benefits, independent of the product as a whole, then it has its own recognizable value for the consumer and can be treated as a kind of product—a product that may have its own bundle of functional benefits. When a feature has no separate functional benefits, but takes on the benefits of the product of which it is a part, then it must be treated as a cue. Consequently, we classify features as either products or cues. Most often, features are cues because they have no functional benefits in their own right and, in the consumer's mind, they are not separated from the product taken as a whole.

Before discussing the research system for determining cue importance, we shall first review the kind of information the research is designed to provide. From the manufacturer's point of view, his need for information on product cues can be summarized as follows.

Which cues are important to consumers because they predict important product benefits and, hence, are prime candidates for enhancing consumer quality perceptions about the product?

Which hardware items (potential cues) are not important to consumers, are not really cues because they do not predict benefits, and, if they are currently featured on products, are candidates for removal and cost reduction?

Which cues signal which benefits to the consumer; what cue strategy is called for to communicate the important benefits of the product?

Research System

How to Develop the List of Cues and Benefits

Cue lists can be assembled from focus groups, or from in-depth interviews with consumers. Typically, in the latter case, consumers are interviewed in a product-clinic setting where several alternative products are on display. The consumer is asked to evaluate each product and to compare them in terms of advantages and disadvantages. The interviewer probes all evaluative comments until specific cues are identified.

Another way to develop cue lists is to work with the product planners and to set down all the things that constitute the product. This approach works at the level of engineering specifications and components and sometimes produces items that may have absolutely no importance for consumers. The cue lists of product planners tend to be longer and perhaps more complete than those developed through consumer interviews. The trouble with some of the cues put up by product planners is that they employ engineering terms that mean very little to the consumer. In these cases, we have found it necessary to demonstrate the cue to the consumer in order to explain something of its function.

Cue lists can be long by consumer research standards—often 100 items or more. In developing a suitable research system, we had to recognize that the interview task must be able to deal with cue lists of this length. Our experience suggests that while interview length is always a problem, it is preferable to make sure the list of cues is complete as possible. Candidates for inclusion in the list should be dropped from consideration only if they clearly can have no meaning or relevance for consumers.

This last point is important. Sometimes particular aspects of a product are glossed over because we assume the consumer will not even notice it or, if he does, it will not mean anything to him. We forget that new cues are being emphasized all the time by the popular culture, and consumers can quickly read important meanings into cues that had been lying dormant. For example, we suspect the problem with aluminum wiring some years ago, which received considerable press coverage at the time, has influenced consumer perceptions about the 'reliability' and 'efficiency' of refrigeration products that use aluminum tubing. The following list shows a number of product areas where cues were identified for the refrigerator study.[4] (Over one hundred cues were used in that study and this is a fairly typical number for a complex appliance.)

Door surfaces	Freezer lights
Handle types	Ice-tray location
Handle trim	Shelf trim
Handle lengths	Size of shelf bars
Amounts of door trim	Shelf bars
Grilles	Amount of door surface
Door openings	Portable containers
Backs	Compartment doors
Freezer shelves	Shelf areas
Inside door surfaces	Assortment of shelves

Door gaskets	Shelf stops
Controls	Shelf supports
Construction lining	Lining material
Shelving material	Bottom shelves
Drawer material	Types of third drawers
Bottom drawers	Location of cold drawers
Size of bottom drawers	Size of third drawers

The other component of the initial work was to specify the list of benefits. Market researchers have their own preferences and conventions for designing benefit lists. In our development of benefit lists for the various quality cues studies, we found it useful to keep the following four points in mind.

1. Benefits are used to describe what products mean to people. They refer to the functional qualities a product has. Benefit statements will be evaluative of the benefit or function, and independent of specific cues; which is to say, reference to cues in the wording of the statements should be avoided.

2. The longer the list of benefits, the more likely will be the problem of interactions between benefits. To cut down on possible interactions we used shorter lists of benefit statements with broad, fairly abstract meanings. Traditional factor analysis was used to reduce longer lists of more specific benefit statements.

3. We used semantic differential scales to capture the benefits because we found respondents can quite rapidly rate different products on several scales. Furthermore, they were able to use such scales to make meaningful comparisons between the products.

4. We made sure the benefit scales were able to differentiate obvious product differences. A more rigorous approach demands that, in conjunction with attribute-utility analysis, the benefit ratings be able to replicate preference behavior. However, such a microsimulation of consumer preference behavior was not a facet of our quality cues work.

How to Gather the Required Information

The information required to do quality cues research was gathered from samples of consumers. Because the research was meant to produce results applicable to the whole market, quantitative methods with a projectable sample were required. In designing the research study, one of the first issues that we needed to resolve was who to interview. Appliance buyers go through an extended buying process as set out in figure 5–3.

Active shoppers in Stage 3 of buying an appliance are obviously ideal candidates for quality cues research, but they are difficult to qualify and expensive to find. The risk one runs in interviewing 'intenders' is that they may not be sufficiently close to their final purchase decision to exercise reliable judgments in the research setting. Nowhere is this more marked than how intenders, removed from an actual decision, deal with price.

To avoid the risk of very expensive or unreliable data, we elected to interview consumers who had just bought the appliance (recent purchasers). Recent purchasers have the merit of recent-purchase decision experience. The values that they used when making their recent purchase are likely to be fairly close to mind.

To reduce the risk of the self-congratulatory kind of answer, we used unbranded products in the research together with some unmarketed products (prototypes of new products) which the consumer would not have had to deal with before. This new information played the role of making the consumer rethink his purchase decision.

In the quality cues studies recently conducted, our purpose was to explain preference for a product, as it appears in the showroom, in terms of features and cues. For this reason, we had no option but to interview the respondent in front of real products—in a product-clinic setting.

Product clinics were set up in a market research interview facility where various products, those to be evaluated and sometimes additional ones exhibiting different features and cues, were installed in what is not unlike an appliance-showroom setting. Respondents meeting the screening criteria were invited to attend the clinics, generally for a sixty- to ninety-minute interview. Trained interviewers conducted the respondents, usually one at a time, through the clinic, administering the questionnaire as they went.

The interview covered various topics and included:

1. familiarity with and attitudes toward brands on the market.
2. record of past purchases of the appliance.
3. ratings of competitive products on benefit scales.
4. reactions to cues and features.
5. trade-off procedures for determining benefit importance weights.
6. product preferences, with open-ended probing of likes and dislikes.
7. questions related to pricing.
8. classification questions related to market and media segments.

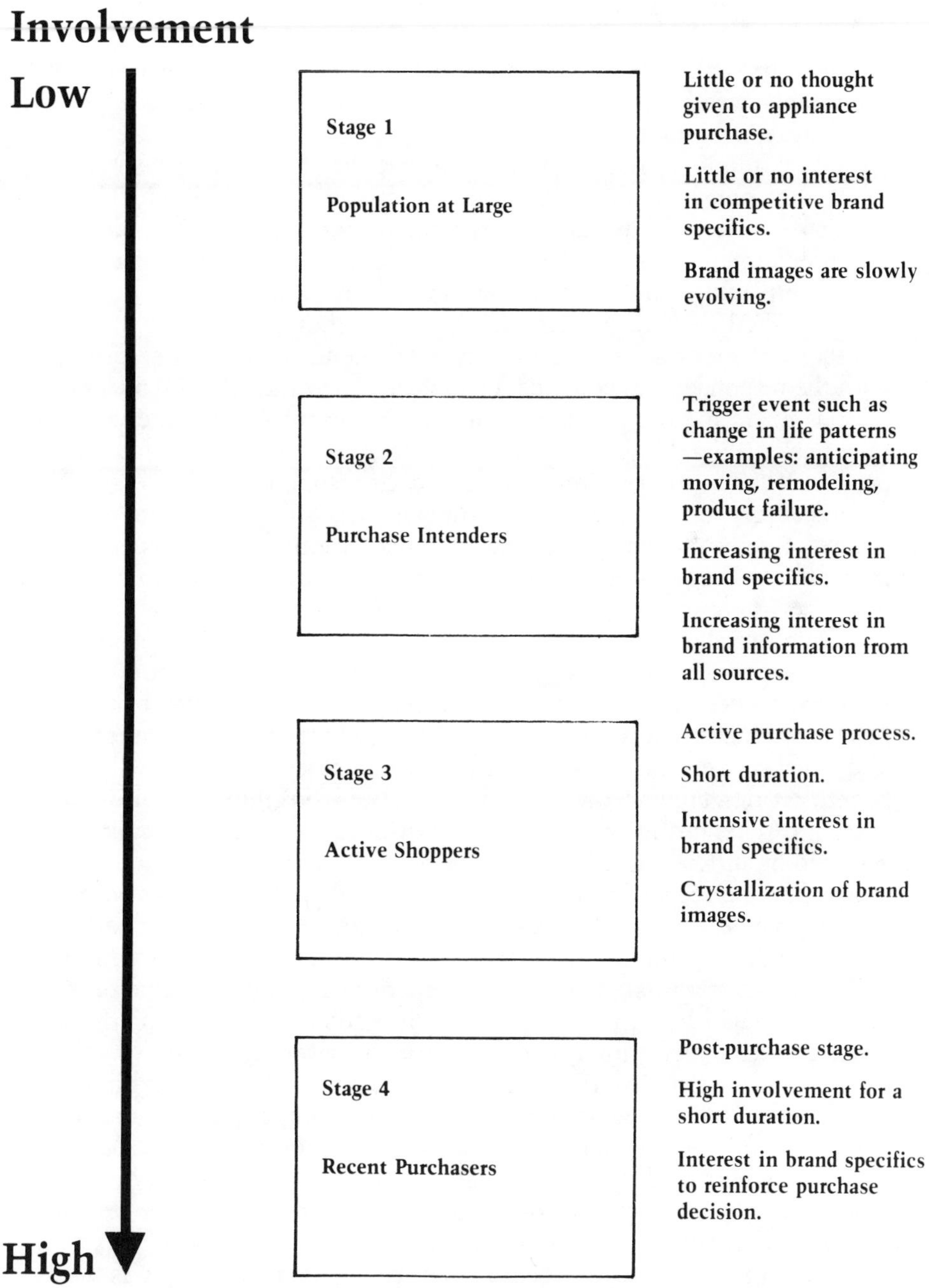

Involvement

Low

Stage 1

Population at Large

Little or no thought given to appliance purchase.

Little or no interest in competitive brand specifics.

Brand images are slowly evolving.

Stage 2

Purchase Intenders

Trigger event such as change in life patterns —examples: anticipating moving, remodeling, product failure.

Increasing interest in brand specifics.

Increasing interest in brand information from all sources.

Stage 3

Active Shoppers

Active purchase process.

Short duration.

Intensive interest in brand specifics.

Crystallization of brand images.

Stage 4

Recent Purchasers

Post-purchase stage.

High involvement for a short duration.

Interest in brand specifics to reinforce purchase decision.

High

Figure 5–3. Stages in Appliance Purchase Process

Analysis Procedures That Are Recommended

At the heart of the quality cues study was a procedure for measuring cue importance weights and explaining quality perceptions in terms of product features and cues.

Olson and Reynolds (q.v.) mention that they favor an analysis technique that maps cognitive structures from aggregated individual-level responses collected using "directed elicitation tasks . . . intended to force consumers to reveal their means-end structures." We have tried a similar procedure ourselves, but with mixed results.

We asked each respondent to first rate different products using a number of benefit scales. The interviewer then reviewed these ratings with the respondent and elicited, in an open-ended way, the respondent's reasons for rating the products as he did. For example, the interviewer might ask, "Why did you rate product X higher on 'easier to clean' than product Y?" The interviewer then probed the respondent's answers until a satisfactory explanation using the language of product cues was elicited. Such a procedure produces a compendium of product cues, rich in consumer language. However, we faced the analysis problem of how to assign importance weights to this open-ended data.

Which product cues are important determinants of the consumer's quality perceptions? How can we identify the means-ends structure—that is, product cues (means) to benefits (ends) links—the consumer uses to judge a product's quality? One method we used was simply to count the frequency of mention of each elicited cue and cross-tabulate it with the benefit ratings. However, we found the analysis too crude to identify important differences in product cues between fairly similar products we knew to be differentiated in terms of overall quality. How should one assign importance weights to this open-ended data: how can we be sure that we have captured the reasons for the consumer's quality perceptions in terms of the cues? Simple counts of frequency of mention of each cue, cross-tabulated against the benefit ratings, gives a kind of importance weight but, in our experience, it is too crude to explain differences between very similar and, hence, competitive products.

It would seem that the consumer's cognitive structure exhibits a great deal of interaction between specific product cues (means) and several different benefits (ends). Some of these links, especially the secondary ones, when held up to close inspection through the interviewer's probings may seem to be trivial or illogical; and consequently the respondent can be averse to verbalizing them.

The "missing data" can cause whatever analysis technique is used to skip over important product cues. Our experience suggests that an interview technique is needed that has every respondent give proper consideration in a controlled setting to every cue, feature, and benefit in the study.

We describe below an approach to data collection analysis that has evolved over several studies. It appears to be generally applicable and to give reliable results. This method has the following essential aspects.

Long cue lists (100 or more cues) can be treated without serious data collection penalties.

A clear distinction is made between functional benefits and product cues; each is treated differently.

The importance of benefits is determined through a full concept trade-off procedure.

The importance of cues is derived from two independent variables: (1) benefit importance; and (2) the strength of linkage or degree of association between a cue and benefit, which measures, from the consumer's point of view, the value of the cue as a means to predict delivery of a functional benefit, an end. How these linkages are determined is discussed below.

In our application of the technique, consumers responded to cues one at a time. The cues were expressed verbally or demonstrated visually as the case required. Respondents were presented with product concepts expressing different bundles of functional benefits. These are akin to the 'full concepts' used in trade-off work. (See table 5–1 for an example of such a concept.) The product concepts were expressed in benefit language which is independent of the cues. Each respondent was presented with a number of concepts reflecting an incomplete, main-effects design of the constituent benefit levels. Respondents were asked to match cues to product concepts. Aggregating the individual-level responses produced a large data matrix (cues by benefits) whose values show the degree to which a cue links to a product benefit. These values were predictive of comments respondents made during open-ended questioning. For ex-

Table 5–1
Example of a Product Concept Used in Heat Pump Quality Cues Study

Terms in which Consumers Were Completely Satisfied	*Terms in which Consumers Were Less-Than Satisfied*
How reliable it is	How long it will last
How energy efficient it is	How easy it is to service
How attractive it looks	How comfortable it keeps the
How much noise it makes	temperature in my house

ample, such comments as "because this product has glass shelves, it will be easier to clean" and "the glass shelves make me more certain that the product will be easy to clean" coincided with a relatively high value in our data matrix linking glass shelves (a cue) to 'easy to clean' (a benefit).

Next, we developed overall importance weights for each cue. Such information is important to the product planner in deciding whether the cost of a cue in manufacturing terms is justified in marketing terms. Our method for developing cue importance weights was to sum the values linking the cue to each benefit, weighted by benefit importance as derived by means of a full-concepts trade-off procedure.

Nature of Information Provided

Information provided by the research was of three kinds:

1. *Degree of linkage matrix.* This information showing links between cues and benefits is set out in table 5–2. The data shows which cues are linked to which benefits. By scanning down a column, one discovers which cues are most instrumental in communicating a particular benefit.
2. *Value of a cue.* In this analysis, we estimate the value of each cue by summing across benefits. This provides a measure of consumer importance which, when compared with the cost of the cue, gives direction for adding on or taking away specific hardware items.
3. *Brand information.* As figure 5–4 shows, Brand X is compared to its competition in terms of twenty or so specific product areas. Each product area stands for a cue, or set of cues, for which we computed importance weights as reflected on the vertical axis.

In figure 5–5 we show the result of actually changing the cues in a few selected areas to improve the brand's competitive position.

Table 5–2
Degree of Association between Selected Cues and Benefits

	Durability	*Workmanship*	*Appearance*	*Ease of Cleaning*
Glass shelves	—	minor	major	major
Porcelain lining	major	minor	—	major
Shelf trim	—	—	major	—
Door hinges	minor	major	—	—
Door panel	minor	—	major	minor
Door handles	major	minor	major	—
Portable containers	—	—	minor	—
Drawer material	major	minor	—	—

Source: Refrigerators Quality Cues Study (Disguised Data)

Competitive Position of Brand *X* (Current Product)

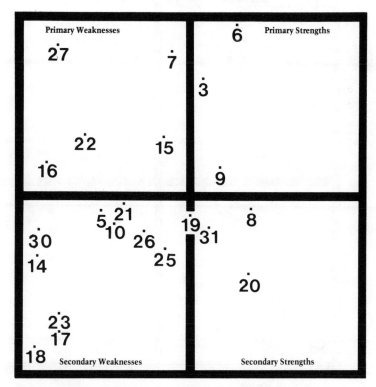

Source: GE Quality Cues Study—Ranges (Disguised Data)

Figure 5–4. Display of Selected Cues for Brand *X*

How to Validate the Research Information

We favor a method of validation using constructed product prototypes featuring some of the important cues. These prototypes are tested alongside other products. The tests are used to confirm predictions made by the quality cues research system. These predictions are of:

1. changes in specific benefit ratings (Example: The prototype will score better on 'cleaning.')

2. changes in preference and intention to buy (Example: The prototype will get a higher preference share than this other production model.)

Competitive Position of Brand *X* (improved product)

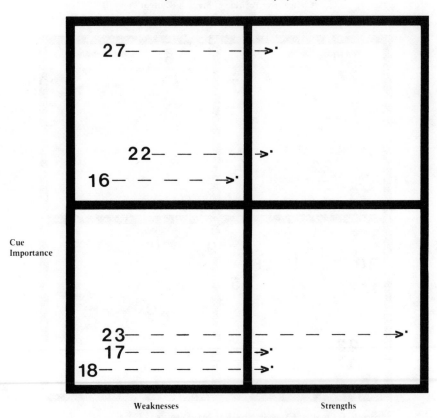

Source: GE Quality Cues Study—Ranges (Disguised Data)

Figure 5–5. Display of Selected Cues for Brand *X* Showing Changes in Perception as Result of Specific Cue Changes

Notes

1. *Product* in this chapter refers to the product itself as opposed to the brand, and is sometimes called 'model.'

2. Excerpts taken from Protocol Interview Transcript, Refrigerator Study.

3. Jerry C. Olson and Thomas J. Reynolds, "Understanding Consumers' Cognitive Structures: Implications for Advertising Strategy," *Advertising and Consumer Psychology* (1983).

4. List taken from Refrigerator Study, GE Research Files.

Part III
Retailer Perspectives on Perceived Quality

6

Adolescents' Cognitive Structures of Retail Stores and Fashion Consumption: A Means-End Chain Analysis of Quality

Jonathan Gutman and
Scott D. Alden

Consumers' perceptions of product quality are generally formed on the basis of an array of cues (Cox 1962). Most notably, these cues have included: product characteristics (Jacoby, Olson, and Haddock 1971; Pincus and Waters 1975; Szybillo and Jacoby 1972, 1974; Wheatley and Chiu 1977; Wheatley, Chiu, and Goldman 1981); price (Berkowitz and Walter 1980; French, Williams, and Chance 1972; Gardner 1971; Lambert 1972; Peterson 1970; Riesz 1978; Wheatley and Chiu 1977; and Wheatley, Chiu, and Goldman 1981); and brand and store name (Berkowitz and Walter 1980; Jacoby, Olson, and Haddock 1971; Rigaux-Bricmont 1982; Szybillo and Jacoby 1974; Venkataraman 1981; Wheatley and Chiu 1977; Wheatley, Chiu, and Goldman 1981).

These cues are often categorized as either extrinsic or intrinsic to perceived quality. Simply, intrinsic cues refer to attributes that cannot be changed or manipulated without also changing the physical characteristics of the product itself; extrinsic cues are attributes that are not part of the physical product (Olson and Jacoby 1972). Price, and brand and store image (or store name) are thus considered to be extrinsic with respect to product quality. In several multicue experiments, it has been shown that intrinsic cues, such as "taste" or "fiber," are more important to the consumer than extrinsic cues in assessing product quality (Olson and Jacoby 1972; Peterson 1970; Szybillo and Jacoby 1974; Rigaux-Bricmont 1982).

In a retail setting, Wheatley, Chiu, and Goldman (1981) have suggested that the physical quality of products is an important element of merchandising strategy. Broadly defined, they say, the product offering is widely regarded as the most important element in the marketing mix.

That the product offering is an important element of retailer strategy cannot be disputed, but there is a difference between a product offering and physical product quality. The product offering of a store includes a number of extrinsic cues (that is, brands, variety, and styles) as well as the intrinsic physical quality of the merchandise.

Additionally, if the focus of perceived quality is a retail store, the dichotomy of extrinsic versus intrinsic cues leads us into still more problem areas. In this sense, the elements of store image are all intrinsic; that is, a change in any one of these cues would be likely to change the "product," the perception of the store. Thus, it seems that there is considerable complexity in the relations among elements determining perceived quality. Variable classifications such as extrinsic and intrinsic seem to break down as their explanatory role is more closely examined.

Olson and Jacoby (1972) have noted that after a substantial amount of experimental effort, we still know very little about which product attributes, from among the many available, are chosen by the consumer as surrogate indicators of product quality; why these particular cues are chosen for use and others are not; once cues are chosen, how they are used (that is, combined) to form a quality judgment; and why the cues are combined in that manner.

Purpose

In an effort to address these issues, this chapter will explore consumers' associations relating to perceived quality. In addition to studying the attributes associated with perceived quality, the outcomes accruing to consumers from their decisions to buy particular merchandise or patronize particular stores will also be a focus. Assuming that these outcomes or consequences are instrumental in moving persons toward or away from important values (Gutman 1982), knowledge of how perceived quality impacts consumers' personal values can increase our understanding of this concept.

One of the underlying concepts relating consequences to personal values is that of knowledge structures in memory. Of direct interest, then, is ascertaining what the contents of memory are in terms of any bearing they might have on the decision-making process, particularly with respect to consequences and relevant values. It is also true that in addition to contents, aspects of structure or linkages between content elements are of concern. That is, we need to understand the basis for the linkages or associations between specific concepts—for example, the types of associations that consumers make between perceived quality and specific attributes of a product or store. By the same reasoning we need to understand the linkages between perceived quality and the positive consequences or benefits implied by those attributes. Thus, perceived quality may be positioned as the critical link between brand and store attributes and consequences and personal values important to consumers.

The goal of this chapter is to study the structural relations among attributes determining perceived quality in relation to outcomes and valued end states produced by consuming products with given levels of perceived quality. Means-end chain analysis (Gutman 1982; Reynolds and Gutman 1983) will be used to develop hierarchical structure maps that explicate these structural relations.

Means-End Chain Model

The means-end chain model posits that linkages between product attributes, consequences produced through consumption, and personal values of consumers underlie their decision-making processes. *Means* are products or services, and *ends* are personal values important to consumers. The means-end chain model seeks to explain how a person's choice of a product or service enables him or her to achieve his or her desired end states. Such a framework consists of elements that represent the major consumer processes that link personal values to behavior.

Two assumptions underlie the model: (1) all consumer actions have consequences; and (2) all consumers learn to associate particular consequences with particular actions they may take. Consumers obtain consequences from the consumption of products or services. Consequences may be desirable (benefits) or undesirable; they may stem directly from consuming or the act of consumption, or occur indirectly at a later point in time or from others' reactions to one's consumption behavior. The central aspect of the model is that consumers choose actions that produce desired consequences and minimize undesired consequences.

Personal values are beliefs people have about important aspects of themselves and the goals toward which they are striving. Personal values are the penultimate consequences of behavior for people, be they feelings of self-esteem, belonging, security, or other value orientations (see Rokeach, 1968 for a more complete listing and discussion of personal values). In this sense, personal values are part of the central core of a person. Thus, personal values as core aspects of self are held to provide consequences (*consequences* refers to the outcomes accruing to the person from behavior, such as consuming a product) with positive or negative valences. That is, personal values determine which consequences are desired by the person and which are undesirable.

Of course, because it is attributes that produce consequences, one must consider the attributes that products or services possess. Therefore, we must also make ourselves aware of attribute-consequence relations. Overall, the attribute-consequence-value interrelations are the focus of the model. Values provide the overall direction, consequences determine the selection of specific behaviors in specific situations, and attributes are what is in the actual products or services that produce the consequences. It is knowledge of this structure that permits us to examine the underlying meaning of perceived quality.

Procedures for Studying Cognitive Structure

The procedure for collecting data to reveal consumers' cognitive structures is to ask respondents to make distinctions within the competitive product or service class (Gutman 1982; Gutman and Reynolds 1979; Reynolds and Gutman 1983). A typical task involves asking respondents to verbalize the important concepts or distinctions they use to distinguish among several sets of three brands of products or service providers. Or, respondents might simply be asked why they buy a certain product or shop at a particular store. However, it is not these elements by themselves that are of primary importance (for this would be like typical qualitative research). Rather, it is the linkages among these and other elements in consumers' cognitive structure that leads to developing an understanding of the consumer's total perceptual framework.

Methodology

The product class chosen for this study is clothing. Clothing is a high-involvement purchase for most people since it is relatively costly and its visibility produces social consequences for the wearer. Additionally, because different clothing is often worn for different occasions and, for some, because of the transitive nature of fashion, clothing is likely to be a product class with which the consumer must be concerned on a reasonably regular basis.

Perceived-quality cues are likely to be differentially important to various groups of consumers in the marketplace. Adolescents have been chosen as the sample for this study because they are highly involved in the consumption of fashion goods. They are, for any of a number of reasons, highly involved in recognizing the consequences their consumption of clothing has upon their feelings of belonging and popularity.

Twenty-five respondents (thirteen men and twelve women) were interviewed singly and in-depth at The University of Southern California campus during June and July of 1983. All respondents were upper-division undergraduates in the business school and were paid $10 for their participation. They were recruited to discuss clothing acquisition and fashion interest.

As a warm-up, respondents were asked about their interest in clothing—buying clothes and keeping up-to-date with changing styles. This was followed with questions about frequency of shopping and whether or not they typically have a definite purchase intention in mind when going shopping. Next, respondents were asked whether they usually choose a particular store or stores, or select a shopping center when considering a major shopping expedition.

To identify the full set of linkages connecting means to ends, consumers were given a laddering task (Gutman and Reynolds 1979; Reynolds and Gutman, in press). The laddering procedure consists of a series of directed probes based on mentioned distinctions the individual has with respect to perceived quality or store choice. The purpose of laddering is to force the consumer up the "ladder of abstraction" to uncover the structural aspects of consumer knowledge as modeled by the means-end chain. The questioning procedure was designed around the unique demands of the laddering procedure.

As one approach to providing a basis for laddering, respondents were asked about the aspects that came to mind for a "high-quality store." Probing proceeded by asking them to explain how they could tell if a store was of high quality or not. This flow of questions was repeated for "low quality." Respondents were then asked to supply the name of clothing stores (department stores, general merchandisers, specialty stores, and so forth) in response to the following store descriptors.

1. the store I shop at most often
2. a store whose clothes I like to wear
3. a store I like but don't shop at
4. a store I used to shop at, but don't shop at any more
5. a store I don't even like to go in
6. a store that's fun to shop at
7. a store whose clothes I wouldn't like to wear

For each store name they supplied, respondents were asked what there was about this store that made it _____ (each descriptor was used to complete the question). The questions on perceived quality and the store-descriptor questions were all used as the basis for probing to uncover key attributes, consequences, and values relating to perceived quality.

An example of laddering, along with a description of the procedure used to elicit the elements should make the methodology a bit clearer.

Let us say that a respondent has told us that she prefers smaller stores to bigger stores (see figure 6–1). When asked why she has this preference, she might reply that smaller stores are more apt to have unique merchandise whereas larger stores are more apt to have more-ordinary merchandise. When asked whether she prefers unique or ordinary merchandise, our respondent says she prefers unique merchandise because it helps her express her individuality. And, when asked why she wants to express her individuality, she replies that she wants to impress other people. Finally, she says she wants to impress others because it gives her a feeling of self-esteem. Thus, what the laddering procedure tries to do is elicit a string of interrelated elements as depicted in figure 6–1. It is not only the elements, but their connections in the consumer's mind that are of importance.

The first step in analyzing the large number of ladders obtained from many respondents is to conduct a thorough content analysis of all the elicited concepts. All the attribute-level respondents are considered so that terms close in meaning can be grouped together. The goal here is to reduce the fragmentation of response that occurs when respondents are using their own language, without losing meaning by grouping elements with widely divergent meanings into the same category. This procedure is repeated at the consequence and values levels. Then, each thought or response from each subject is assigned a category code. All laddering responses are now expressed in a set of standard concepts. This aggregate set represents the content component of consumers' knowledge structures.

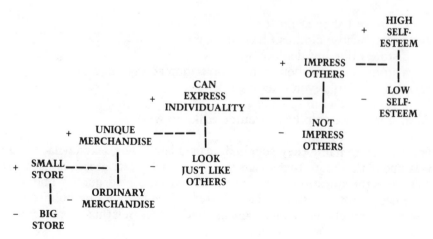

Figure 6–1. Laddering Example

What remains is to identify the linkages between the concepts—the arcs of the network model. The process begins by constructing a square matrix in which the rows and columns are denoted by the concept codes developed in the content analysis. The unit of analysis is an *adjacent* pair of concepts—a linked pair of responses from the laddering task. That is, whenever the row concept was the probe stimulus that elicited the column concept, an entry is made into that cell. Thus, the total entries in any cell of the matrix correspond to the number of times (across all subjects) that a particular concept (row) directly elicited the other concept (column). It is from this data that the overall structure map of means-end relations regarding perceived quality is determined (Olson and Reynolds 1983).

For example, the ladder shown in figure 6–1 would be coded as a vector of numbers, with each number representing the category code the element was given. Say, for purposes of example, that the coded values for the positive elements in the ladder in figure 6–1 were given numerical values as follows.

10—small store

20—unique merchandise

30—express individuality

40—impress others

50—self-esteem

For this ladder, entries would be made in the matrix in row 10, column 20 ($M[10,20]$); similar entries would be made in $M[20,30]$, $M[30,40]$, and $M[40,50]$. Similarly, entries could be made in the matrix for indirect ($M[10,30]$, $M[10,40]$, and so forth) linkages as well as the direct linkages.

Results

Any instance in which a respondent links at least two elements together in an asymmetrical fashion (*A* causes, produces, or leads to *B*) is defined as a ladder. In all, 282 ladders were elicited from the twenty-five respondents, the shortest ladder having a length of two and the longest ladder a length of ten. The typical ladder was comprised of from three to five elements, although there were many two-element ladders (that is, when a number of attributes lead to the same consequence).

Figure 6–2. Content, Analysis of Attributes, Consequences, and Values Obtained From Laddering

Attributes

service

younger salespeople
knowledgeable salespeople
helpful/attentive/not pushy/better service
personal service

brand selection

brand selection/right/popular merchandise/status merchandise fashionable
unique merchandise/exclusive/limited/careful
classic style/conservative/not faddy
good fit

store interior/display

clean/neat/well organized
roomy/uncrowded/quieter
decor/store appearance/atmosphere
layout
good displays/coordinated displays

shopper type

type of shoppers (respondent's type)/high class

well-made

well-made clothes
durable
higher priced
natural fibers

well dressed salespeople
store reputation
high quality
small store
big store

Consequences

lasts longer/stays in style/operational longer
versatile/flexible/can dress for more occasions
fun to shop/less tedious
can shop faster/quicker/saves time
not feel rushed/can take my time
relaxed/calming
more to choose from/not limited in choice
have to buy fewer clothes
saves money/spend less
can maintain a wider wardrobe
convenient
have to shop less
feel comfortable
easier to compare
money for other things
time for other things
can do more/can do better
not ignored/feel cared about
not bored/stays interesting

Figure 6–2. *(Continued)*

in touch/"with it"/hip/in style
easier to make decisions/make up mind
less conflict/safer/more secure
feel important
look good/well dressed
impress others/others think I look good/be admired/makes you better than others
easier to socialize/fit in
can express individuality/stand out
feel good about self
in-control

Values

self-confidence
self-esteem
security
belonging/affiliation/acceptance
accomplishment/success
enjoy life

Contents of Cognitive Structure

Figure 6–2 shows the list of attributes, consequences, and values obtained from respondents. As can be seen, the number of elements obtained is lengthy, with fifty elements being elicited. The figure indicates which elements have been grouped together under a single category code.

The attributes elicited relate to service, brand selection, store interior and display, shopper type, and durability. All but durability can be regarded as extrinsic; durability is an instrinsic aspect of perceived quality.

Consequences extend from the functional (longer lasting, relaxing, saves money, time for other things, and so on) to the psychosocial (feeling important, looking good, making it easier to socialize, expressing one's individuality, an so on). Values include such instrumental values as self-confidence and accomplishment, and terminal values such as self-esteem, belonging, and enjoying one's self.

Hierarchical Value Structure Map

A matrix representing the connections among elements in each respondent's means-end chains was input into a computer program to summarize the number of linkages or connections between elements. A summary matrix output from this analysis representing the frequency of connections is used to build the hierarchical map shown in figure 6–3. The advantage of means-end chain analysis lies in the presentation and subsequent ease of interpretation of complex relationships obtained from in-depth discussions across respondents.

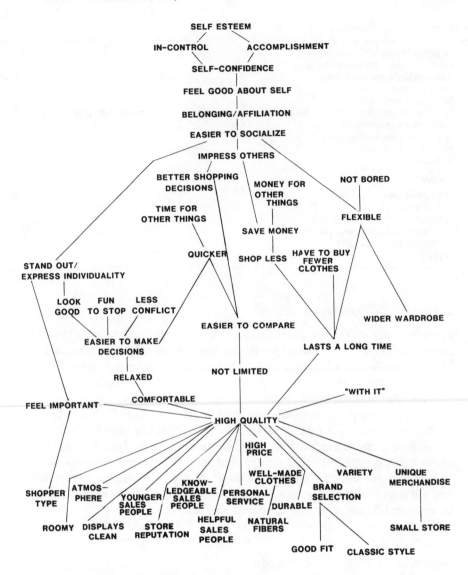

Figure 6-3. Hierarchical Value Structure Map for Perceived Quality of Clothing Fashions

The map in figure 6-3 has some very interesting characteristics. High quality is the gateway between all attributes, consequences, and values because the laddering procedure started by asking respondents what makes a store a high-quality store. This was done to ensure that "high quality" had a central place in the map. It is interesting to note, however, that for these respondents (attending a very fashion-conscious university), all consequences converge on "impress others." This suggests that the goals of these respondents are fairly uniform at this point in their lives (not unusual among adolescents in general).

Also, note that some consequences do not lead to values. Within the context of fashion, "fun to shop," "less conflict," "time for other things," "money for other things," and "not bored" are ends in themselves. That is, when probed as to why these consequences were important with respect to clothing and store choice, no further motives were elicited.

For indicating the major means-end chain embedded within the map, the patterns of relations at the consequence level can be examined. Figure 6–4 shows six major patterns of consequences. Three paths lead to "stand out." The first relates to a feeling of importance one has, the

CONSE- QUENCES / ATTRIBUTES	STAND-OUT FEEL IMPORTANT	STAND-OUT LOOK GOOD	STAND-OUT EASIER DECISIONS RELAXED COMFORTABLE	BETTER DECISIONS COMPARE	SAVE MONEY SHOP LESS LONG LASTING	FLEXIBLE LONG LASTING
SERVICE			"HELP ME OUT" MALES & FEMALES			
BRAND SELECTION	"DRESS TO IMPRESS" MALES & FEMALES	"ASSIMILATE BRAND IMAGE" MALES & FEMALES		"CREATE AN ARRAY" MALES		
STORE INTERIOR/ DISPLAYS			"GOOD FRAME OF MIND" MALES			
SHOPPER TYPE	"WHO ELSE SHOPS THERE" MALES & FEMALES					
WELL-MADE		"TOP GRADE MERCHAN- DISE" MALES			"NOT PLAYING THE GAME" MALES & FEMALES	"MORE BANG FOR THE BUCK" MALES & FEMALES

Figure 6–4. Attribute Consequence Paths from Overall Hierarchical Value Structure Map Shown by Sex

second to looking good per se, and the third relates to the shopping experience—easier decisions from being comfortable and relaxed.

The remaining patterns of consequences are of a more functional nature: better decisions from the ability to compare, saving money from buying long-lasting clothes, and the flexibility from having a wider wardrobe because the items purchased last a long time.

The attributes are shown down the side of the figure. Those of a more extrinsic nature are on top, with the intrinsic attribute "well-made" shown at the bottom. Figure 6–3 shows that many attributes lead to high quality, and that high quality leads to many consequences. However, it does not necessarily follow that all these attributes lead to all these consequences. A consideration of the extent to which each attribute eventually (based on the indirect linkages mentioned above) led to each consequence, yielded the nine interrelations shown in figure 6–4. These patterns are shown separately for men and women.

"Help Me Out." This pattern ties the attributes of good service to the higher-order consequences of looking good and standing out. The service qualities of the retail establishment (knowledgeable and helpful salespeople who give good service) make the shopper feel comfortable and relaxed. This makes it easier for the consumer to make decisions. Both men and women demonstrate this pattern. The males may have less experience or knowledge and therefore need to be set at ease. The women, facing a greater complexity of choices, may also need this support. Both men and women in this group rely in part on the approval of the salesperson, especially if the salesperson is about the shopper's own age and is well dressed.

"Dress to Impress." This pattern links brand selection—having popular brands—to feeling important and standing out. Obviously brand image, an extrinsic attribute, has a strong influence on the ability of the garment to enhance the self-concept of the wearer. Not unexpectedly, both men and women show this pattern of response.

"Assimilate Brand Image." Respondents representing this pattern are more keenly aware of the image and styling properties of the brands they buy. They are the most involved in adopting the symbolic values of the brands and making them part of their self-concepts. These people are apt to be better judges of what looks good than those respondents in the former group.

"Create an Array." In this pattern, a store's having the "right" brand selection contributes to the ability to compare and thus to making better decisions. Only men display this pattern, perhaps because they are not as knowledgeable about what to buy or what is in vogue. Thus, having an array of styles from which to choose, all in one place at one time, is a decided advantage. Women are more apt to go from store to store regardless of any single store's offering.

"Good Frame of Mind." The fact that only men display this pattern might also be related to their lack of knowledge and experience in shopping for fashion clothing. They need more external support from displays than women in order to validate their selections or because it gives them a concrete example of what they would actually look like when wearing the garments under inspection.

"Who Else Shops There." This pattern connects the type of people shopping at the retail store to the feeling of importance and resulting individuality given the respondent from association with these types of people. Having the "right" shoppers in a store, in effect, validates the successful communication value of brand image. Both men and women display this pattern.

"Top-Grade Merchandise." This pattern relates the quality of the merchandise (well made—durable, natural fibers) directly to looking good and standing out. As men, but not women, display this pattern it may be that males in this age group have a longer time horizon for the active life of the garment. Some males' clothing choices may be less subject to short-term fashion considerations (that is, suits), and thus suitable for use over longer periods of time. It may also be a reflection of their use of businessmen as role models and their perceptions of the qualities of business attire. Also, as women's fashions change faster, buying durable items means they are often out of fashion before they are worn out.

"Not Playing the Game." By not playing the game, reference is being made to not reacting to changing styles with continuous purchases of new apparel items. Several respondents (men and women) reacted negatively to fashion pressures resulting from rapid change. Obviously, it takes resources to keep up with fashion, and these respondents are deliberately not keeping up.

"More Bang for the Buck." This pattern reflects a more functional orientation toward staying in fashion. Here, well-made clothes are linked to long-lasting clothes. This gives the wearer added flexibility from having a wider wardrobe. Thus, these respondents can vary the outfits they wear without continuously buying new outfits.

Summary and Applications

This chapter has demonstrated the viability of means-end chain analysis for gaining an understanding of the meanings of perceived quality. The meanings have been elaborated in terms of the attributes implying perceived quality and the consequences and values stemming from perceived quality. En route to this objective, the feasiblity of developing consumer segments for fashion consumers through means-end chain analysis has also been demonstrated.

While the level of effort in gathering data and in analysis for this study has been high, the sample size is too limited to provide for stability in the assessment of segments. A sample size of fifty or larger (depending on the demongraphic breaks built into the sample) is acceptable for this type of research. With a larger sample size it would be possible to construct separate maps for men and women or other sample characteristics such as age, socioeconomic status, geographic location, retail store preference, and so forth. Although this larger-size sample may still not seem to represent a sufficient sample size in the eyes of many researchers or managers, past research for advertising agencies, product manufacturers, and those in various service industries has indicated that there are not that many unique orientations when one examines connections at the consequence-values level. Procedures are available for taking the results from studies such as these and applying them to samples of a much larger size. For example, the perceptual orientations from the overall map in figure 6–3 may be written in the form of scenarios that can be used to obtain self-assessments from respondents.

Using the hierarchical value structure maps constructed through the laddering procedure, it is possible to uncover perceptual orientations that can serve as the basis for segmenting customers based on key characteristics of shopper orientations. Therefore, these segments should be homogeneous with respect to important aspects of retail marketing strategy—store layout and merchandise presentation, brand selection, and advertising strategy (image creation).

These findings show the importance of merchandising strategy in the creation and maintenance of a quality image. This is not to say, of course, that inherent product quality is not also important, but rather that consumers tend to develop their sense of a store's quality from many more of the controllable aspects of store layout and ambience, variety and selection of merchandise, and sales personnel.

With respect to advertising strategy, a model (Olson and Reynolds 1983; Reynolds and Gutman 1983; Gutman 1983) has been developed to translate the structure uncovered in the hierarchical maps directly into advertising strategies that address key connections between attributes, consequences, and values. Furthermore, this can be done for different segments that may be revealed in the analysis. Once this has been done, overall strategies with maximum appeal across segments can be chosen (see Reynolds, Gutman, and Fiedler, in press).

References

Berkowitz, E.N. and J.R. Walter (1980), "Contextual Influences on Consumer Price Responses: An Experimental Analysis," *Journal of Marketing Research* 17 (August):349–58.

Cox, D.F. (1962), "The Measurement of Information Value: A Study in Consumer Decision Making," in *Emerging Concepts in Marketing*, W.S. Decker, ed., Chicago: American Marketing Association, 413–21.

French, N.D., J.J. Williams, and W.A. Chance (1972), "A Shopping Experiment on Price-Quality Relationships," *Journal of Retailing* 48 (Fall):3–16.

Gardner, D.M. (1971), "Is There a Generalized Price-Quality Relationship?" *Journal of Marketing Research* 8 (May):241–43.

Gutman, J. (1982), "A Means-End Chain Model Based on Consumer Categorization Processes," *Journal of Marketing* 46 (Spring):60–72.

_____ (1983), "Segment Consumers, Devise Ad Strategies with Means-End Chain Analysis, 'Ladders'," *Marketing News*, Chicago: American Marketing Association (May 13), 6–7.

_____ and T.J. Reynolds (1979), "An Investigation of the Levels of Cognitive Abstraction Utilized by Consumers in Product Differentiation," in *Attitude Research Under the Sun*, J. Eighmey, ed., Chicago: American Marketing Association, 128–50.

Jacoby, J., J.C. Olson, and R.A. Haddock (1971), "Price, Brand Name, and Product Composition Characteristics as Determinants of Perceived Quality," *Journal of Applied Psychology* 55 (December):570–79.

Lambert, Z.V. (1972), "Price and Choice Behavior," *Journal of Marketing Research* 9 (May):35–40.

Olson, J. and J. Jacoby (1972), "Cue Utilization in the Quality Perception Process," *Proceedings*, 3, M. Venkatesan, ed., Iowa City, Iowa: Association for Consumer Research, 167–79.

_____ and T.J. Reynolds (1983), "Understanding Consumers' Cognitive Structures: Implications for Advertising Strategy," in *Advertising and Consumer Psychology*, L. Percy and A. Woodside, eds., Lexington, Mass: Lexington Books, D.C. Heath, 77–91.

Peterson, R.A. (1970), "The Price-Perceived Quality Relationship: Experimental Evidence," *Journal of Marketing Research* 7 (November):525–28.

Pincus, S. and L.K. Waters (1975), "Product Quality Ratings as a Function of Availability of Intrinsic Product Cues and Price Information," *Journal of Applied Psychology* 60:280–82.

Reynolds, T.J. and J. Gutman (1983), "Developing Images for Services through Means-End Chain Analysis," in *Emerging Perspectives on Service Marketing,*

L.L. Berry, G.L. Shostack, and G.D. Upah, eds., Chicago: American Marketing Association, 40–44.

_____ and _____ (in press), "Laddering: Extending the Repertory Grid Methodology to Construct Attribute-Consequence-Value Hierarchies," in *Personal Values and Consumer Psychology*, R.E. Pitts and A.G. Woodside, eds., Lexington, Mass: Lexington Books, D.C. Heath.

_____ , _____ , and J. Fiedler (in press), "Translating Knowledge of Consumers' Cognitive Structures into the Development of Advertising Strategic Options: A Case History," in *Proceedings: Second Annual Advertising and Consumer Psychology Conference.*

Riesz, P.C. (1978), "Price versus Quality in the Marketplace, 1961–1975," *Journal of Retailing* 54 (Winter):15–28.

Rigaux-Bricmont, B. (1982), "Influence of Brand Name and Packaging on Perceived Quality," in *Advances in Consumer Research* vol. 9, A. Mitchell, ed., Ann Arbor: Association for Consumer Research, 472–77.

Rokeach, Milton J. (1968), *Beliefs, Attitudes and Values*, San Francisco: Jossey Bass.

Szybillo, G.J. and J. Jacoby (1972), "The Relative Effects of Price, Store Image, and Composition Differences on Product Evaluation," in *Proceedings*, vol. 3, M. Venkatesan, ed., Iowa City, Iowa: Association for Consumer Research, 180–86.

_____ and _____ (1974), "Intrinsic versus Extrinsic Cues as Determinants of Perceived Product Quality," *Journal of Applied Psychology* 59:74–78.

Venkataraman, V. (1981), "Price-Quality Relationship in an Experimental Setting," *Journal of Advertising Research* 21 (August):49–52.

Wheatley, J.J. and J.S.Y. Chiu (1977), "Effects of Price, Store Image, and Product Respondent Characteristics on Perceptions of Quality," *Journal of Marketing Research* 14 (May):181–86.

_____ , _____ , and A. Goldman (1981), "Physical Quality, Price, and Perceptions of Product Quality: Implications for Retailers," *Journal of Retailing* 57 (Summer):100–106.

7
Image Representations: An Analytic Framework

Thomas J. Reynolds and
Linda F. Jamieson

After conducting a review of the literature on retail store image, Peterson and Kerin (1983, p. 300) concluded that: (1) not very much is actually known about retail store image, (2) there is an apparent lack of programmatic research, (3) critical managerial questions have yet to be answered, such as: "Are the correct image dimensions being analyzed and are the measurement procedures valid?" and more basically, "Assuming that a reasonably comprehensive set of store image dimensions can be operationally defined and measured, what is the relative importance of the various image dimensions in influencing store choice and shopping behavior?", and (4) the causal link between store image and patronage behavior is weak at best.

To paraphrase, we are not exactly sure what image is, therefore we cannot operationalize it. And we are not sure what relationship it has to perception or to behavior. The goal herein is to get a better handle on the concept of image; in particular, on its measurement and assessment in the real business environment. To begin as generally as possible, we need to develop a consensus on the definition of image. Stated simply, image might be defined as the set of meanings or associations with respect to a particular product or product class that a person has stored in memory. Even though we may feel comfortable in general with the concept of image in the context of stored meanings, a problem arises when we consider operationalization. For example, when we want to ascertain the image of a particular product or service, especially with respect to its competitors, how do we attempt to measure cognitive associations? To do that we need to identify the key descriptors or cues and then ascertain how the various cues are organized and how important each cue is to an individual consumer. In sum, we need to know how to determine the content and structure of the cognitive information upon which consumer perceptions and, ultimately, decisions are based. It is the purpose of this chapter to provide the framework, both theoretically and operationally, that will serve to address these fundamental issues.

To provide the necessary background for positioning this new image perspective, three research areas need to be reviewed. First, the various directions taken by previous researchers will be detailed. The dominant application in the image literature is to retail stores, which will provide the focus of this chapter. Second, the concept of *perceived quality*, defined here as product-class-specific translation of image, will also be presented. Finally, the basis for the theoretical framework in which the general image research paradigm will be developed—the means-end framework (Gutman 1982)—will also be reviewed.

After the summarization of past research efforts, a new operationalization of image will be proposed, based on an extension of means-end theory and research methodology. Additionally, application of recently developed research methods that afford a further understanding of image with respect to the two basic processes of perception and preference will be investigated in a small-scale experiment.

Background

The notion of image in the consumer-research domain most commonly has been defined as a plethora of general characteristics, feelings, and other impressions associated with a product or product class (Jain and Etgar 1976). The reduction of numerous valenced perceptions into a single association construct (image) may be viewed, at least on a surface level, as a cognitive function directed toward reducing the amount of information needed to classify an object. Lindquist (1974) and Marks (1976) reinforce this position by describing image as the result of summarizing many perceptions into a more cognitively manageable form. Assuming that this rationale as to the "why" of image is reasonable, then the translation of image into an operational framework becomes the primary issue.

Although the belief that image is the network of cognitive associations (and their respective valences) that serve to give meaning to a particular product is widely held among researchers, the operationalization of this perspective has taken many directions. For example, image has taken form as: an object's personality (Arons 1961; Martineau 1958); the evaluation of personal advantages and disadvantages associated with a product (Hudson 1974); the linking of factual characteristics and emotional associations relevant to a product (Oxenfeldt 1974); the expected reinforcement a person associates with a particular store (Kunkel and

Berry 1968); and consumers' subjective attitudes toward the functioning business entity (Walters 1978).

Common to virtually all of the ways to operationalize and subsequently assess image is the decomposition into component dimensions, thereby providing a framework for quantifying and understanding perceptual differences. This approach is reviewed in the retail store category by Berkowitz, Deutscher, and Hansen (1978). They note that the number of possible dimensions has included: quality of merchandise, service, price, assortment and variety, locational convenience, clientele, merchandise style, advertising and promotion, credit or billing policies, layout and atmospherics, merchandise display, and exchange and adjustment policies.

Unfortunately, a mere detailing of what are, in effect, attribute descriptors of stores falls short of gaining an understanding of the underlying reasons for their importance to consumers. There may be many reasons for considering the importance and subsequent evaluation of an apparently straightforward concept such as service. For example, consumer *A* may view service as something that is inherently part of the product and its purchase price, particularly in the case where identical goods are offered at various prices in the close physical proximity of a shopping mall. In this case, service justifies the marginal difference in price because it, like the product, satisfies the consumer. Alternatively, service could be considered important to consumer *B* simply because it "saves time." In this case, it could be that the consumer wants to avoid what he or she considers an unpleasant experience. Consumer *C*, however, may see in service some informational value. For that person the benefit may be translated into either time (minimizing the necessity for search) or money (the store bearing some greater portion of the cost, in some sense, of the transaction). Clearly, it is not only the case that a single attribute may be interpreted in more than one way, but also that different attributes may provide essentially the same meaning. Further, if the meanings provide the basis for defining image, we are probably misleading ourselves when we focus solely on the attributes themselves.

The foregoing implies that we not only need to identify the meanings that serve as the bases for conceptualizing image, but to understand as well the structure of the meanings, defined by the network of their associations. Put simply, we cannot understand image without knowing what meanings the consumer is ascribing to the product attributes; moreover, we cannot understand image without knowing the network of links that translate or connect relevant concepts, thereby providing meaning.

Meaning, then, may be seen to have two major components. The first is the series of associations, connections, or links that join one piece of information to another. The other is the resultant substantive interpretation, given to the larger structure comprised of several pieces of information, drawn from their connections. The former refers to a process of association. The latter refers to the content of the interpretation. Thus, if meaning is the fundamental component of image, two subparts need to be identified: (1) the structural part, representing the associational process, and (2) the content part, providing the substance of the interpretation.

In the retail environment, research in the highly image-based area of perceived quality also suggests that consumers differ in their use, comprehension, and judgments of quality cues. Olson and Jacoby (1977) suggest that while some people may perceive quality as pertaining to economic value received, others may link it to a level of physical or socially related benefits expected. Etgar and Malhotra (1978, p. 218) suggest that "each cue may have a better predictive content for one quality facet than for another; thus while price may be (or viewed as) a better predictor of durability, intrinsic measures may be viewed as better predictors of physical performance."

Also, the fact that a consumer might link price, for instance, with quality does not mean that purchase or store-patronage behavior will be influenced to the same degree. For example, Wheatley and Chiu (1977) feel that higher prices might have a tendency to repel persons with limited resources as well as to attract because of their apparent quality implications. Here again it seems that the interpretations that consumers give to a specific attribute can be significantly different. Therefore, to understand perceived quality one needs to know what meaning the consumer is giving to specific attributes of the store or product and the additional associations or linkages that connect relevant concepts.

From an operational perspective, the requirements for investigating image have been summarized by Reynolds (1982) as: (1) an analytic frame at the individual level; (2) a research format that draws on the consumer's own language; (3) an analysis permitting content classification by some version of the means-end perspective (that is, attributes, consequences, and values); (4) a method of recovering the structural associations or linkages between content elements; (5) a way in which products, or in this case retail stores, can be rated or positioned against the levels; and (6) a method of identifying the importance of the various levels in influencing a consumer's perceptual and preference differences across stores.

The basic problems and considerations of image research have been touched upon, and now a framework for interpreting the research problem from a theoretical perspective is required. The research to be outlined here corresponds quite closely to an earlier direction of image research. Weale (1961) and Beardon (1977) personalize the image process by positing that the image of a store is developed by comparison to one's self-image. This suggests that the salience of evaluative attributes is determined by their association to personal descriptors that can be applied to the person. This point of view is expanded by Berry (1969), again relative to store image, where he suggests that the development of image is related to one's personal values. This, of course, corresponds to a means-end orientation where values serve as the control determinant of belief systems (Howard 1977, p. 92).

Means-End Chain Model

Theoretical Framework

In terms of identifying the elements involved in the cognitive process, Howard (1977, p. 50) suggests "choice criteria" as the basis for internal classifications that help to identify objects that satisfy the needs embodied in values and presumably benefits. Basic to the existence of choice criteria are the fundamental tasks of grouping and distinguishing, which permit consumers to extrapolate to the unknown. Howard (1977, p. 28) defines choice criteria as:

> . . . mental counterparts of the attributes [by] which a consumer judges a brand. More specifically, they are a cognitive state of the buyer, which reflects those attributes of the brand that are salient in the buyer's evaluation of a brand and that are related to motives relevant for this product class, in the sense that brands in the product class have the potential for satisfying those motives. . . . It is essential to distinguish between the attributes per se and consumers' perceptions of these attributes, because consumers differ in their perceptions. It is the perception that effects behavior, not the attribute itself. 'Attribute' is often used to mean choice criteria, but this leads to confusion. To use 'attribute,' when you mean not the attribute itself but the consumer's mental image of it, is to reify what is in the consumer's mind.

The means-end chain is a concept relating values important to the consumer with attributes contained in products. It suggests that choice criteria are perceptual in nature and keyed to directing attention to objects that will often, but not always, satisfy the consumer's values. Gutman (1982) further expanded the theory underlying the means-end chain as the connection between product attributes, consumer consequences, and personal values.

Also embodied in the means-end chain model is the concept of *levels of abstraction* (Gutman and Reynolds 1979). Through this concept a consumer's perceptions and evaluations of stimuli can be studied at different levels in the chain (see Olson and Reynolds, 1983, for a review of the various conceptualizations of the means-end chain). Figure 7–1 portrays the model we have adopted in this chapter. These representations are hierarchically ordered from lower to higher levels of abstraction.

Attributes are features or aspects of products, services, or certain retail stores. Attributes that are relatively direct reflections of physical characteristics of the product or store (for example, color or size) may be considered concrete or of low abstraction; whereas reference to such attribute distinctions as "styling" or "pleasant atmosphere" are more subjective or abstract in nature (Olson and Reynolds 1983).

Consequences accrue to people from consuming products, using services, or patronizing certain stores. They may be desirable (benefits) or undesirable. A functional consequence would include such things as "saves me money," "less hassle," and "easier to locate items." A psychosocial level appears as a transition step to the values—that is, "I look

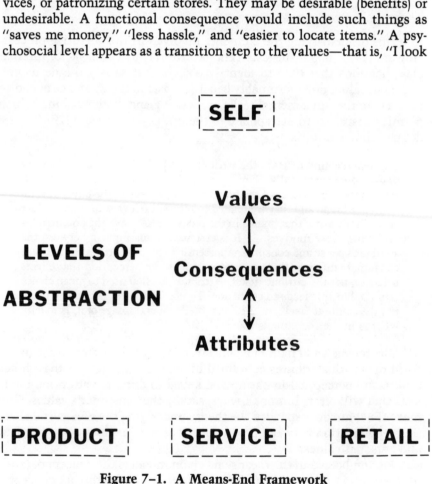

Figure 7–1. A Means-End Framework

better" from "I'm more relaxed" (Reynolds 1982). Gutman (1982, p. 61) also notes that "benefits differ from attributes in that people receive benefits whereas products have attributes." *Benefits* as used here refers to positive consequences.

Terminal and instrumental values are defined within the context of Rokeach's (1973) theory of values. *Terminal values* are defined as the end states of existence toward which people strive (for example, comfortable life, world at peace, happiness, pleasure, wisdom). *Instrumental values* are defined to be more closely tied to "doing" than to the "being" of terminal values. In terms of the means-end chain, terminal values represent the goals toward which one strives.

This structure of linking attributes, consequences, and values provides information on how associational networks are formed and can therefore be used as the fundamental unit of analysis in understanding consumers' perceptions or images.

Methodology

To operationalize image as a research framework presents the researcher with many problems, all centering around the fact that what is needed—the relation of choice criteria to salient values—is clearly personal in nature thereby ruling out a standard questionnaire approach. This problem is further compounded by the realization that attributes do not readily translate into choice criteria. That is, those classifications used as cognitive reference points within the mind cannot be assumed to be identical across individuals. Thus, if research is to be done in this area, what is required is a methodology that directly taps a single individual's choice criteria and then attempts to make the necessary links to values.

To discover consumers' values and their relation to benefits and attributes, some method is needed to force consumers to think in value-related terms about their choices. Gutman and Reynolds (1979) in proposing a technique that combines the triadic sorting procedure associated with the Repertory Grid (Kelly 1955) with a value-linking technique, termed *laddering*, offer such a methodology.

The procedure for gathering data to reveal consumers' cognitive structure, or how they might think of things, is to give respondents simple sorting tasks that permit them to activate the choice criteria or distinctions they use to think about and classify the stimuli (in this case, stores). Typically, subjects are required to specify the bases of the differences or distinctions they perceive between and across the set of stores. To identify the full set of linkages connecting means to ends, consumers are given a laddering task. Laddering consists of a series of directed probes based on mentioned distinctions the individual has with respect to the various stores. The purpose of laddering is to force the consumer up the "ladder of abstraction"—that is, to uncover the structural aspects of consumer knowledge as modeled by the means-end chain.

The individual means-end chains can also be used to create an aggregate composite of these relations. This hierarchical value map (HVM) shows the key elements (attributes, consequences, and values) and their connections. Each distinct pathway can be interpreted as a perceptual orientation or segment.

Research Issues

In the application of this means-end framework and laddering methodology the three following implicit assumptions have been made.

1. *Laddering.* Consumers can and will tell the interviewer the higher-level abstractions that underlie perception and that are the bases for preference. Higher levels should contribute significantly to explaining preference when compared to the contribution of the attribute level.

2. *Analysis.* Aggregation of individual ladders, resulting in a hierarchical representation (the HVM), reflects the dominant orientations that define some combination of the perceptual and preference segments. Which and to what degree each domain, perception, or preference is represented is of issue.

3. *Interpretation.* The hierarchical representation of the means-end chain suggests the relatively increased importance of the higher levels reflecting image differences. Further, these representations should differ significantly for high- and low-image stores.

The major highly interrelated questions that arise with respect to the methodology in establishing the framework for image representations would include:

1. Are the higher levels uncovered by laddering and subsequent analysis real or merely an artifact of the methodology?
2. How do the higher levels of abstraction relate to understanding perceptual and preference differences among, in this case, low- or high-image retail stores?
3. To what degree is the HVM representative of either perceptual or preference segments?

We will attempt to answer each of these issues in our analysis.

Research Design

Sample

Individual interviews of both males and females lasting approximately two hours were conducted with a convenience sample of twenty students, aged 20 to 39, attending a university located in a major southwestern city. To be eligible to participate in the interview all respondents had to be familiar with (that is, have heard about or have opinions about but not necessarily have had to visit or shop at) all the sixteen stores listed in table 7–1. During the analysis four respondents were dropped because of inconsistencies discovered in validity checks of their responses.

Instrument

The research instrument consisted of several sections. After a brief warm-up, basically covering the respondent's shopping habits and reasons for shopping in any of the sixteen stores, each respondent was asked to give preference ratings (using a 0 to 10 scale) for all the stores. The respondent was then asked how many times in a typical year he or she might go to each of the stores. The interview continued using only those low- or high-image stores (of the predetermined groups) that had the highest total number of annual visits for that respondent.

The next step required the respondent to evaluate all twenty-eight pairs of the eight stores with respect to their overall perceived similarity. Two steps were required for the sorting task. The respondent first sorted the pairs into four piles—"very similar," "similar," "a little different," or "completely different." The pairs within each pile were then rank

Table 7–1
Listing of Store Stimuli by Predesignated Image Grouping

Low Image	High Image
K-Mart	Neiman Marcus
Target	Sakowitz
Woolworth	Marshall Field's
Marshall's	Dillard's
JC Penney	Joske's
Montgomery Ward	Lord and Taylor
Walmart	Sanger Harris
Sears	Saks Fifth Avenue

ordered, most similar to least, resulting in a complete rank order for the twenty-eight pairs.

Next, various methods were used to elicit the distinctions that each respondent used to differentiate among the stores. These included: (1) reasons for a store being their "most" or "least" favorite; (2) ideas or mental pictures that come to mind for a high-quality store; (3) reasons for differences between preference and usage ratings; and (4) triadic sorting (Kelly 1955). These distinctions were then used as a basis for laddering (Gutman and Reynolds 1979).

After the laddering procedure was completed, the ladders were rated for their overall importance to the respondent in terms of choosing a store. In this step, the interviewer summarized the four to five ladders elicited, then asked the respondent to choose the two that were most characteristic of his or her general shopping behavior. The respondent was then asked to sort the eight stores in terms of their possession of or their ability to satisfy each of the two sets of attribute, consequence, and value elements corresponding to his or her two chosen ladders. Also, an importance rating (using a 1 to 7 scale) was obtained for each of the six elements with respect to how important that element is in terms of determining each respondent's choice behavior.

The last procedure was a pairwise preference sort to identify fine differences among the stores. Respondents were asked to array the twenty-eight pairs of stores in terms of the relative difference in preference between each pair. The four initial sorting piles were labeled "the pair is equally preferred," "prefer one slightly to the other," "prefer one substantially to the other," and "no comparison—one is clearly preferred." As in the previous similarity/dissimilarity pairwise comparison, a complete rank order of the relative differences was obtained using a two-step sort. This task resulted in a complete order of the pairs with respect to differences in preference, where the first sort yielded an order for overall similarity.

Analysis and Results

Cognitive Differentiation Analysis (CDA)

This analytical technique (Reynolds 1983), based only on ordinal assumptions, was utilized to assess the discrimination power of each individual's descriptors (attributes, consequences, and values) with respect to perceptual distances and preference differences obtained in the pairwise sorting tasks. An index, ranging from -1 to $+1$, is provided as part of the output. This index reflects to what degree each attribute, consequence, and value element accounts for the discrimination judgments—perceptual distances or preference differences—between the respective stores.

An overall index was also obtained for each ladder. This overall attribute-consequence-value (A/C/V) index is analogous to a multiple-correlation coefficient in terms of the ability of the three elements taken in combination (that is, equally weighted) to predict either the perceptual distances or preference discriminations.

CDA Results

The first issue to be addressed was whether or not the respondents could identify the "most characteristic" ladder underlying their preferences. Figure 7–2 relates the ability of each person to assess which of his or her two ladders discriminates most effectively. The "best" criterion was the highest overall A/C/V index for the ladder as a whole.

With the two ladders generated by each respondent, the expected value by chance for correct identification would be 50 percent. In the low-image group the respondents were correct 66.7 percent of the time. In the high-image group they were only correct 28.5 percent of the time. Substantial failure in the high-image group clearly suggests the importance of using a procedure that yields the type of index that determines the respondent's true underlying perspective of the category. Moreover, the significant difference between the low- and high-image groups suggests that people are probably not in touch with their true motivations when choosing among the latter group. We therefore continued our analysis using only those ladders the overall CDA index identified as "best."

Next we will review the contribution level of the individual attributes, consequences, and values in terms of their importance as a basis for similarity and preference judgments. This level of contribution will be represented by a CDA index. The results will be presented here in two ways: first, at the individual level, where we will look at the results of a representative respondent from each of the two store-image groups; and second, on an aggregate basis.

Figure 7–3 shows our representation of the results for respondent 13 for the low-image-store category. The horizontal axis represents the three main elements in her "best" ladder. Moving from left to right, we have the initial distinction or attribute, "lower prices," followed by the consequence determined in the ensuing laddering process, "good value for my money," and finally the resulting value, "live better." The vertical axis represents the corresponding CDA index values that express to what degree the element accounts for differences in preference or overall similarity (perception).

LOW IMAGE:

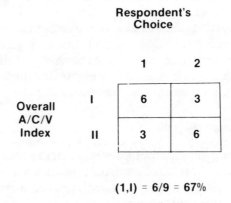

Respondent's
Choice

		1	2
Overall A/C/V Index	I	6	3
	II	3	6

(1,I) = 6/9 = 67%

HIGH IMAGE:

		1	2
	I	2	5
	II	5	2

(1,I) = 2/7 = 28.5%

Figure 7–2. Percentage of Correct Identification by Respondents of "Best" Ladder as Determined by Overall A/C/V Index

In the case of perceived similarity, we observe that for this individual the attribute level "low prices" is dominant. In other words, a majority of the similarity/dissimilarity judgments of the stores made by this individual in her sorting task are based on the attribute of price. However, in the case of preference, the value "live better" has the highest rated index. Therefore, we can say that the value element accounts most for the differences in preferences this individual has among the low-image stores; but, it is true that the value level contributes only slightly more than the attribute level.

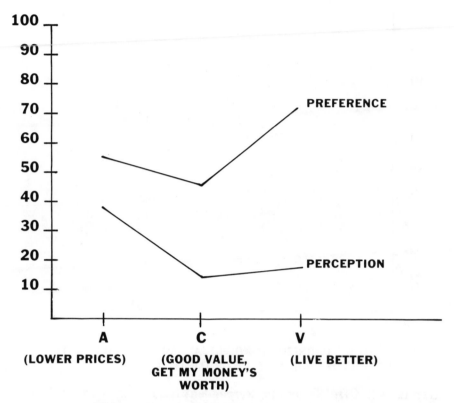

Figure 7–3. CDA Results for Respondent No. 13's "Best Ladder" (Low-Image Stores)

Also very noticeable is the fact that across the content levels there is a higher degree of association between preference and the ratings of the stores on the elements of attribute, consequence, and value, than there is between psychological distance and these same content areas.

The results for respondent (figure 7–4) in the high-image-store category are even more dramatic. The basis for preference discrimination is clearly at the value level. This individual prefers those stores that serve to enhance her own self-esteem, although the conscious level of distinguishing the stores is thought to be on the attribute level—"one-of-a-kind clothes." This value or image can be tapped through the linking elements that "clothes carried are one-of-a-kind" which allows her to dress in such a manner that she "stands out." Moreover, we also note that at a much lower power the attribute level again best explains perceptual distances. Thus, perception operates at a relatively low level,

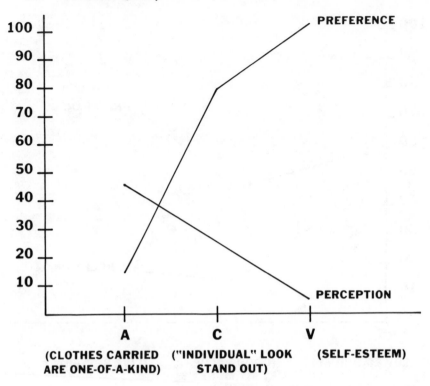

Figure 7-4. CDA Results for Respondent No. 2's "Best Ladder" (High-Image Stores)

while preference appears to be governed by higher levels of abstraction, namely, the values level.

Aggregate results are shown in table 7-2 and table 7-3, along with the overall mean values for each element by store grouping. These results can best be summarized by looking at an aggregate picture (figure 7-5) similar to those for the two individuals. In general, the bases for perceptual differences appear to operate at the attribute level for stores in both groups. With respect to the low-image stores we can see that this element contributes, on average, significantly more than the consequence element or the value element. Importantly, it is also seen that the average association between preference and the element levels becomes stronger as we move up the hierarchical content structure or levels of abstraction. For the low-image stores, the values-level interpretation or meaning contributes slightly more than the attribute level. For the high-image stores, however, the values level contributes substantially to preference discriminations.

Table 7–2
CDA Index for Attribute, Consequence, and Value Corresponding to Best Ladder with Respect to Preference—Low-Image Stores

Respondent	Preference			Distance		
	A_1	C_1	V_1	A_1	C_1	V_1
11	.63	.42	.57	-.08	-.16	-.10
12	.71	.52	.79	.70	.23	.36
13	.53	.42	.71	.38	.10	.13
14	.75	.84	.66	.87	.86	.46
15	-.02	.27	.70	.33	-.13	.11
16	.86	.42	.86	.88	.32	.78
17	.23	.66	.42	.63	.40	.63
18	.13	.22	.18	.01	-.53	-.34
19	.68	.47	.68	.60	.56	.61
Mean Values	.50	.471	.619	.48	.183	.293

Table 7-3
Best Ladder with Respect to Preference—High-Image Stores

Respondent	Preference			Distance		
	A_1	C_1	V_1	A_1	C_1	V_1
2	.11	.77	.97	.41	.21	.02
8	.56	-.19	.66	.27	.27	.30
6	.70	.44	.27	.70	.41	.14
9	.52	.65	.92	.68	.79	.89
10	.57	.77	.12	-.08	.32	.60
5	.10	.03	.78	.01	.38	.18
4	.11	.77	.97	.90	.18	.13
Mean Values	.381	.463	.670	.413	.366	.322

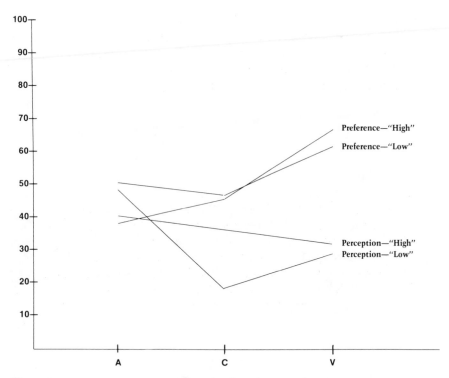

Figure 7–5. Aggregate CDA Results by Element for the High- and Low-Image Groups

This data suggests that appeals to the values that are linked to the product distinctions are stronger than appeals based on attribute distinctions alone. Clearly the higher levels uncovered by the laddering process do provide insight into the bases of preference as is seen in the case for high-image stores. In addition, conventional wisdom would also say that these stores are more closely tied to "self."

Given these results, one might question many of the marketing studies utilizing multidimensional scaling, particularly if a high-image product class is being investigated. Since similarity measures appear to be attribute based, the resulting maps may be misleading if interpretations are made with respect to preference.

Importance Ratings

Figure 7–6 shows the average importance ratings given by the respondents to the elements in their "best" ladder. In effect, these ratings rep-

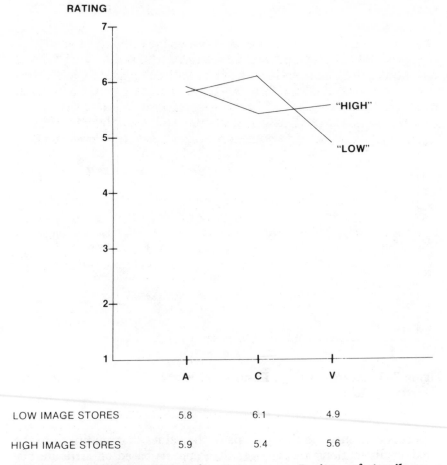

	A	C	V
LOW IMAGE STORES	5.8	6.1	4.9
HIGH IMAGE STORES	5.9	5.4	5.6

Figure 7–6. Aggregate Means for Importance Ratings of Attributes, Consequences, and Values

resent what people tell us is important in a traditional format. In examining these mean levels it is noticed that they all seem to cluster between the five and six rating level, which might indicate that many respondents did not consider each element as distinct from the other when giving their rating scores.

However, a pattern does seem to exist. For both store groups, the average importance rating of the attribute element is higher than the corresponding rating for the somewhat more abstract value element. This suggests that respondents are oriented to the attribute level when asked to assess importance. Recalling the previous results—that value elements on the whole discriminate best with respect to preference—we might therefore conclude that importance ratings are not an accurate or true measure of the actual ability of the element to explain preference. At best, they are questionable.

Since consumers cannot properly assign weights across content categories, this would seem to eliminate the important higher levels of abstraction from inclusion in the traditional attitude models. One might therefore question the usefulness of these models and other research techniques which assume that the content levels are appropriate and that the ratings reflect a true state of affairs.

Hierarchical Value Maps

Having identified the cognitive structures that are the primary determinants with respect to preference for each individual respondent, we next construct a map of the aggregate structures for each group of stores. The hierarchical value map is a "group map." It is reflective of how this group of respondents views the respective stores. The map is intended to highlight the characteristic ways of moving from the attribute to the consequence to the value level. Given the average CDA indices, these paths appear to represent common preference orientations. The key ladders in each map will be discussed, and then we will discuss the differences.

Figure 7–7 shows the value structure map for the low-image stores. The ladders are represented as interconnected sets across levels of abstraction. Also, at the high levels, the merging of the various lower-level distinctions into the same value, "better life," reflects the different meanings or interpretations. Basically this map has three fundamental blocks of relations connected to this one value level. "Clean, neat store," "quality merchandise," "lower prices," and "durable merchandise" all lead to "good value (get my money's worth)." This "good value" denotes "money for other items" and eventually ends in "better quality of life." We consider this block to be a particularly strong basis with respect to preference and subsequent choice behavior. Every respondent had one of their two "most characteristic" ladders fall into this grouping.

On the left-hand side of the map we have "sales help in department" and "wide assortment" leading to "get more done," thereby enabling one to "spend time with the family" which makes "life better." On the right, "have credit" leads to "treat myself" which then leads to "better life."

The high-image-store HVM (figure 7–8) also reveals three major blocks of relations, but these are quite different than those for the low-

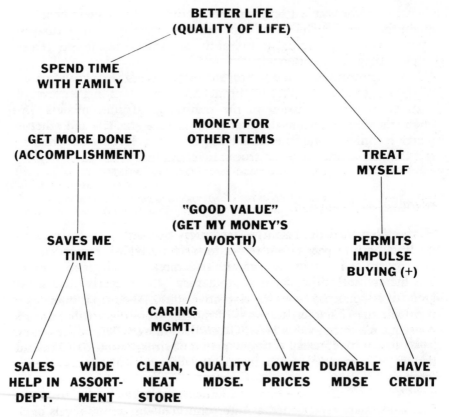

Figure 7–7. Hierarchical Value Map for the Low-Image Stores

image stores. "Friendly, helpful salespeople" and "clean, neat store" lead to "less hassle," which in turn leads to "saves time." "Saves time" is an important node leading to the consequences "in control" and "accomplishment" which are gateways to "self-esteem." This same importance to "self-esteem" can also be seen for "feel special" which has both "clean, neat store" implying an "enjoyable place to shop," and "one-of-a-kind clothing" which allows someone to "stand out," leading to it.

Finally, "feel confident" appears as another important node. It serves as a crossover point for "friendly, helpful salespeople," "quality merchandise," and "have credit" to reach up to "status" and eventually "security." Thus, understanding how to communicate these concepts to the consumer might be critical.

The HVMs for the respective image classifications clearly reveal substantial differences across all levels. One central point here is that the interpretations given the same attribute and benefit level connections are noticeably distinct. In other words, those frequently visiting the low-image stores are driven dominantly by the idea of a better life, while high-image-store visitors are motivated either by self-esteem or the need for security. This is clearly demonstrated if one follows the chain in both ladders starting at the attribute "have credit." Moreover, the relative true importance of each level also suggests that different interpretations can be accorded each HVM, particularly with respect to the relative importance of the higher levels.

Research Implications

The principles underlying this research framework offer several potential applications. First, given that higher levels of abstraction, namely consequences and personal values, contribute substantially to understanding the bases of preference, the means-end framework offers an improvement to current attribute- or benefit-based research. Understanding how inherent product benefits connect with satisfying personal values presents an opportunity for gaining a more complete view of any market.

Second, application of the CDA methodology permits validation of each level derived by laddering. This provides the ability to construct a highly refined HVM.

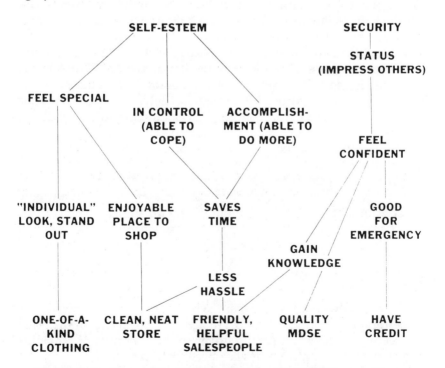

Figure 7–8. Hierarchical Value Map for the High-Image Stores

Finally, the segments represented by the distinct pathways seen in the resulting HVM are preference based, and thus serve as a sound basis for at least the development of strategic advertising options. Olson and Reynolds (1983) detail how the uncovering of perceptual constructs—from choice criteria to terminal values—can be used to define advertising strategy.

Summary

The goal of this chapter was to develop an understanding of what underlies preference. To accomplish this goal, a framework for identifying the various image representations resulting in preference was needed. Essentially this was done by identifying the bases of preference for two groups of department store shoppers in terms of their personal identification with the stores. The framework imposed on the results was that of distinguishing individual responses in terms of three broad classes of elements: attributes, consequences, and value orientations.

The results of triadic and preference distinctions and subsequent laddering elicited the various combinations of attributes, consequences, and values for each person. The results indicate the presence of these types of cognitive elements when dealing with store-patronage behavior.

We identified the underlying individual motivations that provide the impetus for choosing a store by representing the A/C/V orientation in a linking format. The level of contribution for each element was determined by using cognitive differentiation analysis which related the ratings of the respective stores on the individually determined attribute, consequence, and value elements to preference.

Overall averages of the CDA indices for each A/C/V element were obtained. Examination of these indices reveals that high preference discrimination is present at the values level with respect to the low-image stores, and even more so for the high-image stores. However, the attribute level discriminates best only when dealing with similarity judgments. These averages confirm the fact that the respondents are operating at high levels of abstraction when thinking about their store preferences.

Finally, by aggregating the individual points of view, we constructed the two hierarchical value maps which reveal the common preference pathways connecting attributes to values. The respondents who most often go to the low-image stores seem to be driven primarily by the need for a better quality of life. The high-image-store shoppers, on the other hand, seem to be more internally driven, either in terms of providing reinforcement of self-esteem or via a need for security.

We propose, therefore, that image is a valenced construct that is the net result of the content and strength of associations, across levels of abstraction, that link the determinant modifiers for an object (attributes) to the relevant modifers of self (personal values). Put simply, the image of a store is the degree or strength of association of the store with the personal value that serves as the underlying rationale for preference (in a given context). Thus, the means-end research framework provides both the content and structural components that are the bases for understanding and evaluating image.

References

Arons, L. (1961), "Does Television Viewing Influence Store Image and Shopping Frequency?" *Journal of Retailing* 37 (Fall):1–13.

Beardon, W.O. (1977), "Determinant Attributes of Store Patronage: Downtown versus Outlying Areas," *Journal of Retailing* 53 (Summer):15–22.

Berkowitz, E.N., T. Deutscher, and R.A. Hansen (1978), "Retail Image Research: A Case of Significant Unrealized Potential," in S. Jain, ed., *1978 Educators' Proceedings*, Chicago: American Marketing Association.

Berry, L.L. (1969), "The Components of Department Store Image: A Theoretical and Empirical Analysis," *Journal of Retailing* 45 (Spring):4–20.

Etgar, M. and N.K. Malhotra (1978), "Consumers' Reliance on Different Product Quality Cues: A Basis for Marketing Segmentation," in S. Jain, ed., *Research Frontiers in Marketing: Dialogue and Directions, 1978 Educators' Proceedings*, Chicago: American Marketing Association.

Gutman, J. and T.J. Reynolds (1979), "An Investigation at the Levels of Cognitive Abstraction Utilized by Consumers in Product Differentiation," in J. Eighmey, ed., *Attitude Research Under the Sun*, Chicago: American Marketing Association.

—— (1982), "A Means-End Chain Model Based on Consumer Categorization Process," *Journal of Marketing* 46 (Spring):60–72.

Howard, J.A. (1977), *Consumer Behavior: Application of Theory*, New York: McGraw Hill Book Company.

Hudson, R. (1974), "Images of the Retailing Environment: An Example of the Use of the Repertory Grid Methodology," *Environment and Behavior* 6 (December):470–94.

Jain, A.K. and M. Etgar (1976), "Measuring Store Image Through Multidimensional Scaling of Free Response Data," *Journal of Retailing* 52 (Winter): 61–70.

Kelly, G. (1955), *The Psychology of Personal Constructs*, New York: W.W. Norton Company.

Kunkel, J. and L. Berry (1968), "A Behavioral Conception of Retail Image," *Journal of Marketing* 32 (October):21–27.

Lindquist, J.D. (1974), "Meaning of Image: A Survey of Empirical and Hypothetical Evidence," *Journal of Retailing* 50 (Winter):29–38.

Marks, R.B. (1976), "Operationalizing the Concept of Store Image," *Journal of of Retailing* 52 (Fall):37–46.

Martineau, P. (1958), "The Personality of the Retail Store," *Harvard Business Review* 36 (January–February):47–55.

Olson, J.C. and J. Jacoby (1977), "Price as an Informational Cue: Effects on Product Evaluation," in A.G. Woodside, J.N. Sheth, and P.D. Bennett, eds., *Consumer and Industrial Buying Behavior*, New York: North Holland.

_____ and T.J. Reynolds (1983), "Understanding Consumers' Cognitive Structures: Implications for Advertising Strategy," in L. Percy and A. Woodside, eds., *Advertising and Consumer Psychology*, Lexington, Mass.: Lexington Books, D.C. Heath.

Oxenfeldt, A.R. (1974), "Developing a Favorable Price-Quality Image," *Journal of Retailing* 50 (Winter):8–14.

Peterson, R.A. and R.A. Kerin (1983), "Store Image Measurement in Patronage Research: Fact and Artifact," in W.F. Darden and R.F. Lusch, eds., *Patronage Behavior and Retail Management*, New York: Elsevier.

Reynolds, T.J. (1982), "Advertising Is Image Management," Keynote address at the American Academy of Advertising Meeting, Lincoln, Nebraska.

_____ (1983), "A Nonmetric Approach to Determine the Differentiating Power of Attribute Ratings with Respect to Pairwise Similarity Judgments," AMA Educators' Conference, Sarasota, Florida.

Rokeach, M. (1973), *The Nature of Human Values*, New York: Free Press.

Walters, C.G. (1978), *Consumer Behavior: Theory and Practice*, Homewood, Ill.: Richard D. Irwin.

Weale, W.B. (1961), "Measuring the Customer's Image of a Department Store," *Journal of Retailing* 37 (Summer):40–48.

Wheatley, J.J. and J.S.Y. Chiu (1977), "Effects of Price, Store Image, and Product and Respondent Characteristics on Perceptions of Quality," *Journal of Marketing Research* 14 (May):181–86.

8
Forming Impressions of Merchandise and Service Quality

David Mazursky and
Jacob Jacoby

I t is generally agreed that consumers form impressions, or images, of stores. Such images tend to develop over time as the consumer learns about and becomes familiar with a store. The image-formation process is particularly evident in two cases: (1) when a new store opens for business in an established environment (for example, Saks opens in New Orleans); or (2) when it is the consumer himself who moves to a new area and begins to shop at established—but, to him, unfamiliar— stores.

From a practitioner's perspective, what makes store images so important is the fact that, once developed, they are presumed to exert a considerable impact on patronage behavior. Accordingly, it becomes useful to ask: How do store images develop? More specifically, what kinds of information go into the formation of store image and what kinds of information tend to be ignored? Answers to these questions would be of considerable practical worth, since knowing the kinds of information that are used by consumers to form their images gives the practitioner a better idea of the factors he has to operate on in order to shape and influence that image.

Unfortunately, little is known regarding the processes that underlie store-image development (Hirschman 1981). In part, this may be due to the fact that most store-image research has relied on questionnaires that probe post-shopping recall. While this approach permits obtaining an assessment of overall image, it suffers from two major shortcomings. First, recall methods necessarily treat image formation as a static phenomenon rather than the dynamic process it is generally theorized to be. Second and more important, consumers are likely to recall the final or resultant image rather than the objective environmental cues that gave rise to this image. For example, consumers may say that the reason they

Funding for the study described in this chapter was provided by a grant from New York University's Institute of Retail Management.

like a certain store is because "it carries high-quality merchandise," not "they carry Calvin Klein jeans, which I think is a high-quality brand." Retailers interested in understanding just what factors produced the image of high-quality merchandise, or in modifying this image, can make more use of the latter type of information than of the former. In other words, how does a consumer proceed from the information present in the objective external environment (for example, store location, appearance, merchandise, and so forth) to the image that is evoked in the inner, subjective environment (that is, the consumer's perception of the store image)? (See figure 8–1.) Procedures are required that track the inference process from consideration of objective cues (for example, Calvin Klein jeans) to the production of an image (for example, "high-quality merchandise"). This chapter represents an exploratory attempt to address this issue.

In order to study image development, one first needs an idea (or model) of how the image-formation process operates. The existing literature proved to be of little help in this regard. Models that describe the dynamics of the image-development process are seemingly nonexistent. Therefore, the authors developed a model of this process (Mazursky 1983), a revised and condensed version of which appears here as figure 8–2.

With respect to objective reality, store X can be broken down and considered in terms of its specific details. While this can be done in various ways, partitioning in terms of major departments (for example, women's jeans or women's shoes) and elements within these departments seems to make most sense, at least for purposes of an exploratory study.

Perceived reality—the overall image of store X in the mind of that consumer—can also be partitioned into a set of major components. That is, the consumer's overall image of store X is some function of how he or she perceives store X in terms of the major facets of store image. Examples of two such facets are impressions regarding quality of service and quality of merchandise. As figure 8–2 indicates, while overall store image is based on these (and other) aspects, these aspects, in turn, are based on inferences made earlier in the image-formation process. These earlier, basic inferences are tied more closely to specific characteristics of the objective environment. In other words, basic inferences such as "These shoes look like they're made well" and "These jeans are from a top-name designer" are based directly on the information to which the consumer attends in the external environment. These basic inferences then combine to form the higher-order inference such as "This store carries quality merchandise."

With this model of the store-image-formation process, the principal point addressed by this chapter is: Consumers do not use all the available information when forming their impressions of stores; which

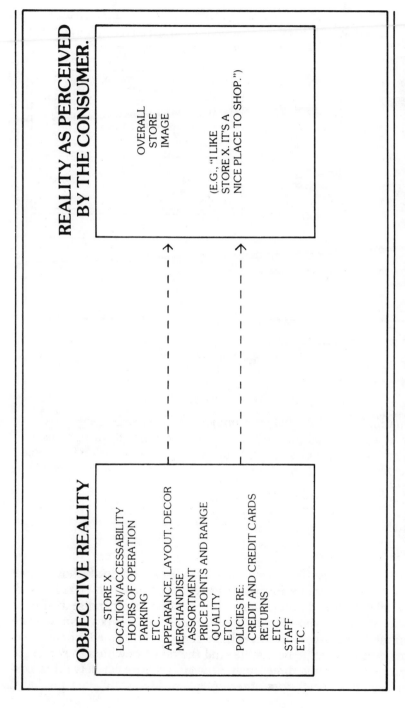

Figure 8–1. How Do the Features of Objective Reality Relate to the Consumer's Perception of that Reality?

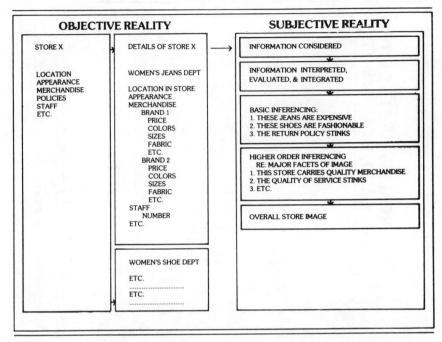

Figure 8–2. A Simplified Model Depicting the Development of Store Image

information in the external environment is likely to be considered (and which is likely to be ignored) when the consumer forms impressions about quality of service and merchandise? What information from objective reality is used in arriving at judgments of service and merchandise quality?

Method

Overview

A behavioral-process (BP) simulation was used to identify how much and just which types of information were used (and which were ignored) when subjects formed impressions of service and merchandise quality in regard to various hypothetical "new" stores.[1] Two types of new-store conditions were used—one in which consumers formed impressions with respect to a single new store, and the other in which they formed impressions regarding three such new stores. Respectively, this corresponds to the "new *store* entering an already established market," and the "new *consumer* entering an already established market." BP simulations involve presenting the subject with a problem (for example, to form an impression of the quality of service offered by store *X*), and then providing him or her with access to a relevant information domain and observing how much, what types of, and in what order information is considered. In the present study, the relevant information environment consisted of 48 different items in the case of the single new store condition; and 144 (or 3 × 48) different items in the case of the three new stores condition (see figure 8–3).

Representing the Objective Information Environment

When one attempts to describe the various objective characteristics of stores, it becomes apparent that the amount of information associated with any single store is enormous. Not only is there information regarding the store itself (its location, hours of operation, size and layout, appearance in general and of each department, services, policies, and so on), but there is also the information regarding each separate item constituting the merchandise assortment. When each detail is considered this could quickly add up to hundreds of thousands of separate items of information. One could not represent all this information, so just which information should be made available?

For the purposes of our study, it was decided that the objective information environment for each store should contain three broad types of information: photographs of the store's interior; general information regarding the store and its policies; and information regarding various products carried by the store. Each store was represented by forty-eight different items of information, as follows:

1. General information regarding store and its policies
   Location
   Number of floors
   Number of salespersons per department
   Number of cashiers per department
   Number of fitting rooms per department
   Which credit cards were accepted
   Merchandise-return policy
2. Photographs of store interior (seven items)
3. Merchandise information on seven products
   Men's wallets (four items)
   Men's shoes (six items)
   Men's jeans (five items)

IMPRESSIONS OF:

NUMBER OF STORES REPRESENTED:	MERCHANDISE QUALITY	SERVICE QUALITY
1	48 ITEMS OF INFORMATION	48 ITEMS
3	144 ITEMS	144 ITEMS

Figure 8–3. Overall Design

Briefcases (four items)
Women's wallets (four items)
Women's shoes (six items)
Women's jeans
  Price range
  Brand names available
  Number of pairs per size
  Percentage of jeans currently on sale
  Size of average discount

Although the stores were given hypothetical names, the information provided in the objective information environment was authentic and, since subjects were drawn from the environs of New York City, was generally for stores some distance away from New York. The photographs were obtained from a company specializing in developing store design and layout. The information regarding the store and its policies was collected via personal visits to each store. Merchandise information that would be of interest to consumers similar to those used in the main study was collected using a separate pretest sample (of twenty-five) drawn from the same population. These pretest subjects responded to two open-ended questions pertaining to six product classes relevant for this age and social group. The six product classes were jeans, shirts, wallets, briefcases, shoes, and cameras. As an example, the first question was: "Have you bought at least one pair of jeans in the past two years?" If the answer was "yes," the second question asked was: "What kinds of things would you want to know about a pair of jeans when you were shopping to buy a pair of jeans?" The number of properties typically mentioned for each of the products ranged between four and six. Since cameras were not available in some of the test stores and the variety of shirts made it difficult to develop a realistic simulation, these two products were later dropped from the study.

Subjects

The sample consisted of 120 students (57 males and 63 females) enrolled in various schools at New York University. They were recruited through announcements in classes and printed calls for participation posted in various campus buildings. The announcements invited students to participate individually in a shopping study. Most subjects (77 percent) were 17 to 22 years of age, with the largest category being 20 to 22 (44.5 percent). Subjects reported having had extensive prior shopping experiences with jeans and shoes (which were two of the four test products). Roughly 97 percent of the sample reported having shopped for these two products at least once during the preceding two years.

Procedure

Subjects were tested individually. Each subject underwent three separate simulations involving forming impressions of either a single store and/or three stores in regard to quality of merchandise and/or quality of service. In each case, each store was represented by a large loose-leaf notebook that contained the relevant information environment. At the outset of a simulation exercise, each notebook was opened at its "graphic index" page which indicated what types of information were available and where each item of information could be found. Subjects were then permitted to look at as much or as little of this information as they desired, in any order they desired. As the subject accessed each item of information, a record was generated of the identity and sequence of information accessing.

Basic Findings

While the available external information environment contained forty-eight different types of information (that is, properties) for each of the stores, several properties appeared more than once (for example, "brand names" appeared four times, once for each of four different products). Since our study focused on the store as a whole and not on the particular products contained therein, aggregation was necessary.

The properties in table 8–1 are rank ordered, from high to low, according to the proportion of total search (that is, all accessed information) that subjects devoted to each property when evaluating quality of service and quality of merchandise. The results show that while the differences in proportions among the two treatments (that is, single- versus three-store evaluations) were marginal, substantial differences exist in the information to which subjects attend when forming different impressions (that is, quality of service versus quality of merchandise). For example, the four most heavily accessed properties when forming service-quality impressions were "number of salespersons per department," "number of cashiers per department," "merchandise-return policy," and "number of fitting rooms." However, the properties that were most heavily accessed when evaluating quality of merchandise were "brand names," "pictures of stores' interior design," "merchandise material," and "price ranges."

Figures 8–4 and 8–5 depict these results graphically. Of particular interest is the "frontier line" (that is, the combination of the properties that had the highest proportions). For example, the first six properties in figure 8–3 (and the first seven properties in figure 8–4) were most fre-

Table 8–1
Types of Information Used in Arriving at Quality Impressions of Service and Merchandise
(percentages)

Property	Quality of Service		Quality of Merchandise	
	Evaluation of a Single Store	*Evaluation of Three Stores Simultaneously*	*Evaluation of a Single Store*	*Evaluation of Three Stores Simultaneously*
No. of salespersons per dept.	17	18	5	5
No. of cashiers per dept.	16	16	4	4
Merchandise-return policy	17	15	6	6
No. of fitting rooms	12	11	3	3
Credit cards accepted	10	10	6	6
Location	9	10	9	9
No. of floors	5	6	5	4
Pictures of stores' interior design	4	4	13	11
Brand names	2	3	13	18
Price ranges	2	2	10	11
Assortment	2	1	4	4
Percentage of stock currently on sale	1	1	4	3
Merchandise material	1	1	11	11
Discount on sale merchandise	1	1	5	2
Merchandise colors	1	1	2	3
Raw Frequency	660	978	856	869

quently associated with evaluating quality of service. The remaining properties were most frequently associated with forming quality-of-merchandise impressions.

Figure 8–6 summarizes the results of Kendall Tau coefficients between the type of impression subjects formed (that is, quality of service or quality of merchandise) and the task they performed (single versus three-store evaluation). The high correlations in the within-impression comparisons (that is, along the marked diagonal) versus the low and non-significant correlations in the between-impression comparisons indicate the high internal consistency of the data.

Discussion

One advantage of the behavioral-process approach over most traditional approaches relates to the question: What is it the subjects saw in

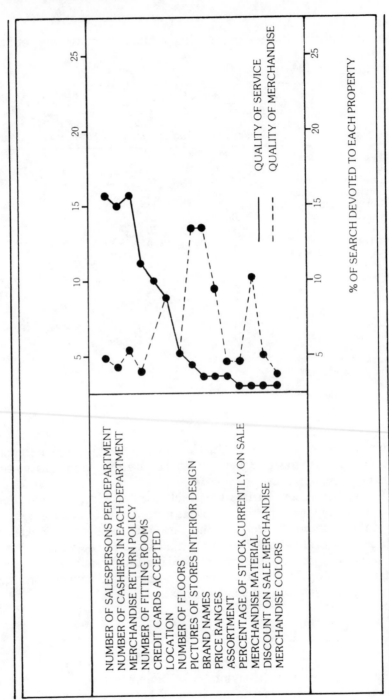

Figure 8–4. Proportions of Search Process Devoted to Accessing Properties in Assessing Image Aspects (A Single-Store Evaluation)

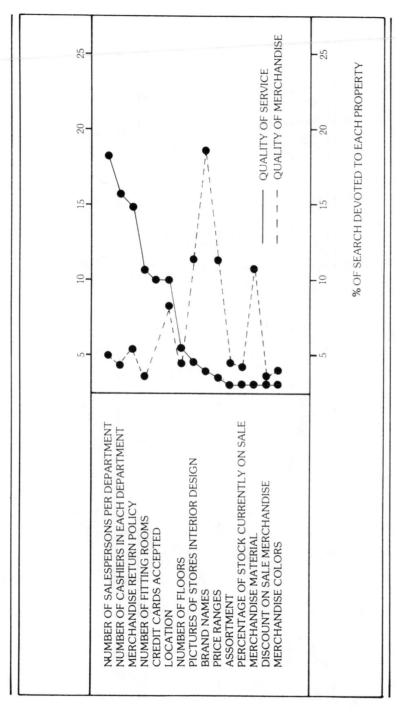

Figure 8–5. Proportions of Search Process Devoted to Accessing Properties in Assessing Image Aspects (A Three-Store Evaluation)

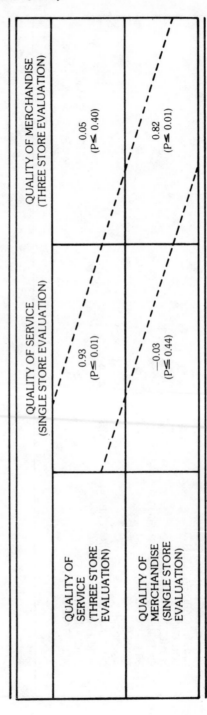

Figure 8-6. Kendall Correlation Coefficients Between Type of Impression and the Performed Tasks

the store that made them believe that the quality of the store's merchandise is high? This has important implications for the manner in which retailers choose to communicate the image they would like to generate in the consumers' minds. Further, since objective cues (such as interior design, brand names, price levels, and so forth) represent the most important channel through which retailers can communicate these images, it is imperative to understand how consumers infer images from those objective cues.

The importance of the inference process is reflected in the findings of our study, which suggest that subjects rely on different sets of objective cues to infer each image aspect. For example, the subjects considered brand name information as the most important cue in forming quality-of-merchandise impressions. In evaluating the quality of service, however, the number of salespersons per department appeared to be the most salient cue. Thus, by learning the fundamental properties, of the stores, that consumers associate with quality of service or merchandise, channels of communication between retailers and consumers may be improved.

In addition, the findings suggest an approach that subjects use in simplifying the complex reality associated with stores—namely, they prefer accessing items that represent "chunks" of information. For example, in forming impressions regarding quality of merchandise, the most frequently accessed property was brand names. Information on brand names may substitute for a much larger set of items of information (Jacoby, Szybillo, and Busato-Schach 1977; Jacoby, Chestnut, Hoyer, Sheluga, and Donahue 1978). Accessing information on brand names may ease the processing of the extensive information associated with stores.

Implications

The major implication that can be drawn from this chapter refers to retailers' strategic considerations when attempting to create a certain image of their department store. Since the findings suggest that consumers associate different fundamental properties of the store depending upon the image aspect for which they search, it becomes necessary for retailers to define their objectives before they design the store and make decisions regarding the physical attributes of the store. For example, if the objective is to create an image emphasizing high quality of service, our findings suggest just which fundamental properties consumers seem to rely upon in forming impressions regarding this aspect of the image. However, if the objective is to evoke an image of the store as carrying high-quality merchandise, the physical attributes of the store should be modified accordingly.

Limitations and Directions for Future Research

One limitation relates to the fact that the information environment was somewhat artificial. In most real-world situations, the information is not as easily accessible as it was in our study. Since in real-life situations the format of information presentation may be different from the one used here, external validity tends to be limited. On the positive side, however, it should be noted that the content of the information made available was collected from actual and relatively typical stores. In that respect, the information presented here possesses higher external validity when compared to many other studies, particularly those that include only two or three factors (which in many cases have hypothetical values) and thereby ignore possible interactions. Our study enabled the subjects to consider forty-eight fundamental properties, all of which were available for accessing.

In addition, the college student sample consisted of a narrow age group that was relatively "up-scale" in terms of education, thereby limiting the generalizability of the findings.

This study was conducted as exploratory research and for demonstration purposes. The method employed represents a crude attempt to recreate the information that shoppers experience when shopping at a store. However, in light of the importance of studying the processing patterns and inferences that shoppers draw from the store's objective reality, it is suggested that efforts to simulate such processes should continue. Pessemier (1980) noted that printed material (such as that used in our study) may be satisfactory as a first step. More technologically advanced methods utilizing cable television and videotapes, would most likely represent a better simulation of the shopping experience and should be considered for future research.

Notes

1. Because this chapter is written with a practitioner audience in mind, the methodology is only briefly described. More complete detail will be found in Mazursky (1983) and in papers now in preparation.

References

Hirschman, E.C. (1981), "Retail Research and Theory," in B.N. Enis and K.J. Roering, eds., *Review of Marketing*, Chicago: American Marketing Association, 120–33.

Jacoby, J., R.W. Chestnut, W.D. Hoyer, D.W. Sheluga, and M.J. Donahue (1978), "Psychometric Characteristics of Behavioral Process Data: Preliminary Findings on Validity and Generalizability," in H.K. Hunt, ed., *Advances in Consumer Research* vol. 5, Ann Arbor, Mich.: Association for Consumer Research, 546–54.

Jacoby, J., G.J. Szybillo, and J. Busato-Schach (1977), "Information Acquisition Behavior in Brand Choice Situations," *Journal of Consumer Research* 3: 209–15.

Mazursky, D. (1983), *A Behavioral Process Approach for Tracking Store Image Development*, an unpublished doctoral diss., New York University.

Pessemier, E.A. (1980), "Store Image and Positioning," *Journal of Retailing* 56: 94–106.

9
The Impact of Linking Brand and Retailer Images on Perceptions of Quality

Jacob Jacoby and
David Mazursky

I t is generally agreed that consumers form impressions (or images) of stores, brands, and manufacturers and that these impressions can later exert a major impact on shopping behavior. Accordingly, retailers and manufacturers have generally been concerned with three basic questions: (1) What images do they (and their brands) evoke in the minds of consumers? (2) How do these images relate to the images of their present or would-be competitors? (3) What can be done to modify or reposition an image?

The latter two questions may be seen to represent *within-level* issues. That is, they compare the images of one retailer with another, one manufacturer with another, and one brand with another. Equally important, though generally ignored, is the corresponding *cross-level* question, namely: What happens when retailer images and manufacturer (or brand) images become linked with one another? For example, how does the consumer react when he or she learns that JC Penney will be carrying the Halston line of designer clothes? Does the combined impression reflect favorably upon both the manufacturer/brand and the retailer, or is there potential for one, or both, of the linked parties to be adversely affected by such an association? This chapter addresses this question with specific reference to the perception of quality.

The vast majority of image-assessment procedures have either been borrowed from or patterned after attitude-measurement procedures developed by social psychologists. Within this set, perhaps no other technique has been as widely used as the semantic differential (Mindak 1961). However, though image researchers borrowed the technique, they

Funds for the investigation discussed in this chapter were provided by a grant from New York University's Institute of Retail Management.

have thus far neglected to consider the theoretical context out of which it evolved. This is unfortunate since this context—particularly that portion known as Congruity Theory (cf. Osgood, Suci, and Tannenbaum 1957)—has considerable implications for retailer and brand/manufacturer image combinations.

Congruity Theory is one of the early social psychological "consistency" theories. The general tenet of all consistency theories is that when an individual's mind contains two related thoughts and these thoughts are somehow inconsistent with each other, psychological tensions will arise that pressure the individual to restore consistency.

Congruity Theory focuses upon what occurs when a source either associates itself with, or disassociates itself from, some other source or object. As applied to the retailing context, an associative link would be reflected by the assertion: "JC Penney sells Halston clothing." In contrast, a dissassociative link is exemplified by: "Bergdorf–Goodman decided to discontinue carrying Halston."

Congruity Theory holds that if the source (in this case, JC Penney) and the object (in this case, Halston) of an associative link are equally valued by the respondent, there should be no incongruity and, therefore, no strain to reestablish consistency. In terms of the standard $+3$ to -3 semantic differential scale, if a source whom the respondent evaluates as being a $+2$ (for example, Saks Fifth Avenue) positively associates itself with an object that the respondent also considers to be a $+2$ (for example, Ralph Lauren–Polo), then the individual should experience no psychological discomfort and, therefore, no strains to restore or establish congruity. This would also be true for the case where a -2 source is positively associated with a -2 object. It seems fitting that those whom we dislike should like things we dislike.

However, Congruity Theory also predicts that all other associations between a source and an object that are not equally valued will generate psychological pressures to restore a state of congruity. As an example, if a $+3$ source (for example, the jeweler Cartier's) became positively linked with a $+1$ object (for example, Bic cigarette lighters), then Congruity Theory predicts that the individual will experience pressures to bring these two elements into a state of congruity. This could be achieved in the present example if the impression of Cartier's moved from $+3$ down to $+2.3$ and the impression of Bic moved up to $+2.3$. Since both source and object are now at $+2.3$ in that consumer's mind, congruity will have been established and the psychological pressures will have been dissipated.

Congruity Theory suggests that there exists potential benefit (and corresponding harm) for both the retailer and the manufacturer/brand in those many instances where a retailer's and a manufacturer's/brand's images are not viewed as being equally positive. These possibilities are outlined in table 9–1. A study was conducted to test these relationships.

Table 9–1
Predicted Impact on Images of Retailer and
Manufacturer/Brand Associations

Case number	Initial Images Of	Likely Impact On
1	Retailer—more favorable Manufacterer/Brand— less favorable	Retailer—lowered image Manufacturer/Brand— raised image
2	Retailer—less favorable Manufacturer/Brand— more favorable	Retailer—raised image Manufacturer/Brand— lowered image

Method

Using a set of 11 seven-point semantic differential scales, one of which was "high quality–low quality," respondents first separately evaluated sets of familiar brand names (in the three product categories of jeans, sneakers, and panty hose) and retail stores. They then evaluated associative linkings between brands with high images and stores with low images, as well as between stores with low images and brands with high images. In all, there were 168 respondents: 77 students and 91 consumers intercepted in two metropolitan New York shopping malls. The data reported here is for the "high quality–low quality" scale. (See Jacoby and Mazursky 1984 for greater detail.)

Results

Table 9–2 provides the means and standard deviations on the quality scale. Table 9–3 indicates the significance of the difference between means.

In the case where a store with a lower image for quality is linked with a brand having a higher quality image, note the following: First, for all three products, respondents began by feeling relatively neutral toward the store; the store evaluations on the quality dimension generally hovered within .5 of the neutral point (4.00). Second, the three brands were all rated quite high on quality. Third, as predicted, the mean evaluation of the linked store and brand image fell between the quality ratings for the separate components. In other words, when a product having a high image for quality is linked with a store having a lesser image for quality, the store's image is helped by this association (significantly so, in the case of two products; see table 9–3) and the brand's image is harmed by this association (significantly so in the case of all three products).

Table 9-2
Quality Ratings of Stores, Brands, and Store-Brand Linkages

| | Low Store Linked with High Brand | | | | | | | High Store Linked with Low Brand | | | | | | |
| | Store | | Store and Brand | | Brand | | | Store | | Store and Brand | | Brand | | |
	$\bar{x}$	S.D.	$\bar{x}$	S.D.	$\bar{x}$	S.D.	n	$\bar{x}$	S.D.	$\bar{x}$	S.D.	$\bar{x}$	S.D.	n
Jeans	3.81	1.17	4.66	1.50	5.75	1.18	65	6.58	.58	4.58	1.34	5.65	1.10	62
Panty hose	3.35	.99	4.76	1.09	6.05	.82	21	6.43	.62	3.81	1.60	4.65	1.15	16
Sneakers	4.42	1.01	4.94	.91	6.05	.78	22	6.21	.89	4.00	1.03	4.35	1.25	16

Note: Means refer to a standard 7-point semantic differential scale. A constant (4) has been added to convert all negative values to positive values. Thus: +7.00 = High Quality; +1.00 = Low Quality.

The situation in which a store with a high quality image is linked with a brand having an image of lesser quality produced a somewhat different pattern of results. First, for all three products, both the store and brand had favorable quality images (that is, above the neutral point), although the store's quality image was considerably higher. Second, contrary to what would be predicted by Congruity Theory, the mean quality rating for the linked image does not fall between the mean of the separate quality ratings. Instead, it falls below the quality image for both the brand and store components, when these were evaluated separately. In other words, when a store with a high quality image is associated with a brand having only a moderately high quality image, both store and brand images are negatively affected (significantly so for all three products in the case of stores, and for one of the three products in the case of the brands; see table 9-3).

Discussion

While this was only a pilot study using convenience samples, the findings are nonetheless provocative. Among other things, they suggest that

Table 9-3
Significance of the Difference between Component Images and Combined Image

| | Low Store Linked with High Brand | | High Store Linked with Low Brand | |
	Store v. Combined	Brand v. Combined	Store v. Combined	Brand v. Combined
Jeans	.001	.001	.001	.001
Panty hose	.001	.001	.001	n.s.
Sneakers	n.s	.001	.001	n.s.

perhaps greater caution needs to be exercised when retailers and manufacturers enter into arrangements, because such arrangements could prove injurious to the party having the more favorable quality image.

References

Jacoby, J. and D. Mazursky (1984), "Linking Brand and Retailer Images: Do the Potential Risks Outweigh the Potential Benefits?" *Journal of Retailing* 60 (Summer), forthcoming.

Mindak, W.A. (1961), "Fitting the Semantic Differential to the Marketing Problem," *Journal of Marketing* 25 (April):28–33.

Osgood, C.E., G.J. Suci, and P.H. Tannenbaum (1957), *The Measurement of Meaning*, Champaign–Urbana, Ill.: University of Illinois Press.

10
The Influence of Social Characteristics on Perceived Quality in Patronage Choice Behavior

William R. Darden and
JoAnn Schwinghammer

Past research on perceived quality has primarily concentrated on products and attribute cues. Olson and Jacoby (1972) for example, showed that the attributes perceived as important in the selection of products differed by product type and suggested that intrinsic cues were more important in the minds of consumers. Etgar and Malhotra (1978) drew upon the work of Olson and Jacoby (1972) and Olson (1977) to set up an experimental design showing that multiple cues were important in the determination of perceived quality. Based on these protocols they attempted to identify consumer groups with respect to perceived quality. They employed both intrinsic and extrinsic cues in their experimental design. Both Olson and Jacoby (1972) and Etgar and Malhotra (1978) hypothesized that extrinsic cues such as price, brand name, and store image did not influence perceived quality as much as intrinsic cues.

While extrinsic product and store cues may not appreciably affect the perceived quality of individual products, this chapter suggests that they may well affect shopper quality perceptions of product categories found in store chains. For example, Render and O'Connor (1976) showed that the image of stores in some cases does relate to the perceived quality of some product categories. They indicated the need for studies that address the issues of the different kinds of chain stores that are available and the impact of their images upon the perceived quality of product sold there.

We suggest that the perceived quality of a product varies by chain type, and that the perceived quality of different kinds of products differs for the same store type. We further think that shoppers are not homogeneous, but that different groups of consumers hold different kinds of quality perceptions. Do these different groups of consumers have different socialization backgrounds and do they have different value systems? In summary, these ideas are predicated upon the belief that social experiences have an impact upon shopping beliefs and perceptions. In other words, *patronage socialization* is defined as the shaping of shopping images, preferences, perceptions, and beliefs through interacting with others at home, on the job, in prior shopping occasions and situations, and through the media. Based on the idea that consumers are differentially socialized, depending upon their backgrounds and their value systems, the following issues concerning perceived quality are examined in this chapter.

1. Consumers perceive the quality of a product differently depending upon whether they are to buy it from traditional department stores, mass merchandisers, discount stores, or specialty stores. These differential perceptions may be the result of various socialization factors.

2. Groups of consumers are believed to differ in how they perceive product quality by chain store and by product category. We suggest that there are discontinuous groups of consumers reflecting essential differences in how they perceive quality across all kinds of outlets and chains.

3. Characteristics such as age, marital status, number of children, income, educational level, and occupation lead to differences in how people perceive the quality of product categories in different chain stores.

4. We feel that the perceived-quality groups differ by the *social visibility* that they ascribe to different kinds of product classes or categories. By social visibility we mean the potential of a product class to be seen and judged by others. We further feel that social visibility is a characteristic that varies by social class and that it is the direct result of patronage socialization, as defined above.

5. Another important characteristic of a shopper is his or her perceptions of the approval from important others of his or her purchase or use of given products from given stores. Because of the same kinds of reasoning advanced above, we suggest that *social approval* for product categories differs across perceived-quality groups. Social approval from others is expected to relate to the kinds of chains at which the consumer feels free to shop. For example, social approval or disapproval from others perceived by the individual about shopping for jewelry at Sears may cause that individual to ascribe certain degrees of quality to the jewelry that he or she may purchase at Sears.

6. The quality that shoppers perceive in purchasing particular types of products at differing types of chains is expected to relate to their value systems. For example, we believe that those individuals who feel all

values are important may well perceive the quality of all products at all types of outlets as higher than do other groups.

In the remainder of this chapter we present evidence that supports at least some of the ideas described, and we discuss the implications of these findings.

Study Approach

Sample

The Arkansas Household Research Panel, a statewide quarterly mail research panel, was utilized to gather data for this study. Three hundred seventy-two usable responses were gathered from the questionnaire. Demographic data of the sample, which is very similar to the demographic data of the state in total, is given in table 10–1.

The data base used was the result of two quarterly mailings of March and June 1983, through which different parts of the data base were gathered. After matching the two mailings, a response rate of only 74.4 percent was available for analysis. From table 10–1 it can be seen that the typical household has approximately one and one-half children; ages of 48.5 and 46.35 years, respectively, for male and female spouses; and educations of a little less than fourteen years for both spouses. Occupational prestige was gathered on a scale ranging from "unskilled" (coded as 1) to "self-employed" (coded as 6). It can be seen that the typical panel respondent was somewhere between clerical and managerial in occupational status.

Research Instrument

Our ideas were investigated using four product classes: shoes, jewelry, televisions, and small household appliances. These product categories were selected because they represented product classes for which product quality could be readily distinguished and for which social approval and social visibility would vary considerably.

Respondents were first asked to indicate how they perceived the quality of each of the four products at different store types (department stores, mass merchandisers, discounters, and specialty stores) known and available to the respondents. Respondents rated their perceptions of quality between 1, for lowest quality, and 5, for highest quality.

Another section of the questionnaire required respondents to indicate their perceptions of the extent to which four product classes possessed

Table 10–1
Panel Sample Demographic Characteristics

Variable	Mean Value
Number of children	1.45 children
Age—male household head (MHH)	48.58 years
Age—female household head (FHH)	46.35 years
Education—MHH	13.85 years
Education—FHH	13.32 years
Occupational prestige—MHH	3.79 [1]
Occupational prestige—FHH	3.51 [1]
Income	$27,002.00

[1]Average position on the rating scale including (1) unskilled, (2) skilled, (3) sales, clerical, office, (4) managerial, (5) professional, and (6) self-employed.

social visibility (as defined earlier). Responses ranged from 1, lowest social visibility, to 5, highest social visibility.

Next, we elicited respondents' perceptions of social approval (how others would react to the respondents' use of each of the four product classes purchased from specified department stores, mass merchandisers, discount stores, and specialty stores). A product class purchased at a store could receive a rating that ranged from 1, social disapproval, to 5, social approval. Also, respondents rated the relative importance of thirty-six values (which contained ratings from 1, not important, to 5, most important) as guiding principles in their lives. Demographic and socieconomic data on each panel household were also used in this study.

Analysis Approach

The raw data were submitted to factor analysis to provide a basis for summating items to form measures of constructs. Split-half coefficients and Cronbach alpha indexes for each construct summate based on the factor structure were sufficiently high (minimum item loading of .6 for all constructs) to warrant confidence in the construct structures. The perceived-quality and social-approval data loaded on shoes, jewelry, televisions, and small household appliances by store type. Two social-visibility constructs emerged: one consisting basically of nonsocial products, those purchased or consumed in relative privacy; and one consisting of social products, those more obvious in social contexts. The values constructs consisted of four terminal value constructs and two instrumental value constructs.

A hierarchical clustering procedure was utilized to group respondents in the product-store quality space. A five-group solution proved to be unique in that error increased dramatically for a four-group solution. Group 2 was distinguishable by the generally highest quality ratings its members gave to all product classes and stores, while Group 5 was its lowest-quality counterpart. Group 3 more frequently gave department stores highest ratings; Group 4 consistently rated discounters as the lowest-quality stores among all product categories. Group 1 maintained moderately low ratings throughout, especially for department stores.

To more fully explain these group differences, discriminant analysis was conducted, grouping by perceived-quality ratings, for demographic data as well as for the social-approval, visibility, and values data.

Analysis

Chain-Product Profiles

The bars in figure 10–1 allow us to visually determine the extent to which different kinds of chains affect the perceived quality of a particular product class. The data provides support for our idea that type of chain store affects the quality perceived by consumers. It is seen that the mean rating on perceived quality for all shoppers is lowest for discount stores, across all product classes. Many of the same brands that were carried at discount stores were also carried at department stores and mass merchandisers. Zales Jewelry, a specialty store, also managed the jewelry department of the traditional department store, Dillard's. Yet, consumers' perceived quality for jewelry at Zales was significantly higher than that for jewelry at Dillard's.

It can also be seen that the perceived quality for large-ticketed items (jewelry and televisions) purchased in specialty stores was much higher than that for small-valued items. This could be due to the fact that specialty stores actually carry products that have been demonstrated to have higher quality. Consumers purchase products at different kinds of chains and discuss the consequences of their use and their reliabilities. These shared patronage experiences provide a basis for the shopper to differentiate among chain types with respect to the quality of their product classes.

Figure 10–1 suggests yet one other finding: For the same kinds of outlet, perceived quality differs among product types. This suggests that the quality perceptions are not due entirely to the kind of outlet that is being considered for a particular product class. Thus, the perceived-quality variations within a product class—which are considerable—may be caused by the kind of retail chain that is assumed to be carrying the product. These conjectures suggest that since individuals have different

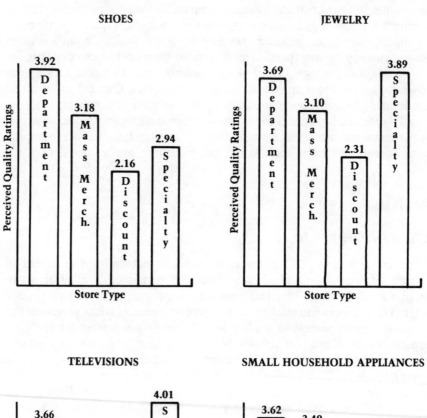

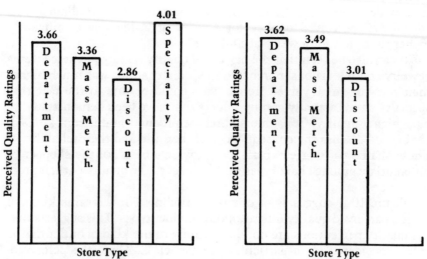

Figure 10–1. Bar Chart of Chain-Product Profiles

socioeconomic and values backgrounds, more than one kind of perceived-quality response pattern may hold for different groups of individuals.

Quality Shopper Types

Five different groups of shoppers, each differing in product-quality perceptions, were found by examining the chain-product class, perceived-quality profiles. The quality profile for each group is shown in figure 10–2. A multivariate analysis of variance among these groups resulted in a highly significant difference among the perceived qualities of the groups. No statistical significance can be assigned to this test, since the group assignment process segmented the perceived-quality profiles in a manner to create differences among groups. Univariate analysis of variance (between the five groups on each of the product-chain dimensions) resulted in highly significant differences ($p \leq 0.000$ for all).

Two groups are of special interest—Groups 5 and 2. Group 5 (15 percent of the total sample) could be described as a generalized low-quality-perceiving group. This group saw the perceived quality of shoes sold at specialty stores to be higher than for any other type of chain. But, these consumers perceived the quality of jewelry sold at specialty stores as much lower than that for discount stores, and no higher than that for department stores. They saw jewelry sold at mass merchandisers as having higher quality than that for specialty stores and department stores. In addition, these consumers, who seemed to ascribe a great deal of perceived quality to products sold in discount stores, also perceived relatively low quality for shoes sold in department stores.

Group 2 respondents (16 percent of the total sample) were characterized by overall high perceived quality for all kinds of chains across all product categories. Yet, relatively speaking, they saw higher perceived quality in shoes, jewelry, televisions, and small household appliances that were sold at mass merchandisers. Also, relatively speaking, they appeared to ascribe less perceived quality to all product classes sold at specialty stores.

Groups 1, 3, and 4 fell somewhere between Group 2 and Group 5. Groups 3 (21 percent) and 4 (18 percent) followed similar profiles, with maximum perceived quality for department chains and minimum perceived quality for discount chains (for all product classes). Group 1 (30 percent) respondents perceived department stores as having minimum quality, while the quality at discount stores was perceived as being greater.

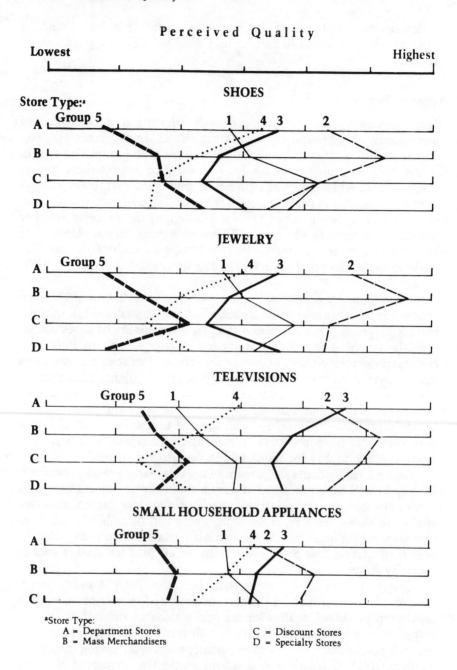

Figure 10-2. Profiles of Shopper Chain-Quality Perceptions

Socially Related

The most striking aspect of the socioeconomic variables was the lack of significant differences (five of the eleven variables were not significant at 0.25) between the perceived-quality groups. Whatever the differences in the geneses of the different product-perception groups, based on the evidence found in this study, differences are unlikely to be from conventional socioeconomic characteristics.

Social visibility did indeed discriminate among the five perceived-quality groups ($p \leq 0.000$). Group 2—the high-perceived-quality group across all products and all chains—perceived higher social visibility for both social and nonsocial products. While Groups 3 and 4 both showed higher social visibility for social products, Group 4 displayed the more extreme difference between social and nonsocial products. An interesting relationship was evident in the social-visibility profiles or Groups 1 and 5, who rated the visibility of nonsocial products higher than that of social products.

The social approval ascribed to product categories purchased at particular chains followed very closely the same patterns of the perceived-quality profiles. For Group 2, the high-quality perceivers, once again, mass merchandisers rated the highest social approval. For Group 5, discount stores were ascribed the highest social approval, with the exception of small household appliances. An interesting feature of Group 5 was the low social-approval ratings given to department stores for shoes and for jewelry. Again, Groups 1, 3, and 4 maintained middle positions on social approval, with Group 4 rating the social approval of specialty stores for shoes and discount stores for jewelry and televisions very much lower than any of the other ratings. Group 1 rated specialty stores higher for shoes and jewelry and discount stores higher for televisions. These relationships throughout were also very significant. Such relationships suggest that social approval is an important variable in helping to explain consumers' perceptions of quality.

The high-quality perceivers of the total sample (Group 2), rated the importance of values higher than did any other group. Group 5, the lowest-quality perceivers, were directly opposite Group 2 in rating the importance of the instrumental values. Group 1 almost exclusively rated all of the values lower than any other group. It was interesting that none of the group profiles were very similar to any of the other group profiles. The distinctiveness of these profiles may offer a better clue to the differences in consumers' perceptions of quality that was provided by demographic data, and may lend support for the consideration of socialization variables in the examination of perceived quality.

Implications

The major implications of this study are that shoppers are not homogeneous with respect to their perceptions of product quality, and that one of the major bases upon which they differentiate the quality of products is the retail outlets through which they are sold. If these conclusions are approximately correct, then retail strategic planners should consider the segmentation of markets on the basis of perceived quality, as operationalized in this study. Retail chain managers should understand that their chain images carry connotations of quality, and either should work to improve them or to modify them to best meet the needs of the particular patronage markets. Some implications for retail strategic planners to consider include the following points.

1. The quality perceptions of shoppers are affected by retail image and, thus, the latter should be considered in the planning of any overall chain image. If a particular chain wishes to reach some quality-perception group, the socialization characteristics of that group should be considered in some detail. For example, Group 2 (the high-quality group) has value systems that are characterized by high importances on most of the value factors in this study. In addition, this group views both social and nonsocial products as more highly visible than do the other groups. Thus, if the patronage target is this group, the store image should incorporate social dimensions in advertising and promotion of all kinds. In more general advertising, the chain should carefully nurture an image of high value, both in terms of integrity as well as in terms of value received.

2. Another implication from this study relates to the kinds of information that can be used in helping the strategic planner to design copy: radio, television, and the print media. Again, using Group 2 as an example, copy should emphasize integrity and social approval from perceived peer groups.

3. Retail strategic planners should carefully select new sites to correspond to the location of those individuals who are similar to the selected target market(s). It is not unreasonable to presuppose that those having similar perceptions of chain product quality may not also have residences near each other.

4. Buyers may find it useful to select products that are considered acceptable by the perceived-quality segment to which they are appealing. It seems likely that a shotgun approach has little chance of success. Purchasing should be trained according to the social character of the major target segment to which the chain is trying to sell products.

5. Particular chains should give attention to the in-store atmospherics, and the environment and motif of stores. In particular, atmo-

spherics should reflect the taste and preferences of the perceived-quality market(s) to which the chain aspires to sell its products. Comfort and overall pleasant motifs may not be enough; it may be necessary to create a social environment that is appropriate for the target market(s).

References

Bearden, William O. and Michael J. Etzel (1982), "Reference Group Influence on Product and Brand Purchase Decisions," *Journal of Consumer Research* 9 (September):183–94.

Bourne, Francis S. (1957), "Group Influence in Marketing and Public Relations," in *Some Applications of Behavioural Research*, Rensis Likert and Samuel P. Hayes, Jr., eds., UNESCO, 207–57.

Darden, William R. (1980), "A Patronage Model of Consumer Behavior," in *Competitive Structure in Retail Markets: The Department Store Perspective*, R.W. Stampfl and E. Hirshman, eds., Chicago: American Marketing Association, 43–52.

Darden, William R., Donna K. Darden, Roy Howell, and Shirley J. Miller (1981), "Consumer Socialization Factors in a Patronage Model of Consumer Behavior," in *Advances in Consumer Research*, vol. 8, K.B. Monroe, ed., Ann Arbor, Mich.: Association for Consumer Research, 655–61.

Darden, William R., Orhan Erdem, Donna K. Darden, and Roy Howell (1979), "Consumer Values and Shopping Orientations," paper presented at the meetings of the Southwestern Marketing Association.

Enis, Ben and James Stafford (1969), "Consumers' Perception of Product Quality as a Function of Various Information Inputs," *Proceedings of Fall Conference*, Chicago: American Marketing Association, 340–44.

Etgar, Michael and Naresh K. Malhotra (1978), "Consumers' Reliance on Different Product Quality Cues: A Basis for Market Segmentation," in *Research Frontiers in Marketing: Dialogues and Directions*, 1978 Educators' Proceedings, Subhash C. Jain, ed., Chicago: American Marketing Association, 143–47.

Jacoby, Jacob, J.C. Olson, and R.A. Haddock (1971), "Price, Brand Name and Product Composition Characteristics as Determinants of Perceived Quality," *Journal of Applied Psychology* 55 (December):570–78.

Lambert, Zarrel V. (1972), "Price and Choice Behavior," *Journal of Marketing Research* 9 (February):35–40.

Lambert, Zarrel V. (1970), "Product Perception: An Important Variable in Pricing Strategy," *Journal of Marketing* 34 (October):68–70.

Mizerski, Richard W. and Robert B. Settle (1979), "The Influence of Social Character on Preference for Social versus Objective Information in Advertising," *Journal of Marketing Research* 16 (November):552–58.

Olshavsky, Richard W. and John A. Miller (1972), "Consumer Expectations, Product Performance, and Perceived Product Quality," *Journal of Marketing Research* 9 (February):19–21.

Olson, Jerry C. (1977), "Price as an Informational Cue: Effects on Product Evaluations," in *Consumer and Industrial Buying Behavior*, A.G. Woodside, J.N. Sheth, and P.D. Bennett, eds., New York: North Holland, 267–86.

Olson, Jerry C. and Jacob Jacoby (1972), "Cue Utilization in the Quality Perception Process," in *Proceedings*, M. Venkatesan, ed., Ann Arbor, Mich.: Association for Consumer Research, 167–79.

Rao, Vithala R. (1971), "Salience of Price in the Perception of Product Quality: A Multidimensional Measurement Approach," in *Proceedings of Fall Conference*, F.C. Allvine, ed., Chicago: American Marketing Association, 571–77.

Render, Barry and Thomas S. O'Connor (1976), "The Influence of Price, Store Name, and Brand Name on Perception of Product Quality," *Journal of the Academy of Marketing Science* 4 (Fall):722–30.

Rokeach, Milton (1973), *The Nature of Human Values*, New York: Free Press.

Stafford, James E. and Ben M. Enis (1969), "The Price–Quality Relationship: An Extension," *Journal of Marketing Research* 6 (November):456–58.

Szybillo, George J. and Jacob Jacoby (1974), "Intrinsic versus Extrinsic Cues as Determinants of Perceived Product Quality," *Journal of Applied Psychology* 59 (February):74–78.

Szybillo, George J. and Jacob Jacoby (1972), "The Relative Effects of Price, Store Image, and Intrinsic Product Differences on Product Quality Evaluation," in *Proceedings*, M. Venkatesan, ed., Ann Arbor, Mich.: Association for Consumer Research, 180–86.

Valenzi, Enzo and Larry Eldridge (1973), "Effect of Price Information, Composition Differences, Expertise, and Rating Scales on Product-Quality Rating," in *Proceedings*, vol. 8, 81st Annual Convention of the American Psychological Association, 829–30.

Vinson, Donald E. and J. Michael Munson (1976), "Personal Values: An Approach to Market Segmentation," in *Marketing: 1776–1976 and Beyond*, K.E. Bernhardt, ed., Chicago: American Marketing Association, 313–17.

Vinson, Donald E., Jerome Scott, and Lawrence Lamont (1977), "The Role of Personal Values in Marketing and Consumer Behavior," *Journal of Marketing* 41 (April):44–50.

Wheatley, John J. and S.Y. Chiu (1977), "The Effects of Price, Store Image, and Product and Respondent Characteristics on Perceptions of Quality," *Journal of Marketing Research* 14 (May):181–86.

Part IV
Regulatory and Economic Perspectives on Quality

11
The FTC's Product Defects Program and Consumer Perceptions of Product Quality

John E. Calfee and
Gary T. Ford

T he consumer-protection laws enforced by the Federal Trade Commission (FTC) include both a general prohibition of "unfair acts and practices" and several highly specific statutes requiring "fair" labeling, nondiscrimination in the granting of credit, and so on. The more general mandate covers, among other things, potentially fraudulent sales and advertising. Within this broad area the FTC is free to emphasize or ignore various market activities, to search for and possibly attack problems previously undiscussed, and finally, to fashion new ways of dealing with old problems that previously were untouched by federal regulation.

The FTC's product defects program is an example of the more creative (and often more controversial) aspect of FTC activity. It attempts to deal with a problem as old as mass retailing: the product that unexpectedly fails shortly after its warranty expires. The commission's approach has been essentially to make firms liable for injury resulting from failure to inform consumers of postwarranty defects that occur systematically and that the firm could have warned consumers about. Thus at its core the defects program is concerned with product quality— or more precisely, with the differences between perceived and actual product quality.

The product defects program has quietly grown to a considerable size; over a dozen cases have either been resolved by consent decrees

The views expressed here are the authors' and do not necessarily reflect those of the Federal Trade Commission or other members of its staff. We thank Marsha Harris who did the background research on the cases discussed in this chapter, and Jeff Karp who provided a careful reading and valuable comments. We are, of course, responsible for any remaining shortcomings.

or are now under litigation after the filing of formal complaints. Redress to consumers has amounted so far to roughly $200 million. In addition, a recent settlement with General Motors (GM) exposes to binding arbitration certain disputes involving more than 10 million vehicles. Other remedies, such as publication of "technical service bulletins" as required in the GM case and the Ford "piston scuffing" proceeding, add to the defects program's total market effects.

The major sections of this chapter provide an overview of the product defects program, present anecdotal and intuitive evidence on the overall need for the program, and discuss in some detail the kinds of issues in product quality that arise in the course of FTC cases. Throughout, we emphasize the set of unresolved research issues that the FTC's approach brings to the surface.

The Product Defects Program

Economic Foundations

The FTC's product defects program can be said to emanate from a belief that if consumers are fully informed, markets can be expected to work well.[1] With fully informed consumers, natural competitive pressures will compel manufacturers to produce roughly the degree and variety of quality and reliability that significant segments of consumers desire.

The potential problem lies in the fact that both common observation and economic theory suggest that information available to consumers will be far from complete. Direct observation on this point is suggestive, although not conclusive. Consumers know little about the workings of complicated objects such as houses, automobiles, room air conditioners, and home computers. Certainly the fact that certain components will turn out to be unusually troublesome is frequently unknown to the buyer at the time of sale. One might therefore argue that the market provides manufacturers with little incentive to make complicated components, such as automobile air conditioners, durable.

But these observations miss the point. Market discipline arises from indirect as well as from direct pressures. A conversation with any home builder or automobile manufacturer will reveal a deep concern with the reputational effects of bad components or unreliable products. Market performance is determined by the sum of these direct and indirect pressures, and the net result is hardly obvious.

The theory, as opposed to the anecdotes, is somewhat more convincing. The economics of information constitutes a significant and increasing portion of contemporary economic theory. Information can be thought of as a commodity like houses and breakfast cereals, and one can ask whether the unregulated market will produce this particular commodity—information about products—at approximately the optimal level. The outlook, at least in theory, is inauspicious. Information as a commodity suffers from severe marketing problems. For example, property rights are incomplete, since the producer of information may lose control over the use of his product as soon as he sells copies to a few people. Also, information dissemination admits of great economies of scale: costs consist of a large fixed base (the initial gathering operation) and low marginal costs (the printing of a few pages of ratings). Thus, even if information producers controlled perfectly the reproduction of what they sold (that is, if the free rider problem were solved), the market would still work imperfectly because sellers could not provide the information at marginal cost while making a profit.

Beyond these problems is the fact that information as a commodity is difficult for potential buyers to evaluate. How can one assess the value of a piece of information until one knows what it is, and then why should one pay for it if one already knows it? Finally, since advertisers are the source of much product information, their claims are often taken at less than face value, because potential buyers are aware of the advertisers' incentives. Thus, purveyors of information face a perpetual problem of credibility, and sometimes cannot disseminate the truth even if they wish to do so.

In the consumer market, the effect of these problems may be to prevent competitive forces from causing useful information to be disseminated from sellers to buyers, even when buyers would be willing to pay the cost of the information. The logical limit would be a "lemons" market (Akerlof 1970), which works as follows. If for one reason or another sellers cannot tell the truth about their products, they have little incentive to provide more quality than what is immediately apparent or is warranted by contract. Buyers, who have no reason to expect better-than-average quality, will pay for no more than that. A vicious circle ensues. Higher-quality products are pulled off the market, average quality falls, the price that buyers are willing to pay therefore also falls, and the process continues until quality descends to the point where nothing can be taken for granted. We reach a market of "lemons," as the used car market is sometimes asserted to be.

Actually, the theory is not so bleak as this. A number of analysts have developed consumer "search" models in which some consumers will try different sellers and punish those who fail to provide quality. Some of the models indicate that the market can work fairly well even with much less than complete information (Salop 1976). In addition, there is the commonsense idea that in a lemons market, sellers as well as buyers lose; neither are as well off as they would be if each side could trust the other. Thus, sellers have an incentive to build up and to guard their reputations, for the establishment of a good reputation makes the provision of high quality and reliable advertising more profitable.

On the whole then, these arguments suggest that the market has the potential to perform poorly in the provision of information to consumers, and that this in turn could lead to inadequate performance in the actual provision of quality. But the arguments are far from conclusive, either on the matter of how badly the market will work or, more to the point here, on the likely effects of an intervention like the FTC's product defects program.

Legal Theory: Liability for Nondisclosure

An obvious problem in a market characterized by imperfect communication is that sellers may have little incentive to tell buyers about specific, unexpected problems that arise over time. Such problems are bound to happen occasionally in the mass production of complicated devices like cars and houses. It is to be expected that sellers will accumulate negative information about their products, and it is at least possible (because of the factors just discussed) that they will tell buyers little of what they know. The result would be both "incorrect" consumer decisions and, in the longer run, a lower level of quality than would obtain if the level of product quality were more perfectly identified.

This is the problem faced by the FTC. Taking for granted its existence, one can imagine two different ways to deal with it. One approach would be simply to require that sellers provide longer warranties. It is to the FTC's credit that it has not taken this approach.[2] Such an approach would suffer from the grave flaw that there is no compelling reason to expect that the commission would be able to specify a trade-off between price and warranty duration more beneficial to consumers than what emerges naturally from the market.

The second approach begins by looking at the cause of the putative problem, which is that sellers who have learned of problems in their products may not have an incentive to provide useful information to past or potential buyers. The FTC's program can be seen as placing upon sellers liability for the harm that consumers suffer in such circumstances. Since this approach involves both product quality and information, the commission typically seeks as remedies some combination of redress to buyers and prospective arrangements for fuller disclosure of information.

This idea is simple in theory but not in application. The FTC has never explained exactly what kinds of activities constitute violations of the law as represented by the product defects program. This is consistent with the commission's overall approach, which involves enforcing a vague standard (the FTC Act plus amendments), the precise meaning of which is left to emerge from the results of individual cases.[3] Unfortunately, in the product defects area no case has ever completed litigation, and things are even more in the dark than usual. However, an examination of the complaints that have been brought by the commission provides insights into the general legal theory being used.

Essentially, a case must satisfy three conditions. The first is that the product included systematic, known defects, where *defect* may be taken to mean (in the words of the 1980 complaint issued against General Motors) "the occurrence or likely occurrence of an abnormal number of failures or malfunctions of a component, group of components or system, where such failures or malfunctions are costly to correct or may substantially affect the quality, reliability, durability, or performance of a motor vehicle." Obviously, this does not mean that every product sold contained the latent defect, merely that an "abnormal" number of them revealed the problem. (How long the product must last before something like a worn-out transmission is no longer considered to be a "failure" is of course not specified.) Not only must the problem exist, but the seller must have known of the problem (or should have known, acting reasonably under the circumstances). Thus it is not illegal—at least so far as this aspect of FTC policy is concerned—to sell a car whose paint peels after eighteen months, if the seller could not reasonably have known at the time of sale that this was likely to happen.[4]

The second requirement has to do with disclosures to consumers. The firm must have been in a position to disclose to buyers something about the problems that were likely to occur, and must have failed to make an appropriate disclosure. Again, what constitutes a "disclosure" is not specified. The FTC has said nothing about what a disclosure must contain, the factual basis that must underly disclosures, or the effects disclosures should have on consumers.

Both these elements can be drawn directly from the wording of the complaints voted by the FTC in past defects cases. A third element is implied (at least in our opinion). The FTC Act requires that commission actions be "in the public interest"—a requirement that seems distinct from and additional to the other parts of the act, which refer to bringing actions to halt "deceptive and unfair" practices. A reasonable interpretation of this requirement is that specific commission actions must increase rather than decrease consumer welfare. The only way to assure this, when constructing defects cases, is to direct the policy only to those situations in which the proscribed actions actually inflicted net injury on consumers. To put this another way, a requirement of a good case is that the "missing disclosure" would have provided more benefits than costs for consumers. This is not a trivial requirement. Preparing for and making disclosures is costly (the cost to be paid by consumers, ultimately), and highly specific information may be misleading or nearly useless, no matter how pure the motives for disclosing it. Thus, one can easily imagine situations in which undertaking to provide the missing information would not have made consumers better off.

Although reliance on these three elements is straightforward conceptually, implementation is beset with difficulties, not the least being the factual burden of determining what the seller knew at the time in question and what would have been the practical consequences of disclosure. These and similar problems lead to an array of research issues, which shall manifest themselves as we discuss the major issues involved in the program. We shall look first at the central underlying question—how bad is the problem the program is designed to solve?—and then at a number of issues that derive from the workings of the program itself.

Representative Cases

A representative list of cases that have been settled or in which a complaint has been filed under the product defects program is provided in table 11–1. The most striking fact is that so far no case has reached a final conclusion, except through the signing of a consent decree. Consent decrees involve no admission of wrongdoing by the respondent, although they usually include some portion of the remedy sought by the FTC. More important, a consent decree produces no public record of the facts and no explanation of legal reasoning. Thus consents cannot contribute significantly to the crucial informational role that completed litigation often provides for those who attempt to understand the working of markets (or the workings of the FTC, for that matter).

An examination of table 11–1 also reveals the following additional points about the product defects program. First, each case involved consumer rather than industrial products. Second, for the most part the cases have involved expensive consumer durables such as automobiles and air conditioners. However, some less-expensive products are involved when consumer safety is at issue. Third, in each case the alleged defect was of a kind that is not observable by consumers before sale, and in fact the defect did not show itself until some time well after the sale of the product. Fourth, most settlements involved notification of substantial numbers of consumers and the transfer of large sums from firms to consumers.

Extent of the Information Problem Addressed by the Defects Program

The FTC has never attempted to gather systematic evidence on the extent to which information problems have caused consumer products to

Table 11–1
Public FTC Product Defects Cases

Manufacturer	Problem	Disposition	Consumers Affected	Remedy
Automobile Cases				
American Motors	Tendency of jeeps to turn over	Consent	Owners of 1972–1981 Jeeps CJ5, CJ6, or CJ7	Disclosure to consumers
General Motors	Transmission, camshaft, and diesel failure	Consent	5 to 6 million trans'ns; 5 million V8s; .5 million diesel engines	Arbitration and publication of technical bulletins
American Honda	Premature fender rusting	Consent	Approx. 700,000 1975–1978 Civics and Accords	Repairs and reimbursement
Ford Motor	Piston scuffing; camshaft rocker arm wear; cracked engine blocks	Consent	Certain 1979 and 1980 models	Repairs, reimbursement, and disclosure of technical bulletins
Chrysler Corp.	Premature rusting	Consent	1976 and 1977 Aspens and Volares (app. 600,000 cars)	Repairs or reimbursement
Chrysler Corp.	Oil filters	Consent	Certain 1971–1982 Chrysler and Mitsubishi cars (approx. 700,000)	Mail notices to current owners
Volkswagen	Excess oil consumption leading to engine problems	In litigation	1977–1981 VW and Audi cars	—
Volkswagen	Oil filer leaks	Consent	1977–1981 diesel VWs and Audis	Reimbursement to owners
Other Cases				
Champion Home Builders	Solar furnace failures	Consent	Approx. 1,600 furnaces manufactured in 1976–1979	Reimbursement to buyers
Figgie Int'l	Inadequate performance of heat detectors	In litigation	Nonpublic	—
Internat'l Harvester	Fuel geysering from fuel intake	Appealed from ALJ to FTC	Owners of various models of I.H. tractors	—
Bayleysuit	Defect in survival suits	Consent	Approx. 4,800 buyers	Upgrade kit for buyers
Mobil Corp.	Use of "Mobil 1" increases rather than decreases oil consumption	Consent	Approx. 750,000 buyers in 1979	Product removed from market
Ward Corp.	Failure to repair defects under warranty	In litigation	Certain developments in Maryland and Virginia	—

be "too defective," however that term may be defined.[5] We shall look at the question of the extent of this problem as a means for introducing the kinds of research issues that the FTC's defects program provides.

One can attack this question either directly or indirectly. The direct approach seeks to examine the relation between product quality (how frequent and how costly are postwarranty defects, and so forth) and consumer knowledge (what perceptions do consumers have about product quality, how accurate are those perceptions, how valuable is the missing information, do people realize how little they know, and so on). One tries to learn the extent to which product quality and information about product quality fall short of consumer "expectations." The FTC has not yet attempted to assess this for an entire market or submarket. The housing study referred to in note 4 is in the spirit of this approach, but it is incomplete since it does not look at consumer information. Other potential sources of information are the FTC defects cases themselves. But as we noted earlier, no FTC cases have yet proceeded far enough to provide significant public information about the extent to which firms fail to disclose the existence of known defects. Precisely because so many issues concerning product quality are generally unresolved, however, FTC cases provide an interesting set of research topics relating consumer perceptions to actual product quality. The first research issue deals with these kinds of problems.

Research Issue Number 1

The issue is: What is the general state of consumer knowledge of product quality? What do consumers generally know and expect about product quality? To what extent do consumers understand the limitations on their own stock of information?

This is actually several research problems, all derived from the central concerns of consumer knowledge and expectations about product quality. These concerns go far beyond the simple question of consumers' knowledge about the technical details of what they purchase. Indeed, no research at all is necessary to show that the vast majority of consumers know little about the workings of a fuel-injection system in an automobile or Dolby sound in an amplifier. But it is no more true that consumers know nothing than it is that they know everything. The challenge is to break the question up into parts that admit to useful answers.

For example, it is obvious that consumers have at least rough perceptions about the level of product quality of items within a class. That is, if a sample of new car purchasers were asked to rank the three automobiles they most considered purchasing on the dimension of overall product quality or reliability, it is not unlikely that these consumers could provide such a ranking. What is not clear is the extent to which consumer perceptions of overall product quality are correlated with actual product quality. Furthermore, we know little about consumers' expectations regarding even the simplest aspects of product quality. For example, no research that we are aware of addresses the large but relatively simple question of whether products do not last as long as, or last longer than consumers expect. Issues such as these are central to the defects program, whose existence rests on the assumption that consumers' expectations about product quality are often significantly higher than the actual quality of the products they consume.

Moving beyond these basic concerns about perceptions of the entire product, the analysis becomes more complex as the focus shifts to consumer perceptions of the quality of product components, such as brakes and transmissions. There is no well-established research that enables the FTC to know whether consumers' expectations center on when a *specific component* will fail or merely on the more general matter of when *something* will fail. In addition, the commission requires knowledge about the extent to which quality perceptions of components are generalized across other similar products and across other components of the same product.

The *direct* approach to ascertaining whether seller nondisclosure is a significant problem looks at the parts and processes of the consumer market, and simply attempts to gauge actual performance in terms of product quality, disclosure, and so forth. The *indirect* approach starts with the defects program's theoretical underpinnings, especially the idea that asymmetric information and the lack of credibility of seller claims provide an inadequate incentive to build quality into products. The central question is whether indirect market forces, such as reputations, are sufficiently strong to limit this problem to a more-or-less negligible amount. In theory, powerful impediments to communication of product information should cause the market to tend toward the lemons equilibrium described earlier. Sellers would not find it profitable to offer products that last longer than the warranty (unless doing so were costless), because buyers would not believe sellers' claims that the product would do so. Thus, product quality would be essentially limited by whatever information consumers could ascertain before purchase, plus explicit guarantees and warranties. Since warranties, like all insurance, are inherently limited by problems of adverse selection and moral hazard, this level of quality would be considerably short of what consumers would pay for if they could be reasonably certain of what they were to receive. Complicated products would be especially prone to this problem, for consumers would have little defense beyond the guarantee. Not being able to evaluate for themselves the technology involved, consumers would have no leverage available with which to force manufacturers to use the latest technology to enhance durability and other qualities that become evident only long after sale.

One might object that casual observation suggests that things cannot be this bad. Televisions, for example, are extremely complex yet obviously last far longer than any known warranty, and indeed, outlast any nonwarranted claim that sellers commonly make. This suggests that the market somehow avoids the worst kinds of lemons outcomes. It is useful to remember in this context that in lemons markets both sellers and buyers lose. Sellers therefore have an incentive to overcome the underlying information problem, which they may attempt to do by creating market signals such as "full" warranties, longer-than-average warranties, brand names (for example, "Diehard"), claims of "satisfaction guaranteed" or "money-back guarantees," and other strategies for building, maintaining, or enhancing reputations (Spence 1973). Yet the fact remains that lemons markets are both possible and serve as justification for a number of regulatory interventions such as the FTC's product defects program.

Research Issue Number 2

The issue is: To what extent does the market diverge from a lemons equilibrium (defined as one in which products include no costly quality beyond what is guaranteed by warranties and consumer search)?

This is a complex and difficult issue for researchers. The work done so far is almost entirely theoretical and of very limited applicability (cf. Heinkel 1981; Leland 1979; Stuart 1981; Salop 1978). Little evidence is available on lemons markets (Bond 1982) and what research exists is inconclusive about the prevalence and severity of lemons markets. Perhaps the best way to investigate this issue is through econometric techniques. For example, the researcher could use secondary data and hedonic price indexes to determine whether product quality is changing over time in a way that is incompatible with a continuing lemons equilibrium.

A final complicating and somewhat more subtle factor involves the perceptions and expectations consumers may have about some of the factors that help prevent a lemons equilibrium. For example, if consumers expect that advertising is truthful, or that price is an accurate cue for quality, lemons markets will not easily occur. The literature on perceived price-quality relationships and cue utilization leads to the conclusion that, although consumers prefer intrinsic cues to extrinsic cues (Olson and Jacoby 1972; Szybillo and Jacoby 1974; Pincus and Waters 1975), they will search for and use those cues that are available

(Jacoby, Olson, and Haddock 1971; Enis and Stafford 1969; Wheatley and Chiu 1977). This research has consistently found that when price is a salient cue, it will be used as a cue for quality (Enis and Stafford 1969). However, if intrinsic cues are available consumers will use them, placing less emphasis on extrinsic cues such as price (Szybillo and Jacoby 1974). The literature on advertising indicates that consumers are quite wary about the truthfulness of advertising (Alter 1981; Greyser 1977). But as long as there is a fairly high level of credibility of advertising or the belief that reliable cues exist, the information market should work well.

The cue-utilization literature also affords a number of questions about the strategies consumers use for assessing product quality. From our perspective, one of the most interesting questions concerns what cue-utilization strategy the consumer uses when the product is so complex that the consumer is not comfortable with the information provided by intrinsic cues. Olson and Jacoby (1982) discuss the concepts of "cue predictive value," that is, the degree to which an individual associates a cue with product quality (p. 174); and "cue confidence value," which refers to the consumer's self-confidence in his ability to distinguish the cue and make accurate evaluations and judgments concerning it (p. 175). With products such as stereo amplifiers or home air conditioners, consumers may not know what cues to use or how to rate products on the available cues. Then extrinsic cues may become more prominent (Olson and Jacoby 1972).

The cue-utilization literature has not shed much light on this question. Most studies have been conducted with inexpensive products such as ball-point pens and women's hosiery rather than with complex durables that make use of intrinsic cues more problematic. Further, the research that does deal with complex products should be considered exploratory (see for example, Olshavsky and Miller 1972; Bearden and Shimp 1982; Shimp and Bearden 1982). Thus, the opportunities for research in this area appear particularly appealing.

Further Research Issues

An important research problem centers on the potential impact on consumers of the types of disclosures that are considered to be missing in FTC cases and therefore are often required as part of settlements. In the Honda fender-lining case, it was alleged that consumers should have been warned of a latent rust problem with fenders, which could have been prevented by installing fender liners. In the "piston scuffing" case, Ford Motors was faulted for failing to warn consumers of an engine problem, and the consent settlement requires Ford to advertise and to make available to consumers a selected set of technical bulletins that previously were sent mainly to Ford dealers. The recent GM settlement contains a similar requirement. The idea is to give consumers access to information with which they can form more accurate impressions of car quality, as well as information that may be useful for special repairs and maintenance. This leads to a third research question.

Research Issue Number 3

The issue is: What are the expected effects on consumer decision making of the types of disclosure contemplated in FTC cases?

It is well known that negative information exerts a disproportionate impact on consumer decision making (Lynch and Srull 1982; Mizerski 1982). For the defects program several questions come to mind. One of the more important is: What is the impact of negative information about one component on the overall evaluation of the product? Suppose, for example, that 10 percent of the models of a certain automobile suffered from a systematic (correctable) defect in their exhaust system that would result in the consumer spending $150 additional over the life of the car to repair this problem. (Thus, the expected extra repair cost is .10 times $150, or $15.) Also, suppose that this car had exceptional gas mileage and relatively low maintenance expenses (other than for the exhaust system), which led to an advantage of $100 over comparable alternatives. In this situation, if the negative information about the exhaust system leads the consumer to choose another automobile, the average consumer will probably be worse off. Therefore from the standpoint of assessing the value of the whole car, the disclosure about the exhaust system would do more harm than good.

This raises some additional questions. Did the negative information lead the consumer to downgrade other attributes of the automobile, to change the weight accorded to the exhaust-system component, or to change his or her assessment of the probability that the stimulus item has the attribute? Or, would the consumer place substantial value on minimizing the time and trouble associated with repairs—that is, to what extent are consumers willing to pay a premium on minimizing inconvenience of repairing a defect? The answers to these and similar questions could have significant influence on any assessment of the workings of defects cases.

These issues have been discussed to some extent in the consumer-behavior literature (Lutz 1975; Scott and Tybout 1981; Weinberger, Allen, and Dillon 1981; Weinberger and Dillon 1980; Mowen, Jolley, and Nickel 1981; Mizerski 1982). For example, the research findings of both Lutz (1975) and Mizerski (1982) are consistent with the notion that negative information affects the subjects' belief that the object possesses the attribute. While this research is suggestive, it has generally been limited by the nature of the sample or the nature of the products used, that is, inexpensive consumer nondurables.

The FTC's product defects program, if it is to be successful, must cause systematic changes in the way products are produced and marketed. Whether this has happened or is likely to happen is an open question. Although the product defects program has been in existence for several years, there is almost no information available about the effects of the program on consumer markets in general. The research problem can be stated as in the next subsection.

Research Issue Number 4

The issue is: What impact has the defects program had on manufacturers' and retailers' disclosures to consumers? What has been the effect on product quality?

Essentially the question is whether there has been a multiplier effect as firms react to the cases brought under the defects program. Although the consumer redress from the defects program is a considerable sum on an absolute basis, it is insignificant relative to total consumer sales in the United States. However, if the defects program has influenced (1) the amount, types, and form of information provided by sellers, (2) the coverage of warranties, or (3) the quality levels of products, the program's effects are considerably larger than any estimate of consumer redress. Added to the total effect is the possibility that an unintended effect of the program may be to make manufacturers more risk adverse. Ultimately this could stifle or at least slow innovation if manufacturers became less willing to introduce new, untried products that may increase liability under the defects program.

Whether much along this line has occurred is open to doubt; certainly no comprehensive effect is evident. The apparently small impact of the defects program can be compared with that of the advertising substantiation program. The latter program has had tremendous effects on the procedures used for developing claims, on the types of claims made, and on other advertising strategy decisions—despite the near absence of such remedies as consumer redress. Of course, the advertising substantiation program has the support of many advertisers (LaBarbera 1981), and a large advertising self-regulation program has augmented the FTC program.

Research Issue Number 5

The issue is: What is the impact of the defects program on consumers' perceptions of product quality? On their perception of sellers' disclosure practices and responsibilities?

Finally, has the defects program had any impact on consumers' perceptions of overall product quality? One can develop conflicting hypotheses about this question. One possibility is that the effects of product defects cases are similar to a commonly hypothesized effect of advertising substantiation cases. That is, consumers become aware that product quality is being monitored by an independent organization, which causes them to have increased confidence in the quality of goods available (LaBarbera 1982). Alternatively, increased awareness of product recalls and defects cases is consistent with the perception that product quality is declining and thus could cause consumers to have less confidence in the quality of products in the market.

Conclusions

The FTC's product defects program, now some six or seven years old, employs a peculiarly informational approach in dealing with potential problems of product quality. The legal rule implied by the commission's defects cases essentially amounts to establishing liability for correctable situations in which product quality is strongly at variance with consumer perceptions of quality.

Thus, consumer perceptions of quality, and consumer uses of product information, form the heart of the program. This approach can be seen as deriving from contemporary economic theory of information. This gives the program a sound intellectual foundation as compared to many FTC and other regulatory innovations, which usually rely upon intuitively unappealing or empirically shaky views of contemporary markets. Nonetheless, the public record so far on the defects program is relatively empty. The existence of those market conditions that would call for a vigorous program of this type is not yet established, partly because of the difficulty of the questions involved. Research on the relevant topics is in its infancy, and likely to be of great interest. Similarly, the mechanics of defects cases themselves—for example, the contention that certain kinds of disclosures would have provided benefits to consumers exceeding their costs—raise a legion of questions. These questions are relatively unexplored in either theory or practice. The answers, which are likely to come from a combination of econometric and consumer-research methods, promise to be of wide interest.

Notes

1. We do not deal in this chapter with the question of "competition" from the perspective of antitrust policy.

2. Section 5 of the FTC Act arguably provides the FTC with the power to regulate the length of warranties. Such a power does not stem from the Magnuson–Moss Act, however: "Congress expressly specified that nothing in the Magnuson–Moss Act was intended to give the FTC power to prescribe the duration of warranties or to require that a warranty be given." (Hobbs and Clayton 1981, p. 21.) In individual cases the commission has occasionally imposed remedies that require manufacturers to extend warranties on certain products or components.

3. In October, 1983, the FTC issued a Statement on Deception, which summarized and synthesized FTC opinions in a large number of deception cases. But this statement did not directly consider the issues raised by defects cases.

4. The defects program is also concerned with situations in which manufacturers could have disclosed new use and care instructions to buyers, but failed to do so. Several of the cases listed in table 11–1 are of this type, the Volkswagen oil filter settlement being an example. In this chapter we shall stick with pure defects cases, and not be concerned with the ways in which the analysis would differ for use-and-care cases.

5. A partial exception to this generalization is a survey conducted for the FTC and the Department of Housing and Urban Development (HUD) by Mathematica, which used interviews and inspections to ascertain the extent to which new houses reveal defects that are not fixed under warranty. This survey, although useful, does not relate product defects to information, as such, and also suffers from the problem of a lack of a baseline—that is, how many problems are "too many" and (a particularly difficult issue with new houses) what exactly is a "problem."

References

Akerlof, George A. (1970), "The Market for 'Lemons': Quality Uncertainty and the Market Mechanism," *The Quarterly Journal of Economics* 84 (August): 488–500.

Alter, Jennifer (1981), "Public Is Still Wary of Ads: Study," *Advertising Age* (June 23):3.

Bearden, William O. and Terence A. Shimp (1982), "The Use of Extrinsic Cues to Facilitate Product Adoption," *Journal of Marketing Research* 19:229–39.

Bond, Eric W. (1982), "A Direct Test of the 'Lemons' Model: The Market for Used Pickup Trucks," *American Economic Review* 72, no. 4 (September):836–40.

Enis, Ben M. and James E. Stafford (1969), "Consumers' Perceptions of Product Quality as a Function of Various Informational Inputs," in *Marketing Involvement in Society and the Economy*, Phillip R. McDonald, ed., Chicago: American Marketing Association, 340–44.

Federal Trade Commission (1980), *Complaint in the Matter of General Motors Corporation*, Docket no. 9145, 7 August, 3 pages.

Greyser, Stephen (1977), *Consumerism at the Crossroads: A National Opinion Research Survey of Public, Activist, Business and Regulator Attitudes Towards the Consumer Movement*, Boston: Marketing Science Institute.

Heinkel, Robert (1981), "Uncertain Product Quality: the Market for Lemons with an Imperfect Testing Technology," Bell Journal of Economics 12:625–36.

Hobbs, Caswell O. and Michael F. Clayton (1981), "FTC Product Liability Program Lacks Guidelines," Legal Times of Washington, 18 May, 21 +.

Jacoby, Jacob, Jerry C. Olson, and Rafael A. Haddock (1971), "Price, Brand Name, and Product Composition Characteristics as Determinants of Perceived Quality," Journal of Applied Psychology 55:570–79.

LaBarbera, Priscilla A. (1981), "The Antitrust Shadow over Advertising Self-Regulation," Current Issues and Research in Advertising, Claude Martin, Jr., ed., Ann Arbor, Mich.: University of Michigan Press, 57–70.

_____ (1981), "Overcoming a No-Reputation Liability through Documentation and Advertising Regulation," Journal of Marketing Research 19 (May): 223–28.

Leland, H. (1979), "Quacks, Lemons and Licensing: A Theory of Minimum Quality Standards," 87 Journal of Political Economy (December):1328–46.

Lutz, Richard J. (1975), "Changing Brand Attitudes through Modification of Cognitive Structure," Journal of Consumer Research 1:49–59.

Lynch, John G., Jr., and Thomas K. Srull (1982), "Memory and Attention Factors in Consumer Research: Concepts and Research Methods," Journal of Consumer Research 9 (June):18–37.

Miller, Ross M. and Charles R. Plott (1982), "Signalling in Experimental Markets," unpublished manuscript, August, 38 pages plus appendixes.

Mizerski, Richard W. (1982), "An Attribution Explanation of the Disproportionate Influence of Unfavorable Information," Journal of Consumer Research 9 (December):301–10.

Mowen, John C., David Jolly, and Gary S. Nickell (1981), "Factors Influencing Consumer Responses to Product Recalls: A Regression Analysis Approach," Advances in Consumer Research, vol. 8, Kent Monroe, ed., Ann Arbor, Mich.: Association for Consumer Research, 405–7.

Olshavsky, Richard W. and John A. Miller (1972), "Consumer Expectations, Product Performance, and Perceived Product Quality," Journal of Marketing Research 9:19–21.

Olson, Jerry C. and Jacob Jacoby (1972), "Cue Utilization in the Quality Perception Process," in Proceedings, Third Annual Conference, M. Venkatesan, ed., Iowa City, Iowa: Association for Consumer Research, 167–79.

Pincus, Stephen and L.K. Waters (1975), "Product Quality Ratings as a Function of Availability of Intrinsic Product Cues and Price Information," Journal of Applied Psychology 60:280–82.

Salop, Steven (1976), "Information and Monopolistic Competition," American Economic Review 66:240–45.

_____ (1978), "Parables of Information Transmission in Markets," in The Effects of Information on Consumer and Market Behavior, Andrew A. Mitchell, ed., Chicago: American Marketing Association, 3–12.

Scott, Carol A. and Alice M. Tybout (1981), "Theoretical Perspectives on the Impact of Negative Information: Does Valence Matter?" Advances in Consumer Research vol. 8, Kent Monroe, ed., Ann Arbor, Mich.: Association for Consumer Research, 408–9.

Shimp, Terence A. and William O. Bearden (1982), "Warranty and Other Extrinsic Cue Effects on Consumers' Risk Perceptions," *Journal of Consumer Research* 9:38–46.

Spence, Michael (1973), "Job Market Signalling," *Quarterly Journal of Economics* 87:355–74.

Stuart, Charles (1981), "Consumer Protection in Markets with Informationally Weak Buyers," *Bell Journal of Economics* 12:562–73.

Szybillo, George J. and Jacob Jacoby (1974), "Intrinsic versus Extrinsic Cues as Determinants of Perceived Product Quality," *Journal of Applied Psychology* 59:74–78.

Weinberger, Marc G. and William R. Dillon (1980), "The Effects of Unfavorable Product Rating Information," *Advances in Consumer Research* vol. 7, Jerry Olson, ed., Ann Arbor, Mich.: Association for Consumer Research, 528–32.

———, Chris T. Allen, and William R. Dillon (1981), "Negative Information: Perspectives and Research Directions," *Advances in Consumer Research*, vol. 8, Kent Monroe, ed., Ann Arbor, Mich.: Association for Consumer Research, 398–402.

Wheatley, John J. and John S. Chiu (1977), "The Effects of Price, Store Image and Product and Respondent Characteristics on Perceptions of Quality," *Journal of Marketing Research* 14:181–86.

12
Quality as a Normative Concept: A Consumer Economist's Views

E. Scott Maynes

T his chapter introduces quality as a normative concept and takes an analytical tour of local retail markets as analyzed from the consumer viewpoint.

In social science, "client" is everything. The client determines the problems addressed and the tools brought to bear upon them. For social psychologists studying consumer preferences, the chief client is the retail seller; and the researchers' tools are appropriate for ascertaining and influencing preferences.

The client in this chapter is the consumer. The objectives here (somewhat simplified) are: (1) to equip consumers with the concepts and understandings that will enable them to function effectively in the market, and (2) to represent them in assessing and proposing policies and institutions that affect consumers. This involves both the utilization of scarce resources and some knowledge of markets—two economic concepts. I am an economist but I have been well associated with both psychologists and retailers.

The Analytical Framework: The Price-Quality Chart

One advantage of the consumer viewpoint is that we are all consumers. As a "vehicle" for this tour of retail markets from the consumer viewpoint, let us suppose there is a consumer who is interested in purchasing a "good" ten-speed bicycle and, more specifically, that he will buy it in Minneapolis. The single, most important aid in helping him choose such a bicycle would be a *price-quality map* of the market for ten-speed bicycles in Minneapolis. No one publishes such a map, but my colleagues and I have prepared one for the purpose here (see figure 12–1). It tells what one needs to know in choosing a ten-speed bicycle. It is also the analytical framework utilized in much of the research that I will describe.[1]

In figure 12–1, price and quality are depicted along the vertical and horizontal axes, respectively. Both are measured cardinally. Money is intrinsically cardinal, $1 being twice as much as fifty cents. Quality is also measured cardinally on this chart, 100 denoting the "best" quality available. A bicycle with a quality score of 75 is 50 percent better than a bicycle with a quality score of 50. Both price and quality are measured cardinally because consumers naturally ask questions of a cardinal nature: Is a bicycle that costs 25 percent more, 25 percent better?

The capital letters on figure 12–1 (A, B, and so on) denote varieties of bicycles, for example, Fuji Road Racer S10S or Raleigh Supercourse MK II DL100.[2] Each black dot (●) denotes a price offer by a Minneapolis retailer, one per retailer; the open dots (+) denote the list price of varieties of bicycles that are available in the national market, but not in Minneapolis. This *product set* includes the varieties that Consumer's

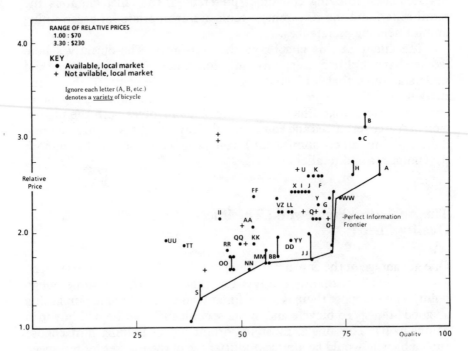

Figure 12–1. Price–Quality Map for 10-Speed Bicycle, Minneapolis—St. Paul, Fall 1976

Union (CU) judged to be representative of the ten-speed bicycles offered in national or major regional markets.

The *market set* consists of the retailers that a middle-class consumer with a car might encounter in normal shopping for this product. The amount of shopping the consumer undertook would depend upon his expected payoffs from the search and the costs of the search, both objective (for example, transportation) and subjective (for example, a distaste for shopping).

Quality can be defined as the extent to which a variety of a product provides the characteristics the individual desires, for example, safety, comfort, and durability. The quality scores depicted in figure 12–1 represent my quantification and cardinalization of data published in *Consumer Reports* (*CR*). CU, publishers of *CR*, measures quality cardinally, but for most products transforms its cardinal measures into orderings or ratings for publication. (Quality is discussed in detail in the next section.)

Intended for normative use, figure 12–1 embodies the fullest information possible, an approach to the economist's "perfect information." The chart displays all the price–quality combinations available to the consumer, whether he is aware of them or not.

The central normative concept in figure 12–1 is the *perfect-information frontier*, defined as the set of points—and the line segments connecting them—for which a given quality may be purchased at the lowest price. The rational consumer who is given this chart and accepts its data as complete and accurate (a strong assumption that we will relax later), would purchase varieties on or near the perfect-information frontier. Why pay more? In choosing a particular point on the perfect-information frontier, the consumer would presumably want to equalize the ratios of marginal utility-to-price (or quality-to-price) across various product categories. In other words, he would allocate his income so that each dollar spent yields approximately the same utility, or quality.

The various uses of this chart lead naturally to various "stops" on this tour through my research. The chart also poses some interesting, but as yet unanswered research questions that I will note along the route.

The Concept and Measurement of Product Quality

The specification of quality is a problem that economists have carefully eschewed. Kelvin Lancaster in his seminal characteristics approach to demand theory (Lancaster 1971, 1966) came close to defining quality, but stopped short, unwilling (in my judgment) to violate utility space, the domain of social psychologists. However, the functioning of markets cannot be assessed validly without taking account of quality, and economists have a responsibility to provide an answer to students and consumers when asked, "What is quality?"

My efforts to say how quality should be conceptualized and measured are represented in Maynes (1976a). Quality is a weighted average of characteristics, given by the following formula.

$$
G_k^{ij} = \frac{\displaystyle\sum_{m=1}^{M} W_m^{ij} \cdot Ch_{km}^{ij}}{\displaystyle\sum_{m=1}^{M} W_m^{ij}}
$$

where: G_k^{ij} = the quality of the kth variety of the jth product class as assigned by the ith individual

W_m^{ij} = the weights assigned to the mth characteristic in the jth product class by the ith individual

Ch_{km}^{ij} = the characteristic score assigned to the mth characteristic of the kth variety in the jth product class by the ith individual

Some comments are in order. Weights represent the relative importance of various characteristics. Within a product class, weights are constant across varieties. Characteristic scores range from 0.00 to 1.00. For each characteristic, 1.00 denotes the utility of a hypothetical "ideal" variety of that product, embodying the best technology. Characteristic scores for particular varieties express the utility obtained from that variety as a ratio to that conferred by an ideal variety. For example, if a Dodge Aries is assigned a value of 0.80 on the characteristic of "Carrying Capacity: Things," this means that the Dodge provides 80 percent as much utility as that afforded by the ideal variety, regardless of the amount of carrying capacity in the Dodge. Hence, my characteristics enter utility space (unlike those of Lancaster) and are subjective, nonuniversal, and personal (again, differing from Lancaster). As noted earlier, my characteristics represent services that consumers want, such as comfort, durability, and safety. Why so? First, because the number of these types of characteristics is likely to be manageably small, facilitating measurement. Second, the relationship between objective characteristics (for example, the glass lining and copper pipes of a hot-water heater) and the services they "produce" in a product (durability, in this example), is likely to be complex. Third, it is the services that consumers want.

An individual can assess quality under different degrees of informedness. For my normative purposes, it is appropriate to assume that the quality assessments are made under full information.

In the research reported in this chapter, quality is assessed for varieties of products and hence does not reflect retailer's characteristics such as locational convenience. The implications of this omission are discussed in the next section.

Formally, as marketers will note, this model is equivalent to the multiattribute model though, of course, my interpretation of the terms differs.

I propose a single index of quality for three reasons. First, a single index facilitates information processing by consumers.[3] Second, a single-valued measure (like a price index or disposable personal income per capita) simplifies analysis and allows for graphical presentations. However, I have no quarrel with those who would also wish to make available separate information regarding the ingredients of quality, for example, the desirability of characteristics, data on performance, and so forth. Finally, it is worth noting that the quality scoring systems utilized by Consumers Union and all its counterparts conform in essence, though not to form, to the model proposed here.[4] (For a critical review of Consumers Union's entire quality assessment and quality publication activities, see Maynes 1976b, chapter 5.)

The Documentation of Informationally Imperfect Consumer Markets

Presumably, all researchers of consumers' perceptions would follow Adam Smith in believing in the efficacy of market mechanisms. It is my belief that Adam Smith, given a price-quality chart, would prefer a market where all prices stood on the perfect-information frontier (assuming that fully informed consumers made uniform assessments of quality).

It is the thesis of Maynes et al. (1983a) that local consumer markets are informationally imperfect—that is, characterized by substantial price variation, quality constant. In such markets many consumers pay higher prices than necessary, thus reducing their level of living. There are three reasons for this: affluence, which makes for more choices and information overload and also for less shopping (time is too valuable); technically complex goods that make assessment of quality and sometimes price difficult; and urbanization which makes for too many choices.

The evidence in support of this thesis comes from price–quality charts for twenty-five products, thirteen of uniform quality and twelve of variable quality, collected in either Syracuse, New York or Ann Arbor, Michigan in 1976 and 1978.[5] The data collected embodies the concepts described earlier, and the results are displayed in table 12–1. They are emphatic. Looking first at "products of uniform quality," for 61 percent of such products the highest price exceeds the lowest price by 50 percent or more; for 38 percent, the highest price is more than double the lowest price; and for 23 percent, the highest price is more than triple the lowest price. We place particular emphasis on these results because they largely avoid the controversial problem of taking account of quality.

For "products of variable quality" the results are even more emphatic: for 91 percent, the highest price exceeds the lowest by 50 percent or more; for 50 percent, the highest price is more than double the lowest price; and for 25 percent the highest price is more than triple the lowest price.

There exists the possibility, for products of variable quality, that some fully informed consumers might make different quality assessments. Here a judgment is unavoidable: Of the price dispersion depicted in table 12–1, how much is properly attributable to differences in quality assessments by fully informed consumers? "Not much," was the authors' judgment. We would note, though, that the greater observed price dispersion for variable-quality products may in part be attributable to consumers' difficulties in assessing quality.

Another objection is that characteristics of retailers—locational convenience, easy return, and so on—may account for some of the observed price dispersion. Prices far above the frontier could reflect consumers' willingness to pay extra for greater amounts of such services that some retailers (we shall call them "good" retailers) offer; prices near the frontier could be those of "bad" retailers who offer few such services. Table 12–2 tests this hypothesis. The test product is single-lens reflex cameras; the test statistic is the *price ratio*, defined for each price a retailer offers as the ratio of that price offer to the corresponding frontier price. As an example of price ratio: for variety B on figure 12–1 the highest *relative* price charged is 3.23; its corresponding *frontier* price (the lowest relative price for approximately the same quality, in this case for variety O) is 1.77; hence, the price ratio in this example is 1.83 (or 3.23 divided by 1.77).

Table 12–2 displays for each retailer the price ratio of each camera that retailer sells. Were the "good–bad" retailer hypothesis correct, the former would have high price ratios with a small variance, and the latter would have low price ratios with a small variance. No formal test is necessary. Inspection of price ratios across retailers tells us that there are neither "good" nor "bad" retailers in this sense. Instead, all retailers offer some cameras at prices far above the frontier and some others

Table 12–1
Observed Price Dispersion, Quality Constant, in Medium-Sized Cities: A Summary

Percentage by Which Highest Price, Quality Constant, Exceeds Lowest Price	Products of Uniform Quality		Products of Variable Quality		Both	
	Number	*Percentage*	*Number*	*Percentage*	*Number*	*Percentage*
Less than 30	3	23	0	0	3	12
30 to 49	2	16	1	9	3	12
50 to 99	3	23	5	41	8	32
100 to 199	2	15	3	25	5	20
200 or more	3	23	3	25	6	24
Total	13	100	12	100	25	100

Table 12–2
Price Discrimination: Evidence from Sales of Single-Lens Reflex Cameras in Ann Arbor, Michigan

Type of Store	Number of Prices	Price Ratios[c]
Camera Specialists[a]		
Quarry Photo, Campus Store	12	1.00, 1.05, 1.35, 1.36, 1.91, 2.33, 2.37, 2.49, 2.50, 3.01, 5.21, 5.50
Quarry Photo, Stadium Blvd.	10	1.00, 1.20, 1.53, 1.91, 2.04, 2.24, 2.37, 3.01, 4.43, 5.20
Lobby Hobby	10	1.29, 1.35, 1.70, 1.78, 1.79, 1.92, 2.17, 2.74, 2.80, 4.06
Purchase Camera	4	1.45, 1.96, 1.97, 2.42
Lafayette Radio–TV	4	1.53, 2.10, 2.67, 3.66
Sun Radio	4	1.27, 2.36, 2.58, 3.55
Discount Houses[b]		
Big George	7	1.00, 1.15, 1.78, 2.15, 2.22, 3.50, 4.16
Century House	4	1.53, 2.07, 2.53, 3.66
K-Mart	2	1.00, 3.53
Meijers' Thrifty	5	1.43, 1.48, 2.09, 2.11, 3.22
State Discount	2	2.06, 4.68

[a]For camera-specialist stores, the mean number of prices = 7.33; the mean low = 1.26; the mean high = 4.07; the mean range = 2.81.

[b]For discount houses, the mean number of prices = 4.00; the mean low = 1.40; the mean high = 3.85; the mean range = 2.46.

[c]The numbers listed under "Price Ratios" run from low to high; that is, the first number listed is low, the last is high.

either on or close to the frontier. Consumers do not in fact obtain ancillary services by paying high prices; they obtain such services by choosing the "right" retailer.

Our general conclusion is that most markets are informationally imperfect, characterized by extensive price dispersion that is not utility conferring. This result does not stand alone. Other research (Duncan 1981; Maynes 1983b) applying the same approach in Minneapolis and Ithaca, New York in 1976, gave highly similar results. Numerous studies (Geistfeld 1982; Lesser and Masson 1983; Morris and Bronson 1969; Riesz 1978; Sproles 1977) confirm a low correlation between CU's quality rankings or ratings and list prices for large samples of products tested by CU. Finally, the subject of informationally imperfect markets has been an important topic for economic theorists who have constructed numerous models of informationally imperfect markets that yield, like the data here, a distribution of prices as their outcome. See Stiglitz (1979) and Salop (1978) for a summary of this literature.

What are the implications for consumers? Informationally imperfect markets are dangerous to financial health; it is easy to pay 50 percent, 100 percent, or even 200 percent more than necessary to obtain a given level of quality.

Unanswered research questions remain, such as: Do fully informed consumers make uniform assessments of quality? Are there consumers who consistently purchase on or near (or far above) the frontier? If so, who are they? Will other investigators and other methods confirm the existence and persistence of informationally imperfect markets?

Perceptions of Price Dispersion, Quality Constant

Maynes and Assum (1982b) focus, in part, on a mechanism helping to account for the existence and persistence of informationally imperfect markets. The mechanism is: misperceptions of prices, quality constant. The argument is straightforward. If consumers substantially underestimate price dispersion, with quality constant, they will undershop. The net effect of large-scale undershopping is that markets are undisciplined and that price dispersion persists.

The study involved twelve products and was conducted in Syracuse in 1978. Misperceptions were studied by "feeding" a probability sample of consumers information regarding the lowest price, quality constant, at which a particular product was sold, and asking respondents to name the highest price that would be charged for the same product. The wording of the critical question is as follows.

> Let's start with questions about particular products. The first one is DISHWASHING DETERGENT—the kind you use for washing dishes by hand. For a 22-ounce bottle of dishwashing detergent, the LOWEST PRICE charged in Syracuse in February was *sixty-nine cents*. What do you think was the HIGHEST PRICE charged—for the SAME SIZE BOTTLE, but ANY BRAND, from ANY STORE in Syracuse? Again, the LOWEST PRICE was *sixty-nine cents*.

> Let us make sure I got that right. You think that _____ cents was the HIGHEST PRICE charged for the *same size* bottle from *any store*. Is that right?

The results were again emphatic. For eleven out of fourteen products, perceptions of price dispersion were inaccurate. Among those products where inaccurate perceptions were dominant, there existed a very strong tendency to underestimate price dispersion. Similar results were obtained in the small town of Ithaca.

A Missing Institution: The Local Consumer-Information System

If local consumer markets are indeed informationally imperfect, it follows that existing information channels are unsatisfactory and need either to be improved or supplemented. Maynes et al. (1977) provide a blueprint for a "missing institution"—the local consumer-information system. The heart of the system would be a data bank to which the consumer could address questions and receive answers regarding prices and quality of products in the local market.

This new institution would help identify the "best buy" variety of a product, quickly and at low cost. It would tell the consumer from what local retailers and at what local prices this best-buy variety—or any brand model in which he is interested—can be purchased. This new institution would serve all consumers in a given community by lowering many prices, with quality constant. By reproducing itself in different locales, as the product-testing organizations have, it might be expected to serve consumers in many communities. Maynes et al. (1977) discuss the types of information to be provided, methods of information collection and dissemination, means of ensuring accuracy and fairness, and ways it might be financed.

There are no operating models of a local consumer-information system, but the *Michelin* and *Mobil* guides to restaurants and motels and *Washington Checkbook* are models that come close.

The New Information Technology: A Critical Review of Prestel

One consumer-information system—not local—embodying the new information technology is Prestel, the British variant of videotex. Prestel is an information system in which users seek answers to their questions on almost anything by calling up onto their home or office television screens items of information that are stored in a central computer. Prestel started commercial operation in January 1980, and by the end of 1981 had 15,000 subscribers who had access to 175,000 pages of information provided by all sorts of organizations—airlines, government agencies (the Central Office of Information and Social Security Administration), Consumers Association, travel agents, and so forth—totaling 650 in all.

Prestel has been a marketing and consumer-behavior fiasco. Instead of the 200,000 subscribers forecast for the end of 1981, it had 15,000; instead of 95 percent of its receivers being sited in homes, 95 percent were located in businesses. For research on and a critical review of Prestel, see Maynes (1982a).

Large, Medium, and Small Consumer Markets Compared

Drawing on the price–quality framework introduced earlier, Maynes (1983b) asks the general question: How well, or how badly, do consumers fare when they deal in local markets of different sizes? Specific questions asked and answered in this three-way comparison are: *How well can* the consumer do in this market? *How well does* the *average* consumer fare? *How badly* might a consumer fare? *How badly* might the *average* consumer fare? *How rich* is the choice offered in terms of numbers of (1) retail outlets, (2) types of stores, (3) brands and models available, and (4) price offers?

My general conclusion is that local markets are chaotic, posing huge informational problems for consumers. There are few patterns on which one can rely and simple rules such as "price is an indicator of quality" do not work.

Consumption and Inequality

The thesis of Maynes's (1983c) paper is that differing efficiencies in consumption should be a central concern of those interested in inequalities in the distribution of economic well-being. The first part reviews time series and international comparisons of shares of income and wealth and concludes that this is *not* where the action is or is likely to be. The second part reviews data from the Survey Research Center's fifteen-year Panel Study of Income Dynamics (Hill, Hill, and Morgan 1981) that shows poverty to be more pervasive and less persistent than previously thought. Specifically, about one-quarter of U.S. citizens were "poor" for one year or more during the 1968–1978 decade, while an unexpectedly small 2 percent were poor for eight or more years out of ten. The third part reviews data on observed price dispersion and asserts that this may be the greatest source of inequality.

Consumerism and Consumer Protection

My views on the origins and research implications of consumerism are recorded in an article (Maynes, 1973) where consumerism is identified as a permanent and growing feature of our economic landscape. Its rise is attributed to consumer grievances (delivery failures, performance failures, communication failures, safety concerns, and so on), the under-recognized problem of informationally imperfect markets, and the under-representation of the consumer interest. Among the research implications is a call for annual surveys of consumer grievances, foreshadowing the consumer satisfaction–dissatisfaction "industry" that developed soon thereafter.

In "Consumer Protection: The Issues" (Maynes, 1979a) and "Consumer Protection: Corrective Measures" (Maynes, 1979b), I sought to organize the discussion of the issues and possible corrective measures. The emphasis in these articles is more on the attainment of consumer *sovereignty* than on what is usually understood as consumer *protection*.

Finally, *Decision-Making for Consumers* (Maynes, 1976b) collects in one place the price-quality framework developed here and ideas and views expressed elsewhere. All of the works cited here reflect one economist's views of a research program growing out of his consciousness of the consumer as his primary client.

Notes

1. The arguments and evidence from my research are reported in compressed form in this chapter. The concepts described in this section are discussed in detail in Maynes, 1976a; 1976b, chapter 3. Greg J. Duncan of the University of Michigan, Loren V. Geistfeld of Ohio State University, Robin A. Douthitt of the University of Saskatchewan, and Terje Assum formerly of the State Institute for Consumer Research, Olso, Norway, have been my collaborators in collecting and analyzing the data cited in this chapter.

2. *Variety* of a product will be used here to indicate the brand and model combination—for example, a Dodge Aries sedan.

3. Perhaps reflecting this idea, a survey of subscribers to *Consumer Reports* revealed that 74 percent of those buying automobiles and 61 percent making other purchases reported "looking up the ratings" (Benson and Benson 1970, tables 20 and 21).

4. About fifteen countries have major consumer product-testing organizations like Consumers Union. In terms of the scope and sophistication of their quality testing and reporting, the three leading organizations would be the U.S. Consumers Union, Stiftung Warentest of West Germany (publishers of *Test*) and Consumers' Association of the United Kingdom (publishers of *Which, Motoring Which, Holiday Which,* and so forth).

5. The sample of products of *uniform quality* included: heating oil, eggs, milk, participating term life insurance, nonparticipating term life insurance, participating whole life insurance, nonparticipating whole life insurance, white bread, gin, grease or oil change, beer, aspirin, and Kodak Pocket Instamatic 18

(a single brand of pocket camera). The sample of products of *variable quality* included: washing machines, dishwashing liquids, microwave ovens, porch and deck paint, dishwashers, "low-priced" stereo speakers, men's ten-speed bicycles, "medium-priced" stereo receivers, mini tape recorders, wool blankets, single-lens reflex cameras, and pocket cameras (all varieties).

References

Benson and Benson (1970), "Survey of Present and Former Subscribers to Consumer Reports," unpublished report, Consumer's Union, 256 Washington St., Mt. Vernon, N.Y.

Duncan, Greg J. (1981), "The Dynamics of Local Markets: A Case Study of Cameras," *Journal of Consumer Affairs* 15 (Summer):64–74.

Geistfeld, Loren V. (1982), "The Price–Quality Relationship Revisited," *Journal of Consumer Affairs* 16 (Winter):334–46.

Hill, Martha S., Daniel S. Hill, and James N. Morgan, eds. (1981), *Five Thousand Families, Patterns of Economic Progress,* vol. 10, Ann Arbor, Mich.: Institute for Social Research.

Lancaster, Kelvin J. (1971), *Consumer Demand,* New York: Columbia University Press.

———— (1960), "A New Approach to Consumer Theory," *Journal of Political Economy* 74 (April):132–37.

Lesser, William H. and Robert T. Masson (1983), "Quality Signaling and Oligopolistic Overcharges," *Policy Studies Review* 2:474–84.

Maynes, E. Scott (1976a), "The Concept and Measurement of Product Quality," in *Household Production and Consumption,* Nestor E. Terleckyj, ed., New York: Columbia University Press for National Bureau of Economic Research, 530–59.

———— (1979a), "Consumer Protection: The Issues," *Journal of Consumer Policy,* (2), 97–109.

———— (1979b), "Consumer Protection: Corrective Measures," *Journal of Consumer Policy,* (3 and 4), 191–212.

———— (1973), "Consumerism: Origin and Research Implications," in *Family Economic Behavior, Problems and Prospects,* Eleanor B. Sheldon, ed., Philadelphia: Lippincott, 270–94.

———— (1983c), "Consumption and Inequality," unpublished paper, Department of Consumer Economics and Housing, Cornell University, Ithaca, N.Y.

———— (1976b), *Decision Making for Consumers, An Introduction to Consumer Economics,* New York: Macmillan.

———— (1982a), *Prestel in Use, A Consumer View,* London: National Consumer Council.

———— and Terje Assum (1982b), "Informationally Imperfect Consumer Markets: Empirical Findings and Policy Implications," *Journal of Consumer Affairs* 16 (Summer):61–87.

————, Robin A. Douthitt, Greg J. Duncan, Loren V. Geistfeld (1983a), "Informationally Imperfect Markets: Implications for Consumers," in *The Collec-*

_____ (1983b), "A Tale of Three Cities: Large, Medium and Small Consumer Markets Compared," unpublished paper presented at the American Council on Consumer Interests, Ithaca, N.Y., Department of Consumer Economics and Housing, Cornell University.

_____ , James N. Morgan, Weston Vivian, and Greg J. Duncan (1977), "The Local Consumer Information System: An Institution-To-Be?" *Journal of Consumer Affairs* 11 (Summer):17–33.

Morris, Ruby Turner and Charlotte S. Bronson (1969), "The Chaos in Competition Indicated by Consumer Reports," *Journal of Marketing* 33 (July):419–26.

Riesz, Peter C. (1978), "Price versus Quality in the Marketplace, 1961–1975," *Journal of Retailing* 54 (Winter):15–28.

Salop, Steven (1978), "Parables of Information Transmission in Markets," in *The Effect of Information on Consumer and Market Behavior*, Andrew A. Mitchell, ed., Chicago: American Marketing Association.

Sproles, George B. (1977), "New Evidence on Price and Quality," *Journal of Consumer Affairs* 11 (Summer):63–77.

Stiglitz, Joseph E. (1979), "Equilibrium in Product Markets with Imperfect Information," *American Economic Review* 68 (May):339–43.

Washington Checkbook, periodical published quarterly by the Center for the Study of Services, 1518 K Street, N.W., Suite 206, Washington, D.C.

Part V
Price and Perceived Quality

13
The Effect of Price on Subjective Product Evaluations

Kent B. Monroe and
R. Krishnan

Although price plays an important role in everyday economic activities, it remains an enigma to the decision maker. For the marketing manager, price is a key decision variable affecting the profitability of individual products, as well as the firm. For buyers, price represents the value of something they have to give up to obtain something else of value.

Buyers may use various cues or types of information in forming an evaluation of a product or in choosing among alternatives. Of the several types of product evaluations that have been investigated in the past, price effects on the perception of product quality have been one of the most frequently examined.

Economists have considered price as an indicator of the cost or sacrifice one has to make to acquire a product or service. While the economic view recognizes that preference for a higher-priced item might occur, nevertheless, such an occurrence is considered as a minor deviation of the traditional demand theory. That buyers might prefer a higher-priced product, simply means that the utility derived from the product is enhanced because others are purchasing it, or because the product carries a higher price tag. Normally, demand for a product is assumed to result from the qualities inherent in the product. Thus, aside from external reasons for purchasing a higher-priced product, demand is not a function of buyers' perceptions of the product. And since buyers are assumed to know the attributes of products and the utility to be obtained from acquiring each unit of each product, the issue of quality perception cannot arise.

However, behavioral-science researchers have shown that evaluation and choice are related and involve two separate mental processes. Further, it has been shown that price can affect the evaluation as well as the choice of a product. As used here, *evaluation* refers to a judgment of product quality, while *choice* refers to the willingness to purchase a product at a particular price. Also, buyers neither have perfect information about product attributes nor are they perfect-information processors. If buyers do not possess perfect information about product attributes, then they must make some inferences from the information cues available, one of which is price. Thus, price might be used as an indicator of the qualities inherent in the product, and, if so, a higher price might lead to the perception of higher product quality.

Interest in the price–perceived-quality behavioral research can be traced to Scitovsky's (1945) essay, in which he outlined economic and social consequences of the increasing tendency for consumers to use "indexes" such as price and size of the firm when evaluating product or brand quality. However, much of the price research that has followed seems intended merely to demonstrate that price could influence the perception of product quality. Early research typically examined the effects of price as the only informational cue available to the consumer subjects, while later studies tended to consider multiple cues. In general, all of the past studies tested the hypothesis that price is positively related to perceived quality.

An Overview of the Price–Perceived-Quality Relationship

Past price–perceived-quality research rarely attempted to explain the influence of price on the perception of product quality. This section will briefly concentrate on the relationship between price, perceived quality, perceived value, and willingness to buy. It will be argued that *perceived quality* and *perceived value* are two separate constructs. Perceived quality is viewed purely as an evaluative measure, whereas perceived value is considered a trade-off between perceived quality and affordability, within a choice condition.

As mentioned above, the price of a product may play two different roles in buyers' decision processes. That is, price may represent a measure of what must be sacrificed to obtain a product; but, price may also influence the perception of product quality. In the former situation, the higher the price, the greater will be the sacrifice one needs to make and, therefore, the less will be the inclination to purchase the higher-priced product. But in the second situation, the higher the price, the greater will be the perceived quality of the product and the greater will be the inclination to purchase the higher-priced product. So, the buyer in a purchase situation makes a value judgment by trading off the utility of the sacrifice against the utility inferred from the perception of quality. This trade-off represents the value of the product as perceived by the consumer.

If the utility inferred from the perception of quality is greater than the utility sacrificed, then there is a positive perception of value. Other things remaining the same, the more positive the buyers' perception of value, the greater will be the buyers' willingness to purchase.

To understand the relationship between perceived quality and willingness to buy, it is helpful to introduce the concept of the *acceptable price range*. Buyers generally have a set of prices that are acceptable to pay for a considered purchase rather than a single price. Therefore, a price may be unacceptable to pay if it is perceived to be too low, or if it is perceived to be too high. The implication is that if a price is unacceptable to pay, then there must be little or no perceived value in the offer. Within the narrow confines of this conceptualization, such a situation would occur when the utility inferred from the quality perception is not greater than the utility sacrificed by paying the price. Thus, even if there is a positive relationship between price and perceived quality, we cannot make a direct inference between perceived quality and willingness to buy. Rather, the effect of both the positive influence of perceived quality on the perception of value, and the direct negative influence of price on the perception of value must be assessed prior to making the inference about willingness to buy. Moreover, it has been suggested that while a positive perception of value may be necessary to induce a willingness to buy, it is insufficient to produce this effect (Della Bitta, Monroe, and McGinnis 1981).

The important point derived from this conceptualization is that the perception of quality and willingness to buy are separate behavioral responses. Moreover, the relationship between these two responses is indirect. In some previous research, the perception of quality has been induced from respondents' choice behavior (willingness to buy). For example, Leavitt (1954), Tull, Boring, and Gonsoir (1964), and McConnell (1968) inferred the price–perceived-quality relationship from a choice situation. However, as argued above, the influence of perceived quality on perceived value and, therefore, willingness to buy (choice), is counterbalanced to some extent by price itself. Also, Deering and Jacoby (1972) and Szybillo and Jacoby (1974) showed "willingness to buy" to be unrelated to "perceived quality." Also, Raju (1977) observed a monotonic relationship between price and perceived quality even beyond the unacceptable high price. These findings suggest that price cues may have differing effects upon behavior tendency (willingness to buy) and evaluation (perceived quality). Therefore, it is questionable to induce quality perception from buyers' choices.

The objectives of this chapter are to review previous research on the price–perceived-quality relationship and to isolate some of the persistent, unresolved research issues. Instead of cataloging past findings, previous research will be reviewed on an issue-by-issue basis.

Selected Review of Price–Perceived-Quality Research

Defining Perceived Quality

The meaning of perceived quality has not been carefully defined in previous research, resulting in different operationalizations of the construct. *Perception* is the process of organizing, interpreting, and deriving meaning from stimuli through the senses. *Sensation* is the process of receiving these sense impressions. However, individual needs, memories, and experiences also influence perception. The *Dictionary of Psychology* (Chaplin 1981) defines quality as:

> 1. A basic aspect of a sensation by means of which it is distinguished from all other sensations. Quality as used in this sense implies a difference in kind and not in degree. 2. The relative level of goodness or excellence of anything.

In short, perceived product quality is the perceived ability of a product to provide satisfaction 'relative' to the available alternatives.

Several different definitions and operationalizations of the perceived-quality construct can be observed in previous research. Rao (1971) argued that unconstrained preference is akin to product evaluation, that is, perceived quality. Valenzi and Andrews (1971), McConnell (1968), and Lauridsen (1973) measured taste quality and, therefore, assumed that perceived quality and taste quality are equivalent. Other studies have implicitly defined quality in terms of product engineering (Raju 1977; Rao 1971). However, unless the respondent is an expert, he or she has no direct point of reference to make a judgment. So, it is possible that buyers may use a smaller set of attributes (easily available and interpretable) to judge product quality.

The Price–Perceived-Quality Relationship

Perception is an important determinant of buyer behavior. Buyers use cues such as product characteristics, store images, brand names, and prices to differentiate among products and to form impressions of product quality. It is important to understand not only how buyers use such cues, but also which cues they actually perceive. Cues that are not perceived cannot influence customer decision processes. Essentially, differences in perceptions lead to different in-store decisions and buying behavior. Thus, an examination of the role of cues in forming quality impressions has obvious implications for both theoretical and managerial perspectives.

The basic notion underlying the behavioral approach to understanding the effect of price on buyers is that price serves as a cue whereby a buyer can predict the quality of the product. The notion of this price–perceived-quality relationship was introduced in 1945 by Scitovsky, and he argued that judging quality by price merely implies a belief that price is determined by the competitive interplay of the forces of supply and demand. Following Scitovsky's thinking, several researchers have empirically tested the hypothesis that price is positively related to perceived quality. The review of this past research will be presented by classifying previous studies according to:

1. conceptualization of the relationship;
2. stimulus presentation (single or multisensory stimuli presentation);
3. products studied;
4. type of price treatments used;
5. methodological issues; and
6. findings.

Conceptualizations

Leavitt's "Arm-chair" Thinking. Several studies have relied on Leavitt's (1954) hypothesis that when price is the only available differential information, then consumers would feel some conflict in making a choice; and, therefore, they would sometimes select the higher-priced product. Leavitt identified several variables leading to maximum consumer conflict and, consequently, leading to a significant number of higher-price choices:

1. the price level of the products;
2. the frequency of purchase;
3. the buyers themselves and their perceived roles in society; and
4. the products which may carry with them stereotyped notions about their own quality—for example, consumers may feel that certain products are alike from brand to brand, while other products are really different from one another.

Most studies in some way have considered the influence of these variables, as shown in table 13–1.

Theory of Perceived Risk. Several price–perceived-quality studies have relied on the theory of perceived risk by arguing that buyers would tend to select a higher-priced product when they perceive a substantial degree of uncertainty in the purchase situation. Shapiro (1972) extended the

Table 13-1
Leavitt's Conceptual Variables

Variables	Study
Price levels	Gardner (1970, 1971); Deering and Jacoby (1972)
Frequency of purchase	Gardner (1970, 1971); Raju (1977)
Consumer himself and his role in society	Lambert (1970, 1972); Bettman (1973); Shapiro (1970)
Products—similarities, dissimilarities among different brands	Leavitt (1954); Tull, Boring, and Gonsoir (1964); Shapiro (1970); Jacoby, Olson, and Haddock (1971); Valenzi and Andrews (1971); Wheatley, Chiu, and Goldman (1981); McConnell (1968); Lauridsen (1973)

notion of perceived risk by suggesting that consumers perceive a product as a set of information cues. Each cue is evaluated as to whether it has predictive value (how close the cue matches a desired product attribute) and confidence value (consumers' ability to evaluate the cue itself). Since price is considered to be a high confidence cue, it would be used to impute quality to the product.

Intrinsic versus Extrinsic Cues. Olson and Jacoby (1972) proposed that any informational stimulus or cue may be considered to be derived either from the actual physical product (that is, the cue is intrinsic to the product) or from product-related attributes not part of the physical product (that is, the cue is extrinsic to the product). Following their suggestion, several studies manipulated intrinsic cues while testing for the price–perceived–quality relationship (see table 13-2).

With one exception, all of the studies found significant intrinsic-cue effects. Four of the studies found a significant price main effect; and two studies found an interaction between price and product samples. Based on these results, one may hypothesize that intrinsic cues are likely to have a greater impact on product evaluations than extrinsic (price) cues.

A critical problem in using intrinsic cues when studying quality perceptions is how to manipulate these cues. Using a seller's classification of the levels of these cues, while providing a method of determining intrinsic-cue levels, does not indicate that buyers perceive differences in these cues. Therefore, unless separate testing confirms that buyers' perceptions of differences in these cues match the sellers' claims, it cannot be assumed that the cue stimuli are perceived by the buyers to be different.

Table 13–2
Intrinsic versus Extrinsic Cues

Study	Main Effects		Interaction: Price and Intrinsic Cue
	Price (Extrinsic)	Intrinsic	
Valenzi and Andrews (1971)	yes	yes	yes
Jacoby, Olson, and Haddock (1971)	no	yes	yes
Rao (1971)	no	yes	no
Valenzi and Eldridge (1973)	yes	no	no
Cimbalo and Webdale (1973)	yes	yes	no
Szybillo and Jacoby (1974)	no	yes	no
Pincus and Waters (1975)	no	yes	no
Wheatley, Chiu, and Goldman (1981)	yes	yes	no

Some additional observations regarding the manipulation of intrinsic cues are worth noting:

1. Experimental manipulation of intrinsic cues as a within-subject factor might produce strong carry-over effects from one product experience to another. Such carry-over effects are unlikely in real-world product experiences that involve rather large intertrial time periods, thereby allowing for the dissipation of carry-over effects (Olson 1977).
2. Presence of a product may intrigue a subject more than any extrinsic cue, that is, domination of a visual cue in an experimental situation. Thus, the manner in which experiments on quality perceptions are conducted may influence the outcome.

Summary. The effects of intrinsic cues on quality perceptions are not clear. The results are likely to be sensitive to the specific physical characteristics of the product used, the range of variation of intrinsic cues, and ambiguity involved in discriminating these differences. While the dichotomy of intrinsic and extrinsic cues provides one point of departure, and offers a means of predicting relative utilization of price in the product-evaluation process, it does not explain how buyers perceive price, nor how such perceptions affect their judgments.

Stimulus Presentation

To investigate the relationship between price and perceived quality requires a careful manipulation of the qualities or attributes of the test product. In some experiments, subjects were presented hypothetical product descriptions; in other experiments subjects were able to see and either taste or feel the product. As observed earlier, perceptions are formed from information received through the senses (sensations), information acquired from past experience, and other information available in the experimental situation. Thus, the observed variance in any experiment will be due not only to the manipulations of the independent variables, but also to sensory variability, memory variability, or response variability (Sandusky 1974). Although several studies attempted to control one or more of these sources of variance, no study has separated these sources of variance from the overall variance found in the experiment. Since the multicue studies tended to vary more stimuli in the experimental situation than the single-cue studies, a plausible explanation for the general lack of statistically significant findings is that the error variances were larger because of the above variances that were not separated in the analysis. Until a research effort attempts to isolate these other sources of variance, a methodological explanation for the differences between the results of single-cue versus multicue studies remains plausible.

Products Studied

Some studies have used multiple products to study the price–perceived-quality relationship. Leavitt (1954), and Tull, Boring, and Gonsoir (1964) selected the products based on perceived similarities and dissimilarities among the brands of each product. Gardner (1970, 1971) used frequency of purchase and search time criteria to select the products, Shapiro (1970) used five criteria: (1) low importance; (2) difficult to judge; (3) broadly interesting; (4) consequential decision; and (5) varied with regard to price of the product, the nature of the product (durable versus nondurable), and the relevant product attributes and sensory organs used in the evaluations. No other research studies provide any explanation for product selection.

Although the products used in price–perception research have inherent confounds, these confounds can be better controlled through careful selection of the population of products eligible for a particular experiment, and then use of a random-selection procedure to determine the products to be studied. Following such an approach will, over time, promote the generalizability of this area of research.

Price Treatments

One of the problems associated with price–perception research is the number of potential confounds that may influence the observed results. Some of these confounds relate to the manner in which the price variable is manipulated. Other confounds relate to the purchase situation or context prevailing at the time of judgment. This section will review several perceptual issues revolving around the manipulation of price, and the implications of these issues for price–perceived-quality research.

Price Level. Leavitt (1954) argued that the relative price level of the product may influence the difficulty and direction of choice. For example, a buyer may feel quite differently about purchasing a higher-priced brand of peas than about purchasing a higher-priced television set. *Price level* refers to the absolute amount of money one needs to give up to get something of value.

In some studies, the results suggest that price level does influence the perception of quality (Deering and Jacoby 1972; Leavitt 1954; Shapiro 1970; Gardner 1970, 1971). For example, in Gardner's (1970) study, the overall perception of quality for men's suits, shirts, and toothpaste, followed the general price level of these products; that is, quality perceptions were highest for men's suits, and lowest for toothpaste, which also corresponds to the price levels used for these three products. Since price level and product represent a confound, the suggestion that perceptions of quality vary over price level implies also that perceptions of quality carry over products (as observed above). Therefore, since the majority of studies has used relatively inexpensive products, future research needs to broaden the price and product combinations studied.

Price Differentials. Another variable that may influence buyers' perceptions of quality is differences in prices. Leavitt (1954) argued that when price was the only differential information available, price differences would create conflict in a buyer's mind, and as a result, the buyer would select a higher-priced alternative. Although Leavitt used choice as an indicator of buyers' quality perceptions, nevertheless, buyers may use price differences as a cue to infer quality differences. Therefore, the issue is how much of a difference in prices is necessary for an inference that there must also be differences in quality? If prices manipulated in a price–perceived-quality experiment are not perceptually different, then not finding a statistically significant price–perceived-quality relationship is inconclusive.

Most studies of this type appear to have manipulated prices without paying much attention to price differences. It is important to note that even if the numerical prices are different, it cannot be assumed that the prices are perceived to be different. Thus, the problem becomes one of determining the effect of perceived price differences on product evaluation.

Acceptable Price Range. It is natural to recognize that the widening of price differentials, ceteris paribus, leads to the extension of the range of prices available for evaluation. As conceptually argued earlier, the concept of the range of acceptable prices helps to link the perception of quality to willingness to buy (choice), through the moderating variable "perception of value." Four studies have used the acceptable price range for testing the price–perceived-quality relationship (Gardner 1970, 1971; Deering and Jacoby 1972; Raju 1977). Except for Raju, these studies selected prices within the acceptable price range. Gardner argued that selecting prices only from the acceptable price range is essential because eliminating extremely low and high prices removes a bias in favor of finding a price–perceived-quality relationship. However, selecting prices only from the acceptable price range might result in a narrow price-differential condition and thus might remove a condition where price might have a positive effect on perceived quality. Raju's study found perceived quality to be monotonically related to price even in the unacceptable high-price range. Deering and Jacoby (1972) found that willingness to buy is relatively low when price is unacceptably low or high, and is higher for acceptable prices. Thus, another situational price variable influencing quality perception is the range of prices available for evaluation.

Order of Presentation. Della Bitta and Monroe (1973) found that presenting prices for judgment in order of increasing magnitude produced significantly higher price acceptability than when the price series was presented in decreasing order of magnitude. Rexeisen's (1982) findings corroborate these earlier results. Order of presentation is very important in price–quality research, since most studies expose the subjects randomly to the price treatments. But as noted by Monroe (1982), a randomized presentation of prices simply produces a different, perhaps, unknown order effect. Therefore, either the order of presenting prices must be constant across treatment conditions or it must be specifically manipulated in future research.

No-Price Condition. Some studies have manipulated the price cue by providing subjects with different actual prices. Olson (1977) argued that from a theory-generating perspective, it might be more profitable to focus on the relative effects of price in general, rather than with specific levels of price. Accordingly, Olson suggested that future research should manipulate the presence and absence of specific price information. That is, to interpret the effects of the price cue as a generic item of information, it is necessary to have a baseline or reference point (provided by the price-absent condition). In line with this suggestion, several price–perceived-quality studies used a no-price condition either as a control group or by incorporating the price-absent condition into the design. Of the studies reviewed, seven studies used a no-price condition and not one of them reported a significant price main effect. Twelve studies using specific-level prices reported a significant price main effect, while two other studies reported very weak effects (Wheatley, Chiu, and Allen 1982, found $p < .4$; Peterson and Jolibert 1976, found $p < .333$).

While the price-absent condition provides a baseline for examining the role price may play in buyers' evaluations of products, it does not per se help answer whether and to what extent price is used to judge product quality. The price–perceived-quality hypothesis suggests that buyers will infer that higher-priced products are also of higher quality. This hypothesis specifies a direction of relationship and also implies a comparative form of evaluation. Subjects exposed only to a no-price condition and asked to evaluate a product have no basis for judgment except through the information provided by the researcher and information available from memory. Similarly, subjects exposed only to one price-present condition have little marginal information available on which to render a product evaluation. Testing the mean values in these two conditions evaluates only the marginal contribution of price to buyers' evaluations of a product, it does not test whether buyers will impute greater quality for products that are higher priced than other products.

For example, Pincus and Waters (1975) did not find a statistically significant effect between price-present and price-absent conditions, and therefore, concluded that there was no statistically significant relationship between price and perceived quality. However, looking at their results only for the price-present condition, there is reason to question their conclusion. Subjects rated pens on a nine-point scale with the value "one" having a semantic anchor of "extremely low-quality pen," and "nine" having a semantic anchor of "extremely high-quality pen." A second factor in the design was presenting the pens either in a cellophane package, or in an unpackaged condition. In the unpackaged condition, mean quality ratings were 4.83 (49-cent pen), 5.57 (98 cents), and 6.37 ($1.98), all of which are statistically different at $p < .05$. For the packaged condition, mean quality ratings were 3.82 (49 cents), 5.70 (98 cents), and 6.33 ($1.98), all of which are statistically different at $p < .06$ or less. These results do support the hypothesis that there is a positive relationship between price and perceived quality.

Although Rao (1971) did not report support for the price–perceived-quality relationship, Olson (1977) suggested that Rao's results reveal that while test reports may have an effect on quality saliency, price also may have an effect. Furthermore, these two factors interacted for electric shavers. In summation, the findings of studies using a price present or absent condition are not conclusive. Also, it can be argued that the present–absent condition studies do not directly test the price–perceived-quality relationship. Instead, they directly test the marginal contribution of price to buyers' product evaluations.

Price as a Between- or Within-Subject Factor. The price cue has been manipulated both as a between- and as a within-subject factor. Those studies with a specific price manipulation used price as a within-subject design factor except for five studies (Gardner 1970, 1971; Peterson and Jolibert 1976; Enis and Stafford 1969; and Wheatley, Chiu, and Goldman 1981). Studies manipulating a price present or absent condition typically adopted a between-subject factor design, except for Rexeisen (1982). But for the price-present condition, prices were treated as a within-subject condition—that is, subjects were exposed to all the specific price levels.

Deering and Jacoby (1972) suggested that demand characteristics are particularly likely when within-subject manipulations are used. That is, when subjects receive multiple product samples with different prices, there seems to be an implicit "demand" in such procedures to assign different ratings to the samples (Olson 1977). However, it must be recognized that certain factors have inherently within-subject effects. If price information is manipulated by presenting subjects with actual prices for different product samples to be judged, then a within-subject design is appropriate, since the experimental situation thus created is analogous to the real-world situation of examining and evaluating several different brands at different prices. Thus, the appropriateness of a between-subject design for the studies, manipulating specific price levels can be questioned, since a subject who has been exposed to several cue levels (or cue combinations) is unlikely to react the same as when exposed to only one cue (Olson 1977). In the future, researchers must choose a price-manipulation procedure that clearly operationalizes the type of price-cue effect being examined.

Methodological Issues

Measurement Issues. The outcome of price–perceived-quality research depends upon how the dependent variable "perceived quality" is measured. Of the twenty-two reviewed studies, twenty reported using rating scales assumed to have interval scale properties. Seven studies used a five-point scale; four studies used a seven-point scale; six studies used a nine-point scale; one study used a twenty-five-point scale; and one study used a hundred-point scale. While category scaling of the type used in these studies has several serious weaknesses, the variation in scale categories used (five to one hundred) increases the opportunity to find differences in responses. By offering a fixed number of categories, however few or many, the responses either may be artificially constrained, or expanded (Lodge 1981). Regardless, responses are inadvertently affected. Consequently, a plausible explanation for the variation in results of the price–perceived-quality studies is the variation in rating scales used.

Also, most studies treated perceived quality unidimensionally. McConnell (1968) and Lauridsen (1973) measured taste quality using different methods, but the reliability and validity of the measures were not provided. Rexeisen (1982) used semantic scales, Likert scales, and ratio scales to measure perceived quality; but all three scales involve similar methods and, therefore, are not as useful for testing convergent validity as claimed.

In addition to including multiple measures of the dependent variable "perceived quality," in future experiments researchers should also include multiple indicators of the variable. Such a procedure would allow for the examination of the effects of the price cue on several evaluative criteria that may be components of the product quality construct. Also, use of multiple indicators and multiple measures would facilitate establishing the convergent validity of the dependent variable.

Manipulation of Independent Variables. Many studies have not clearly documented the rationale used for determining the levels of the independent variables. It has been argued conceptually that the price–perceived-quality relationship is more likely to occur when buyers perceive that brands within a product category are heterogeneous with respect to quality. Thus, Leavitt (1954), Tull, Boring, and Gonsoir (1964), and Wheatley, Chiu, and Goldman (1981) used several products arranged according to how pretest subjects rated brands within the product category in terms of quality differences. However, how the pretest subjects made their similarity–difference judgments is unclear, and whether study subjects had similar perceptions is also unclear.

Many potential confounds related to the manipulation of the price variable have been treated here. To overcome the problems discussed earlier, more attention needs to be given to the design of the study as well as to the selection of the actual prices used.

Care needs to be exercised also when actual brand names and store image or names represent a part of the manipulation. Each of these other cues represents additional differential information available to subjects. However, the magnitude of this differential information to individual subjects may vary because of previous experiential information in memory. Thus, potential confounds must be considered as the manipulations are being determined, and as much as feasible, be controlled so the contributions to response variation can be accounted for.

Findings

Some studies have considered situations when the only differential information available was price. Generally, these single-cue studies have found a positive and statistically significant price–perceived-quality relationship. However, other studies have varied other cues in addition to price, including actual product samples, promotional, store, and brand information. Although the multicue studies have found a positive price–perceived-quality relationship, generally, such a relationship was not statistically significant.

Our review thus far has isolated a number of concerns about both the conceptualization and the empirical methodology of past price–perceived-quality research. When findings have been discussed, it has been on an individual study basis. While it is clear that the results obtained from these studies may vary because of some methodological problems, the extent to which these problems account for the inconsistent results between, for example, single-cue and multicue studies has not been assessed. However, it is possible to compare results across studies, and isolate some reasons why results in previous research have not been consistent. Although a number of the concerns raised cannot be explicitly answered except through more rigorously designed research, by quantitatively integrating some of the previous results, we can begin to address the significance of these concerns. In the next section we provide an initial assessment of the research results.

A Quantitative Assessment of Selected Price–Perceived-Quality Research

To quantitatively assess the results requires an examination of (1) the probabilities at which the results were statistically significant, and (2) the magnitude of the effect of price on perceived quality (effect size). This assessment is described below.

Table 13–3 provides a distribution of p values for twenty-eight price–perceived-quality results. An examination of the table reveals that sixteen of the twenty-eight studies support the price–perceived-quality

Table 13–3
Distribution of Main Price Effects: Price–Perceived-Quality Studies

p value	Frequency	Cumulative Frequency
.001	4	4
.005	1	5
.010	7	12
.050	4	16
.300	2	18
.333	1	19
.380	1	20
.400	1	21
.470	1	22
.500[a]	6	28

Note: $\Sigma\ f_i(p_i) = 5.462$

$$\frac{\Sigma f_i(p_i)}{\Sigma fi} = 0.195$$

[a]Insignificant and unreported p values assumed to be equal to .500.

relationship at the 0.05 statistical significance level or less. However, using this counting method, it is not possible to assess the strength of the relationship; thus, a better procedure is to compare the results by determining whether the results are consistent across studies.

Comparing Studies

When comparing studies, the basic objective is to identify sources of variation, if there are any. The variations may be due to the quality of the methodology, sampling error, measurement error, or differences in the range of the independent variable investigated. A test for homogeneity alerts the reviewer to one or more of the possibilities. For the twenty-eight results, table 13–3 provides the data necessary to test for homogeneity. With the assumption that reported statistical insignificance without a corresponding p value was at a p level of .50, and assuming all statistical significance of less than .01 to be equivalent to a p level of .01, the significance test was conducted. The statistical significance test of heterogeneity of Zs is (Rosenthal 1982):

$$\Sigma(Z_i - \bar{Z})^2 \text{ is distributed as } \chi^2 \text{ with } N - 1\ df. \tag{1}$$

For the data of table 13–3, $\Sigma(Z_i - \bar{Z})^2$ is 28.85. The probability of this chi-square value with 27 *df* is approximately 0.50. Thus, these 28 p values appear to be relatively homogeneous.

It is also possible to test the statistical homogeneity of the effect-size estimates. However, it was not always possible to compute the effect sizes because many studies did not provide sufficient descriptive data for the computations. Both the effect size $d = (X_1 - X_2)/s_y$ and the correlation coefficient r were computed for those studies providing the descriptive data. One approach to testing for statistical significance of the homogeneity of results requires transforming the correlations to their associated Fisher zs and conducting a chi-square test (Rosenthal 1982):

$$\Sigma(N_i - 3)(z_i - z)^2 \text{ is } \chi^2 \text{ with } k - 1 \; df.$$

where:

z_i is the transformed r, and
$\bar{z}$ is the weighted mean z,
$\bar{z} = \Sigma(N_i - 3)z_i/\Sigma(N_i - 3)$.

It was possible to compute the effect size for several results, and generally, the results do vary across studies. Thus, until we can find an explanation for this variation, we should not combine the individual results.

Checking for Moderating Variables

The above review isolated several issues that may substantially influence the observed relationship between price and perceived quality. It has been suggested by several researchers that a no-price treatment ought to be included in price–perceived-quality studies. The argument is that this "control" treatment provides a baseline for comparing the effect of price treatments on subjects' perceptions of product quality. Three studies were found with a price-absent treatment for which effect sizes could be computed (Gardner 1970; Jacoby, Olson, and Haddock 1971; Szybillo and Jacoby 1974).

Comparing the effect size of price-present versus price-absent treatments, for the brand-name-absent condition, the test of homogeneity of effect size produced a chi-square value of 8.27 with 14 *df*, implying homogeneity of magnitude effects. A chi-square value of 2.18 with 8 *df* was found for the brand-name-present condition, also implying homogeneity of results. While there is some variation in the effect sizes across the two conditions (eight of the twenty-four effects were negative), this variation is well within the possibility of chance. Also, unexpectedly, the price-present treatments produced stronger positive effects in the presence of brand name information than in the absence of brand name information. But, as expected, the price-absent treatments produced stronger effects when brand name information was present.

This first finding was unexpected because those multicue studies that varied brand information along with prices generally found a statistically significant brand name effect on quality perception, and a statistically insignificant price effect. Thus, it has been previously concluded that brand name information dominated price information in the perception of quality. However, finding a more positive effect for price when brand information is present than when brand information is absent suggests that the interaction of price and brand information not only is stronger, but that the influence of price on quality perception is stronger in the presence of brand information than by itself. Thus, the implication is not that brand name dominates the influence of price, but rather, increases the influence of price on quality perceptions.

Another issue discussed above concerned whether perceptions of quality positively increased as price increased. Some studies presented price information at several different price levels. Since the actual prices used varied depending on the products examined and the date of the study, it was necessary to categorize the prices from each study into low or high for a two-level price treatment, and low, medium, or high for a three-level price treatment. Then some comparisons across studies could be made. These comparisons were made regardless of whether manipulation for the price treatment was a between- or within-subject design.

As would be expected, the largest average effect size occurs in the high price versus low price comparison, followed by the high price versus medium price comparison. Further, of the thirty-seven effect sizes, only two were negative, with both occurring in the medium versus low price comparison, and these negative effects are the smallest in absolute value of any calculated. The largest effect sizes occurred in the within-subject research designs. From a methodological perspective, it would be expected that stronger effects would be observed from a within-subject design since the imputation of quality is more likely to occur when subjective price comparisons are possible. The results indicate that the between-subject design results are homogeneous and the within-subject design results are heterogeneous. Again, a possible source of variation may be attributable to the large effect sizes obtained by the Szybillo and Jacoby (1974) study. A closer look at their study reveals that the larger effect sizes might be attributed to:

1. the use of a 100-point scale (subjects, probably, were able to express their impressions more freely), or

2. the manipulation of physical composition characteristics (the use of the product) in an experimental situation, which may have resulted in strong carry-over effects.

Also, interestingly, the largest average effect sizes occur in the high price versus low price comparison, followed by the high price versus medium price comparison. These results confirm the hypothesis that perception of quality increases as price increases. Also, as would be expected, stronger effect sizes occurred in the within-subject research designs. This observation agrees with the logic that an inference of quality is more likely to occur when subjective price comparisons are possible, and also strengthens the argument for a within-subject design for testing the price–perceived-quality relationship. Further, it is generally agreed that within-subject designs are more powerful than between-subject designs.

Combining Studies

After the results of the set of studies have been compared, the next step is to combine the probability levels of these studies. The objective is to obtain an estimate of the overall probability that these probability levels could have occurred if the null hypothesis of no relationship between the two variables were true. There is a variety of methods available for combining studies (Rosenthal 1980).

The method of adding Zs requires converting all probability levels to the appropriate normal deviate Z values, summing, and dividing by the square root of the number of studies being combined. For the data in table 13–3, the sum of the Zs is 36.7. Therefore,

$$Z_m = \Sigma Z_i \sqrt{N} = 36.7/\sqrt{28} = 6.94$$

is distributed as Z and is significant at the .01 probability level, one-tailed test. This combined probability supports the majority of the studies that found a significant, positive price–perceived-quality relationship.

An alternative approach of combining results is to test the mean probability value using: $Z = (.50 - p)(12N)$. For the data of table 13–3, Z equals 5.50, which again is significant at the .01 probability level.

Returning to the method of adding Zs, another question of interest is how many additional studies reporting a p value of .50 (Z equals 0) would be required to reduce the significant Z value of 6.94 to just significant at the .05 p level. It was determined that 470 additional studies reporting a p value of .50 would be necessary to lower the overall probability level to .05. Thus, overall, there is evidence of a significant, positive price–perceived-quality relationship.

Since we are also interested in the combined estimate of the effect size, we should also perform a similar analysis. The effect sizes were computed for the basic two-variable relationships utilizing the r effect size estimate and the Fisher r-to-z transformation to compute: $z = \Sigma\, z/N$ (Rosenthal 1982). Again, the combined effect sizes for the price-present versus price-absent conditions are relatively small, r equals .05 and $-.01$. For the direct price comparisons, the combined effect sizes are considerably larger; r equals .45, .30, and .245, for the high versus low price, high versus medium price, and medium versus low price comparisons.

Testing Interactions

In addition to price, some studies manipulated brand name, store name, and product familiarity to study their effect on quality perception. Underlying each of these studies is the conceptual expectation that subjective evaluation of product choice depends on other cues as well as the price cue. In addition to a substantive review of these interactions, the results will be compared and combined for those studies that did manipulate brand or store name.

Price and Brand Name Interaction. Table 13–4 presents the results of the six studies that examined brand name (image) and price. The significant interaction effect obtained in the Andrews and Valenzi (1971) study is consistent in that price cues should have an increasingly powerful effect on product evaluations as brand familiarity decreases. That is, in cases of low brand familiarity or absence of a brand name, the price cue should provide additional, useful information not available through the brand name cue. In addition, brand image is also a function of price. This effect would be evidenced as a price and brand name interaction. Out of the six studies, three studies showed significant interaction effects and an additional two exhibited weak effects. The price effect was found to be significant in three studies while relatively weak price effects were found in two other studies. In contrast, five studies showed significant brand main effects and one study showed a very weak effect.

Analysis of interaction effects can be carried out in a similar manner as described for the price main effects. The purpose here is to determine the magnitude of the interaction effects. Past studies show that price and brand name do interact to form the perception of quality, but the magnitude of the interaction effect is not known.

The test for homogeneity showed that these interactions are relatively homogeneous, that is, the variations across the studies are within

Table 13–4
Price and Brand Name Interaction Results

Study	Brand Name Manipulation	Main Effects		Price and Brand Interaction
		Price	Brand	
Andrews and Valenzi (1971)	unknown, moderately known, very well known	yes	yes	yes
Gardner (1971)	present/absent	no	yes	no
Jacoby, Olson, and Haddock (1971)	present/absent	no	no	no
Peterson and Jolibert (1976)	American/French brand names	no	yes	no
Raju (1977)	three brand names	yes	yes	yes
Wheatley, Walton, and Chiu (1977)	two brand levels	yes	yes	yes

the statistical probability limit. The Z value of the price and brand name interactions were combined and this result supported the conclusion that brand name interacts with the price cue to enhance the perception of product quality, further strengthening this observation made when analyzing the price-present or -absent studies.

Price and Store Name Interaction. Five studies manipulated store name (image) in addition to price, while testing for a price–perceived-quality relationship. The results shown in table 13–5 reveal that the effects of store name cues are not at all clear. It seems reasonable to expect a relatively strong store main effect in within-subject design experiments as compared to between-subject design experiments since store cues are likely to affect consumers' product evaluations in natural settings. Also, it is reasonable to expect an interaction effect since the stores are often apparently classified on the basis of price level, for example, discount stores and department stores. However, only two of the five studies statistically support the existence of interactions.

The store name and price interaction effects were analyzed for homogeneity of the results before obtaining an overall probability estimate

Table 13–5
Price and Store Name Interaction Results

Study	Brand Name Manipulation	Main Effects		Price and Brand Interaction
		Price	Brand	
Enis and Stafford (1969)	actual names	yes	no	yes
Andrews and Valenzi (1971)	actual names	yes	yes	yes
London and Shafer (1974)	high and low store image	yes	yes	no
Szybillo and Jacoby (1974)	actual names	no	yes	no
Rexeisen (1982)	actual names	no	no	no

of the interaction. The test for homogeneity revealed that the interaction effects are fairly homogeneous, and the combined test supported the existence of a positive price and store interaction effect. Thus, like brand name, store name also interacts with the price cue to enhance the perception of product quality.

Conclusions

This selected review of the research on the price–perceived-quality literature has isolated a number of issues that influence the degree of confidence we may have about previous research findings. Based on this review, several recommendations seem worthwhile.

We have not been able to identify conceptually or empirically when buyers will infer product quality on the basis of price. From the limited data available, the quantitative integration of research evidence strongly suggests, that in general, people do make positive inferences about product quality on the basis of price. However, this integration of research results is based on a limited number of studies, and the conclusion must be considered tentative. For this reason, efforts need to be made to acquire additional data for a more comprehensive integration of results.

Considering the previous studies individually, it is troubling to find such inconsistency in the results across studies. It is obvious that a reasonable argument can be made that many of the methodological and substantive criticisms discussed in this chapter offer plausible alternative explanations for the results obtained in these individual studies. In essence, most of the past price–perceived-quality research can be categorized as exploratory in nature, contributing little toward resolving the question of when buyers might use price to infer product quality. Moreover, the interactive role price may play with other information cues such as brand and store name to enhance quality perceptions needs more research effort.

To systematically resolve the critical issues raised in this review will require a program of research, rather than several isolated studies. Careful research design and measurement procedures can isolate sources of variation attributable to biases present in how different people acquire sensory information and utilize information stored in memory. Confounds present in product and price treatments can either be held constant across treatment levels or systematically varied over a series of experiments. Efforts to improve the quality of measurement procedures must become routine.

Substantively, the implication that brand name, rather than dominating the price cue, serves instead to enhance the effect of price on quality judgments is worthy of additional research. Further, the additional effect of store name (image) on quality judgments needs to be incorporated into future research. Finally, the effect of quality judgments, however influenced, on product and brand choice and on store choice needs specific research attention.

References

Andrews, I.R. and Enzo K. Valenzi (1971), "Combining Price, Brand and Store Cues to Form an Impression of Product Quality," *Proceedings*, 79th Annual Convention of the American Psychological Association, 649–50.

Bettman, James R. (1973), "Perceived Price and Product Perceptual Variables," *Journal of Marketing Research* 10:100–102.

Chaplin, J.P. (1981), *Dictionary of Psychology*, a Laurel Edition, New York: Dell Publishing Co., Inc.

Cimbalo, Richard S. and Adrienne M. Webdale (1973), "Effects of Price Information on Consumer-Rated Quality," *Proceedings*, 81st Annual Convention, American Psychological Association, 831–32.

Deering, Barbara J. and Jacob Jacoby (1972), "Price Intervals and Individual Price Limits as Determinants of Product Evaluation and Selection," in M. Venkatesan, ed., *Proceedings*, 3rd Annual Conference of the Association for Consumer Research, Iowa City, Iowa, 145–66.

Della Bitta, A.J. and Kent B. Monroe (1973), "The Influence of Adaptation Levels on Subjective Price Perceptions," in Scott Ward and Peter Wright, eds., *Advances in Consumer Research*, vol. 1, Ann Arbor, Mich.: Association for Consumer Research, 353–69.

_____ , _____ , and John M. McGinnis (1981), "Consumer Perceptions of Comparative Price Advertisements," *Journal of Marketing Research* 18 (November):416–27.

Enis, Ben and James E. Stafford (1969), "Influence of Price and Store Information upon Product Quality Perception," *Southern Journal of Business* 4 (April): 90–94.

Gardner, David M. (1970), "An Experimental Investigation of the Price–Quality Relationship," *Journal of Retailing* 46 (Fall):24–41.

_____ (1971), "Is There a Generalized Price–Quality Relationship?" *Journal of Marketing Research* 8 (May):241–43.

Jacoby, Jacob, Jerry C. Olson, and Rafael A. Haddock (1971), "Price, Brand Name and Product Composition Characteristics as Determinants of Perceived Quality," *Journal of Applied Psychology* 55 (6):570–79.

Lambert, Zarrel V. (1970), "Product Perception: An Important Variable in Pricing Strategy," *Jounal of Marketing* 34 (October):68–71.

_____ (1972), "Price and Choice Behavior," *Journal of Marketing Research* 9 (February):35–40.

Landon, Laird, Jr. and Kurt B. Shafer (1974), "Risk Style and the Price–Quality Relationship," unpublished manuscript.

Lauridsen, M.L. (1973), "The Relationship Between Price and Perceived Quality: An Experimental Study," *Markeds Kommunikasjon* 2:1–12.

Leavitt, H.J. (1954), "A Note on Some Experimental Findings about the Meaning of Price," *Journal of Business* 27:205–10.

Lodge, Milton (1981), *Magnitude Scaling: Quantitative Measurement of Opinions*, Beverly Hills, Calif.: Sage Publications.

McConnell, J. Douglas (1968), "Effects of Pricing on Perception of Product Quality," *Journal of Applied Psychology* 51 (4):331–34.

Monroe, Kent B. (1979), "Research Opportunities in Pricing," *Proceedings*, Southeastern Conference of the American Institute for Decision Sciences, 93–96.

_____ (1982). "The Influence of Price on Product Perceptions and Product Choice," in A. Mitchell, ed., *Advances in Consumer Research* vol. 9, Ann Arbor, Mich.: Association for Consumer Research, 206–9.

Olson, Jerry C. (1977), "Price as an Informational Cue: Effects on Product Evaluations," in Arch G. Woodside, Jagdish N. Sheth, and Peter D. Bennett, eds., *Consumer and Industrial Buying Behavior*, New York: North Holland, 267–86.

_____ and Jacob Jacoby (1972), "Cue Utilization in the Quality Perception Process," in M. Venkatesan, ed., *Proceedings*, 3rd Annual Conference, Association for Consumer Research, Iowa City, Iowa: 167–79.

Peterson, Robert A. and Alain J.P. Jolibert (1976), "A Cross-National Investigation of Price and Brand as Determinants of Perceived Product Quality," *Journal of Applied Psychology* 61 (4):533–36.

Pincus, Steven and L.K. Waters (1975), "Product Quality Ratings as a Function of Availability of Intrinsic Product Cues and Price Information," *Journal of Applied Psychology* 60 (2):280–82.

Raju, P.S. (1977), "Product Familiarity, Brand Name and Price Influences on Product Evaluation," in W. Perreault, ed., *Advances in Consumer Research*, vol. 4, Ann Arbor, Mich.: Association for Consumer Research, 64–71.

Rao, Vithala (1971), "Salience of Price in the Perception of Product Quality: A Multidimensional Measurement Approach," in Fred C. Alvine, ed., *Proceedings*, Chicago: American Marketing Association, 571–77.

Rexeisen, Richard J. (1982), "Is There a Valid Price–Quality Relationship? in A. Mitchell, ed., *Advances in Consumer Research*, 9, Ann Arbor, Mich.: Association for Consumer Research, 190–94.

Rosenthal, Robert (1980), "Summarizing Significance Levels," in R. Rosenthal, ed., *New Directions for Methodology of Social and Behavioral Sciences: Quantitative Assessment of Research Domains*, no. 5, San Francisco: Jossey-Bass, 33–46.

――― (1982), "Valid Interpretation of Quantitative Research Results," in D. Brinberg and L. Kidder, eds., *New Directions for Methodology of Social and Behavioral Science: Forms of Validity in Research*, no. 12, San Francisco: Jossey-Bass, 59–75.

Sandusky, Arthur (1974), "Memory Processes and Judgment," in Edward C. Carterette and Morton P. Friedman, eds., *Handbook of Perception*, vol. 2, New York: Academic Press, 61–83.

Scitovsky, T. (1945), "Some Consequences of the Habit of Judging Quality by Price," *The Review of Economic Studies* 12:100–105.

Shapiro, Benson P. (1970), "Price as a Communicator of Quality: An Experiment," unpublished doctoral diss., Harvard University, Cambridge, Mass.

――― (1972), "The Pricing of Consumer Goods: Theory and Practice," working paper, Marketing Science Institute, Cambridge, Mass.

Szybillo, George J. and Jacob Jacoby (1974), "Intrinsic versus Extrinsic Cues as Determinants of Perceived Product Quality," *Journal of Applied Psychology* 59:74–78.

Tull, Donald S., R.A. Boring, and M.H. Gonsoir (1964), "A Note on the Relationship of Price and Imputed Quality," *Journal of Business* 37:186–91.

Valenzi, Enzo R. and I.R. Andrews (1971), "Effect of Price Information on Product Quality Ratings," *Journal of Applied Psychology* 55 (February):87–91.

――― and Larry Eldridge (1973), "Effect of Price Information, Composition Differences, Expertise, and Rating Scales on Product-Quality Rating," *Proceedings*, 81st Annual Convention, American Psychological Association, 829–30.

Wheatley, John J., Richard G. Walton, and John S.Y. Chiu (1977), "The Influence of Prior Product Experience, Price and Brand on Quality Perception," in W. Perreault, ed., *Advances in Consumer Research* vol. 4, Ann Arbor, Mich.: Association for Consumer Research, 72–77.

――― , John S.Y. Chiu, and Arieh Goldman (1981), "Physical Quality, Price, and Perceptions of Product Quality: Implications for Retailers," *Journal of Retailing* 57 (Summer):100–16.

――― , ――― , and Allen Douglas (1982), "Generics: Their Impact on National and Private Brands," in A. Mitchell, ed., *Advances in Consumer Research*, vol. 9, Ann Arbor, Mich.: Association for Consumer Research, 195–200.

14
The Effects of Price, Package Design, and Brand Familiarity on Perceived Quality

Raymond C. Stokes

The cues that consumers use to judge the quality and value of products have been of interest to students of marketing and consumer behavior for about forty years. Beginning with Scitovsky (1945), the cue that has received the most research attention is price.

While price is of considerable importance to the marketing practitioner and to most people who purchase the products, it probably is not as important as brand name, which communicates a great deal of information from the marketer to the consumer through the "bundle" of information with which it has become associated through advertising, word of mouth communication, and previous usage of the brand. A few studies have recognized the importance of this cue but have studied it by manipulating the presence or absence of the brand name—a purely academic exercise in that few products are marketed without brand names in today's marketplace, even with basic commodities like sugar, salt, and flour. A more realistic experimental manipulation of the brand name variable would be to present the consumer with a choice between competing brands that differ in their degree of familiarity.

Another important variable in the marketing mix whose major purpose is to project an image of quality is the package design. Marketers of consumer packaged products spend millions of dollars annually on designs to achieve this objective, yet this variable has been totally ignored in quality-cue research.

Another weakness in most experiments has been that the brand itself was not physically presented or was unrealistically viewed in isolation. When a brand is perceived apart from the others with which it normally competes for the consumer's favor, it is difficult to generalize the results and use them for practical purposes.

One other difficulty faced by most previous researchers has been that of budgetary limitations and availability of subjects, which usually forces the investigator to use college students. In most instances, the researcher has been wise enough to choose products that are purchased and consumed by college students, but certainly such a sample is atypical of the general population and projection of obtained results requires extreme caution.

The objectives of this chapter are to investigate the effects of: (1) the price, (2) the package design, (3) brand familiarity, and (4) the familiarity of a background array of brands on three dependent variables—familiarity with the brands (a manipulation check), perceived quality, and purchase intentions. To achieve this a $2 \times 2 \times 2 \times 2$ completely crossed-factorial experimentation design was executed among a reasonably representative sample of typical consumers for the product class.

Price

It was originally shown through survey research (Gabor and Granger 1964, 1965) that consumers typically attribute higher quality to brands that have a relatively high price, demonstrating presumably that consumer's believe that "you get what you pay for." Early experiments involving the manipulation of price were single-cue studies that generally demonstrated a positive cause and effect relationship between price and perceived quality. The first reported by Leavitt (1954) was followed by many others including Tull, Boring, and Gonsior (1964), Cunningham (1967), Olander (1969), Newman and Bucknell (1970), McConnell (1968), Peterson (1970), Lambert (1970), Rao (1971), Della Bitta (1971), and Deering and Jacoby (1972).

An early multicue study reported by Smith and Broome (1966) manipulated price, share of market, and familiarity of brands. This was followed by Stafford and Enis (1969) who varied price and high- and low-prestige stores. Gardner (1970, 1971, 1973) published several multicue studies which were criticized by Olson (1973). Many other studies involving a price variable have appeared. Some of interest are Andrews and Valenzi (1970), Shapiro (1970, 1973), Rao (1972), Valenzi and Eldridge (1973), Cimbalo and Webdale (1973), Jacoby, Olson, and Haddock (1971), Szybillo and Jacoby (1972), Granger and Billison (1972), Pincus and Waters (1975), Peterson and Jolibert (1976), Raju (1977), Wheatley and Chiu (1977), Berkowitz and Walter (1980), and Venkataraman (1981).

In summary, the majority of the experimental investigations involving the manipulation of price found a significant main effect for price; however, a number of studies found no such effect. Price was shown to interact with other cues in some studies and not in other studies, a finding that is not adequately explained.

The Package Design

The packaging of consumer products has a number of functions. It must have a protective quality to get the product from the manufacturer through channels of distribution to the point of purchase and to the point of consumption, in good condition. It may also serve as a storage container and be used to communicate weight, ingredients, nutrition information, manufacturer, cooking directions, storage instruction, and so forth. But perhaps the most important characteristic of the package to the marketing manager is the design, because this aspect of the package carries the primary responsibility for moving the product through the last foot of the distribution channel. The package design, ideally, will instantly communicate an image of a brand that is "friendly." It would say "Here is an old friend," or for a new product it would say "Here is something you would like to try." Outstanding consumer packages have superior sales power. They have distinctive personalities, offer intrigue, are highly visible as compared to their competitors, and give a composite impression of quality, dependability, and style.

One of the first organizations to become interested in researching package design was the Seagram's Distilleries in Louisville, Kentucky where Giradot (1947) wrote an article entitled "Can Package Design Be Evaluated?" At that time Seagram's, in evaluating their package designs, measured legibility, recognition, memory, and attractiveness. Legibility was measured by the use of a shadow box; recognition and memory, by the use of a tachistoscopic device; and attractiveness was determined by word-association tests.

Cheskin (1971), long active in researching package design, measures visibility because the shoppers must be able to see the package and recognize it, readability because the brand and main copy items must be legible, and eye movement to determine which elements are seen first and how the eye moves from element to element on the package. But most important to Cheskin is what he calls "controlled association." Since he feels that the most important reaction to the package is at the unconscious or subconscious level, he uses nondirective techniques to determine the affect of or feeling toward the package without making the respondent act as a packaging expert or an art critic.

Faison (1961, 1962), package-design researcher, measures four key characteristics: (1) visibility—is the package easily distinguished in the visual competition of actual shelf display, (2) content communications—does the package quickly signal the nature of its contents, (3) psychological connotations—does the package have an image that is consistent with the product marketing strategy, and (4) function—is the package easy to open, close, and store, and does it adequately protect its contents.

Faison believes that it is appropriate to measure the distance at which the package can be identified, the extent to which it attracts and holds attention, the angle at which the package can be identified, the speed at which it can be recognized, the apparent contents relative to competition, and the legibility of the copy.

Perception Research Services, Inc. and Telcom, both located in New Jersey, offer package-design evaluation using the eye camera; and both claim success. However, research studies of acceptable quality involving the eye camera are rare.

Schwartz (1971) reviewed techniques frequently used in package-design research and found that there are:

1. visibility and legibility testing by means of a tachistoscope
2. measures of impact and relative legibility in simulated supermarket displays
3. distance legibility tests, variable illumination-level tests
4. test for the "time-to-find" the test package from a typical supermarket display
5. image studies
6. simulated shopping trips
7. indirect measures by preference testing of identical products in two different package designs

Schucker (1959) conducted the most comprehensive research study on package design to date. He believed the package should have *attention-drawing* power—that is, it should draw the eye away from competitive packages to the test package. If the package is not seen or perceived, it cannot achieve any other objective. After the package is seen, it should have maximum *brand name readability* in order to capitalize on advertising and other promotional expenses. The package should also quickly *communicate a good economic value;* and one of the main components of this is the apparent package size or content of the package relative to the competition. And last, the appeal of the package or the *psychological connotations* of the design are important. The main purpose in Schucker's research was to measure the reliability of various methods of measuring these four aspects of packaging design and to determine the extent to which they measure unique attributes. The methods Schucker developed for measuring these four aspects have a high level of reliability ranging from .81 for attention-drawing power, up to .97 for apparent size. These aspects are also relatively independent as reflected by generally low intercorrelation coefficients except for the coefficient of 5.7 between attention-drawing power and package appeal. This indicates that the eye tends to be drawn to packages that are attractive or appealing.

The Experimental Design

The experimental design shown in figure 14–1 is a $2 \times 2 \times 2 \times 2$ completely crossed-factorial fixed model with unequal cell frequencies ranging from four to eleven. Twelve questionnaires were mailed to respondents in each of the sixteen cells. Of the 192 who received questionnaires, 128 returned them, for a return rate of about 67 percent.

Sample

Too frequently, convenience samples of college students are selected for research involving price–quality perception. In order to avoid this weakness and to facilitate the manipulations of the familiarity of various brands of rice, it was decided to conduct the research among female heads of households in the West Coast states of California, Oregon, and Washington.

One convenient and relatively inexpensive way to conduct field research involving a fairly complicated research design is by means of a mail panel-survey technique. Home Testing Institute (HTI) is an independent market-research organization which maintains a large sample of families subdivided into panels of 1,000 each. The panels are representative of the population of the United States within census regions with respect to four key demographic characteristics: annual family income, size of family, age of the housewife, and size of the market area.

HTI selected the 192 subjects for the study at random from one of the 1,000-member panels from the West Coast census region. The 192 subjects were further divided at random into 16 groups of 12 each; and the 16 groups were then assigned at random to the 16 cells in the experimental design. The number of usable returned questionnaires was 128. The demographics of the 64 who did not return questionnaires were not different from the 128 respondents who did; thus no apparent bias was introduced from this source.

Independent Variables

The independent variables were: (1) a familiar or strange array of background packages, (2) a 39-cent or 49-cent price of the test brand, (3) a familiar or strange test package, and (4) a new or old package design of the test brand.

Operationalization of Dependent Variables

The dependent variables were: (1) familiarity with the brands—this was essentially a manipulation check on the degree of success in presenting brands that would be viewed as relatively familiar or strange; (2) the perceived quality of the brands; and (3) the stated likelihood of purchasing the brands.

The dependent variables were operationalized as follows. Familiarity was measured on a five-point scale of highly familiar, quite familiar, somewhat familiar, slightly familiar, or not at all familiar. Quality was measured on a five-point scale of high quality, above-average quality, average quality, below-average quality, or low quality. Purchase intentions were operationalized by ranking the brands, assigning "1" to the brand that would be most likely purchased, "2" to the brand as the second choice and so forth down to "9" as the brand that would be least apt to be purchased.

Selection of Stimuli

The manipulation of price was no problem but, in accordance with the experimental design, it was necessary to manipulate the familiarity of a

		FT_1		FT_2	
		D_1	D_2	D_1	D_2
FB_1	P_1	$N = 8$	$N = 10$	$N = 7$	$N = 8$
	P_1	$N = 8$	$N = 10$	$N = 7$	$N = 9$
FB_2	P_1	$N = 10$	$N = 9$	$N = 5$	$N = 8$
	P_2	$N = 9$	$\cdot N = 4$	$N = 11$	$N = 7$

Independent Variables
  FB—Familiarity of background brands
    FB_1—Familiar
    FB_2—Strange
  P—Relative price of test brand
    P_1—High
    P_2—Low
  FT—Familiarity of test brand
    FT_1—Familiar
    FT_2—Strange
  D—Package Design
    D_1—New
    D_2—Old
Dependent Variables
  1. Familiarity of brands
  2. Quality perception of brands
  3. Purchase intentions

Figure 14–1. Design of the Experiment

test brand as well as the familiarity of an array of background brands, and also to manipulate a new and old package design of a test brand. To accomplish this, it was necessary to select a product category that allowed these manipulations. Lengthy experience in the rice market as described later, allowed me to select brands of rice that would be well known and familiar to food shoppers on the West Coast and also to select brands of rice that had never been sold in that region of the country and, therefore, should be totally strange to all who had not lived in other areas of the country. Old package designs and newer, more-modern rice packages designed by myself were also available. Therefore, the rice product category was selected.

The Selection of Specific Brands of Rice

Table 14–1 lists the familiar and strange brands presented in the background array. In the familiar category, Rice-A-Roni, Minute Rice, and Uncle Ben's brands are highly advertised, nationally distributed, and therefore, familiar on the West Coast; MJB White, MJB Instant, and MJB Brown have long been sold and advertised only on the West Coast. Those brands intended to serve as relatively strange background packages have never been sold on the West Coast.

The Selection of Test Brands of Rice

Uncle Ben's Quick Rice was developed under my supervision at Uncle Ben's, Inc. and has been sold on the West Coast for more than twenty-five years. I designed the original package in which the product was sold, but it was subsequently modified and presumably improved. This brand, familiar to those on the West Coast, was therefore available in two different package designs—an old and a new one.

Table 14–1
Price of Brands of Rice

Familiar Background	Strange Background	Price
Rice-A-Roni	River	41¢
Minute Mix	Peacock	41¢
MJB White	Blue Ribbon	43¢
Minute Rice	Dragon	45¢
MJB Instant	Riceland	45¢
MJB Brown	Carolina	47¢
Uncle Ben's Converted	Adolphus	55¢
Uncle Ben's Wild Mix	Comet	69¢

The test brand of Uncle Ben's Quick (familiar) and Wonder (strange) were priced at either 39¢ or 49¢; that is, the lowest or third from the highest price in the array.

A Comet Rice Mills brand that has good sales in the Southwest is Wonder Rice, which has never been sold on the West Coast. This product was sold for many years in an old-fashioned package with a cellophane window with no vignette on the package. Upon becoming senior vice-president at Comet with responsibility for the marketing function, I redesigned all of the company's packages including Wonder's. A new package with a more-modern, simple design, a bright green color, and a rice-dish illustration was shown through research to be superior to the old design. This brand, strange to those on the West Coast, was available in extremely different designs—an old one and a new one.

The Selection of Prices of Test Brands

A price difference of 10 cents per package would be reasonable in the rice product category, and a difference of this magnitude could reflect differences in quality. It was decided to price the test brand either at the lowest price in the array which was 39 cents, or at the relatively high-price condition of 49 cents. These prices were close to actual prices at the time the data were collected. At the high-price condition, the test brand would be exceeded in price only by Uncle Ben's Converted and Uncle Ben's Wild Rice Mix, both of which are of high quality and are recognized as being expensive.

The Presentation of Stimuli to Subjects

Since it was impractical to present nine actual packages to respondents either face-to-face or through mail-survey interviewing techniques, it was decided to present 8- by 10-inch color photographs.

The quality of these photographs was such that the brand names and the package-design details were easily perceived by the respondent and thus should have had an impact similar to that which the actual packages would have when seen in a similar array on the supermarket shelf. The test package was, in each case, in the center of the display—that is, in the middle of the second of three rows—and was, therefore, surrounded by other packages.

The price was presented for each brand on the photograph by means of a pressure-sensitive white circle of paper which was three-eighths of an inch in diameter. The pressure-sensitive marker was placed in the extreme lower-right corner of the package and the price was printed in black ink.

Results

Familiarity Dependent Variable

The analysis of variance of familiarity shown in table 14–2 confirms that the manipulation of brand familiarity was successful:

> The test brand sold on the West Coast was rated higher in familiarity than the test brand not sold in that area.

> The background brands sold on the West Coast were rated higher in familiarity than those not sold in that area.

Quality-Perception Dependent Variable

The ANOVA of the quality-perception dependent variable is also presented in table 14–2. As expected, all main effects were significant with familiarity of background brands significant beyond the .01 level, and package design at the .05 level. An examination of the marginal means in table 14–3 shows the quality ratings to be in the expected directions:

1. The test brand is rated higher in quality when viewed against a strange background of brands than it is when seen in an array of familiar brands.
2. The test brand is rated higher in quality when it is shown at the higher 49-cent price than when shown at the 39-cent price.
3. The familiar test brand (Uncle Ben's Quick) is rated higher in quality than is the strange test brand (Wonder).
4. The test brand presented in the new design is rated higher in quality than when presented in the old design.

Purchase-Intentions Dependent Variable

The ANOVA results of the purchase-intention data is also given in table 14–2. Two of the main effects were significant at the .01 level or beyond, while the other two—found significant on the quality-rating dependent variable—were not; that is, familiarity of background brands and familiarity of the test brand are significant, while price or package design alone had no effect on purchase intention. An examination of the marginal means in table 14–3 shows that the test brand is much more apt to be purchased when available in a strange array of brands than in a familiar group of brands. These consumers were also more likely to purchase the familiar test brand than the strange one wherever it is seen. It is interesting that neither price nor package design was related to the probability of purchase, while familiarity has great influence.

Table 14–2
Analysis of Variance of the Three Dependent Variables for the Complete Design

Source	df	Familiarity		Quality Perception		Purchase Rank	
		MS	F	MS	F	MS	F
Total	128	2.456	—	.975	—	6.974	—
Between	15	14.381	—	2.982	—	18.181	—
FB	1	30.421	34.830[a]	6.489	9.162[b]	155.996	28.435[a]
P	1	.083	.095	4.140	5.845[b]	1.276	.233
FT	1	145.580	166.678[a]	16.270	22.973[a]	36.285	6.614[b]
D	1	1.357	1.554	2.676	3.778[c]	4.488	.818
FBxP	1	.003	.003	2.924	4.128[c]	10.753	1.960
FBxFT	1	29.297	33.513[a]	1.960	2.767	12.179	2.220
FBxD	1	.108	.124	.257	.368	15.117	2.156
PxFT	1	.313	.393	1.490	2.104	2.355	.429
PxD	1	.049	.056	.025	.036	.032	.006
FTxD	1	1.841	2.108	2.638	3.725[c]	2.483	.453
FBxPxFT	1	.028	.032	1.537	2.171	.271	.049
FBxPxD	1	3.379	3.868[c]	.686	.969	3.107	.556
FBxFTxD	1	.694	.795	3.568	5.038[c]	26.355	4.804[c]
PxFTxD	1	.412	.471	.035	.049	.808	.147
FBxPxFTxD	1	2.119	2.426	.031	.044	1.205	.220
Within	113	.873	—	.708	—	5.486	—

[a] $p < .001$
[b] $p < .01$
[c] $p < .05$

Table 14–3
Marginal Means

| | Dependent Variable | | |
	Familiarity	Quality	Purchase Rank
FB_1	1.87	3.35	6.14
FB_2	2.87	3.82	3.87
P_1	2.35	3.77	4.91
P_2	2.40	3.40	5.11
FT_1	3.47	3.95	4.46
FT_2	1.28	3.22	5.56
D_1	2.48	3.73	4.82
D_2	2.27	3.44	5.20

There were significant interactions found in the ANOVA of all three dependent variables, which will not be discussed in detail here. It can be seen, however, that:

1. Price and package design do not interact.
2. Familiarity interacts in complex ways with package design on quality perception and intentions to buy.

Discussion

Based upon most of the research on price–quality-perception, it was expected that the price main effect would be significant on the quality-rating dependent variable. The confirmation of this expectation lends some additional support for a generalized price–quality-perception hypothesis.

Previous research has shown that price is used more as a quality cue in situations where uncertainty exists, such as with unfamiliar brands. This was found to be true in this experiment, supporting results found in previous research.

The significant main effect of package design on quality perception was also anticipated, and the significant interactions with familiarity are not surprising. It is clear that package design is used more as a quality cue when uncertainty exists, that is, when the test brand is unfamiliar within the array of brands. In this regard, package design has effects similar to price as a quality cue. Package design and price do not interact.

It is also not surprising that both the familiarity of the test brand and the familiarity of the background array should have significant effects on quality perception. But the fact that the magnitude of the effects of familiarity are so large, especially with the background or context in which the brand is perceived, should demonstrate to future researchers in this area that the perception of brands should be studied under realistic conditions if the results are to have meaning in the real world of consumer behavior.

This is even more apparent when the results of the purchase-intentions dependent variable are examined. The fact that neither price nor package design had significant effects and familiarity did, lends additional emphasis to the importance of the consumers' familiarity with brands. Brand familiarity does affect consumer behavior and indicates that those who spend large sums on advertising, promotion, couponing, and giving away free samples in order to increase familiarity are not wrong. These results indicate that those who introduce new products and new brands against familiar, established ones have an uphill battle. This, of course, is not a surprising conclusion to the marketing practitioner, who often fails in his attempts to introduce novel products or new brands.

The fact that neither price nor package design has significant effects on purchase intentions in this experiment also points up the need for the inclusion of a dependent variable that is a measure of value anticipated for the money spent in addition to or perhaps in place of mere quality perception. Shapiro (1970) showed that perceived worth is a better predictor of purchase intentions than perceived quality. In other words, the results of this experiment indicate that it is the *ratio* of quality to price that has the major influence on purchase intentions and not the perception of greater quality because of a higher price.

References

Andrews, I.R. and E.R. Valenzi (1970), "The Relationship between Product Purchase Price and Blind Rated Quality: Margarines and Butters," *Journal of Marketing Research* 7 (August):393–95.

Berkowitz, Eric N. and John R. Walter (1980), "Contextual Influences on Consumer Price Responses: An Experimental Analysis," *Journal of Marketing Research* (August):340–58.

Cheskin, L. (1971), "Your Package: Marketing Success or Disaster?" *Package Engineering* (April):16f–16g.

Cimbalo, R.S. and A.M. Webdale (1973), "Effects of Price Information on Consumer-Rated Quality," *Proceedings*, 81st Annual Convention of the American Psychological Association.

Cunningham, S.M. (1967), *Risk Taking and Information Handling in Consumer Behavior*, D.F. Cox, ed., Boston: Graduate School of Business Administration, Harvard University.

Deering, B.J. and Jacob Jacoby (1972), "Price Intervals and Individual Price Limits as Determinants of Product Evaluation and Selection," in M. Venkatesan, ed., *Proceedings*, 3rd Annual Conference of the Association for Consumer Research.

Della Bitta, A. (1971), "An Experimental Examination of Conditions which may Foster the Use of Price as an Indicator of Relative Product Attractiveness," unpublished Ph.D. diss., University of Massachusetts.

Faison, E.W.J. (1961), "The Application of Research to Packaging," *Business Horizons* 4 (February):39–40.

Faison, E.W.J. (1962), *Package Design: An Aid to Deisgn*, Chicago: Visual Research, Inc.

Gabor, A. and C. Granger (1964), "Price Sensitivity of the Consumer," *Journal of Advertising Research* 4 (December):40–44.

_____ and _____ (1965), "The Pricing of New Products," *Scientific Business* 2 (August):141–50.

Gardner, D.M. (1970), "An Experimental Investigation of the Price–Quality Relationship," *Journal of Retailing* 46 (Fall):25–41.

_____ (1971), "Is There a Generalized Price–Quality Relationship?" *Journal of Marketing Research* 8 (May):241–43.

_____ (1973), "Factors Affecting the Price–Quality Relationship," *Proceedings*, 81st Annual Convention of the American Psychological Association.

Giradot, N. (1947), *Can Package Design Be Evaluated*, New York, American Management Association.

Granger, C.W.J. and A. Billison (1972), "Consumers' Attitudes Toward Package Size and Price," *Journal of Marketing Research* 9 (August):239.

Jacoby, J., J.C. Olson, and R.A. Haddock (1971), "Price, Brand Name, and Product Composition Characteristics as Determinants of Perceived Quality," *Journal of Applied Psychology* 55:570–79.

Jones, E.E. (1964), *Integration: A Sociopsychological Analysis*, New York: Appleton-Century-Crofts.

Lambert, Z.V. (1970), "Product Perception: An Important Variable in Pricing Strategy," *Journal of Marketing* 34 (October):68–71.

Leavitt, H.J. (1954), "A Note on Some Experimental Findings about the Meanings of Price," *Journal of Business* 27 (July):205–10.

Lippincott, J.G. and W.P. Margulies (1956), "Packaging in Top-Level Planning," *Harvard Business Review* 35 (September–October):46–54.

McConnell, J.D. (1968), "The Development of Brand Loyalty: An Experimental Study," *Journal of Marketing Research* 5 (February):13–19.

Newman, D. and J. Bucknell (1970), "The Price–Quality Relationship as a Tool in Consumer Research," *Proceedings*, 78th Annual Conference of the American Psychological Association.

Olander, F. (1969), "The Influence of Price on the Consumer's Evaluation of Products and Purchases," in B. Taylor and G. Wills, eds., *Pricing Strategy*, Princeton, N.J.: Brandon-Systems Press.

Olson, J.C. (1973), "Cue Properties of Price," *Proceedings*, 81st Annual Convention of the American Psychological Association.

Peterson, R.A. (1970), "The Price–Perceived-Quality Relationship Experimental Evidence," *Journal of Marketing Research* 7 (November):525–28.

_____ and A. Jolibert (1976), "A Cross-National Investigation of Price Brand Determinants of Perceived Product Quality," *Journal of Applied Psychology* 61 (July):533–36.

Pincus, S. and L.K. Waters (1975), "Product Quality Ratings as a Function of Availability of Intrinsic Product Cues and Price Information," *Journal of Applied Psychology* 60:280–82.

Raju, P.S. (1977), "Product Familiarity, Brand Name and Price Influences on Product Evaluations," *Advances in Consumer Research*, vol. 4, William D. Perreault, Jr., ed., Association of Consumer Research, 64–71.

Rao, V.R. (1971), "The Salience of Price in the Perception of Product Quality: A Multidimensional Measurement Approach," paper presented before the Fall Conference of the American Marketing Association, Minneapolis, 30 August to 1 September.

_____ (1972), "Marginal Salience of Price in Brand Evaluations," in M. Venkatesan, ed., *Proceedings*, 3rd Annual Conference of the Association for Consumer Research.

Schucker, R.E. (1959), "An Evaluation of Methods for Measuring Consumer Reactions to Retail Packages," unpublished Ph.D. diss., Purdue University.

Schwartz, D. (1971), "Evaluating Packaging," *Journal of Advertising Research* 11 (October):29–32.

Scitovsky, T. (1945), "Some Consequences of the Habit of Judging Quality by Price," *The Review of Economic Studies* 12:100–105.

Shapiro, B.P. (1970), "The Effect of Price on Purchase Behavior," paper presented before the American Marketing Association Fall Educators' Conference, Boston.

_____ (1973), "Price Reliance: Existence and Sources," *Journal of Marketing Research* 10 (August):286–94.

Smith, E.M. and C. Broome (1966), "Experimental Determination of the Effect of Price and Market-Standing Information on Consumers' Brand Preferences," *Proceedings*, American Marketing Association Conference.

Stafford, J.E. and B.M. Enis (1969), "The Price–Quality Relationship: An Extension," *Journal of Marketing Research* 6 (November):456–58.

Szybillo, G.J. and Jacob Jacoby (1972), "The Relative Effects of Price, Store, Image, and Composition Differences on Product Evaluation," in M. Venkatesan, ed., *Proceedings*, 3rd Annual Conference of the Association for Consumer Research.

Tull, D.S., Boring, R.A. and M.H. Gonsior (1964), "A Note on the Relationship of Price and Imputed Quality," *Journal of Business* 37 (February):186–91.

Valenzi, E. and L. Eldridge (1973), "Effect of Price Information, Composition Differences, Expertise, and Rating Scales on Product Quality Ratings," *Proceedings*, 81st Annual Convention of the American Psychological Association.

Venkataraman, Vik (1981), "Price–Quality Relationship in an Experimental Setting," *Journal of Advertising Research* 21 (August):49–52.

Wheatley, John J. and John S.Y. Chiu (1977), "Effects of Price, Store Image, and Product and Respondent Characteristics on Perceptions of Quality," *Journal of Marketing Research* 14 (May):181–86.

Zajonc, R.B. (1968), "Attitudinal Effects of Mere Exposure," *Journal of Personality and Social Psychology* 9, Monograph Supplement (June), 1–27.

15
Perceived Risk and Price-Reliance Schema as Price–Perceived–Quality Mediators

Robert A. Peterson and
William R. Wilson

T he role of price in the process by which a consumer arrives at an overall judgment of product quality is an issue that has generated much research as well as theoretical discussion since it was first introduced by Scitovsky (1945). This chapter attempts to provide neither a comprehensive review of past findings nor a critical assessment of theoretical progress regarding what is commonly termed the price–perceived-quality relationship (see, for example, Monroe 1973; Olson 1974). Rather, it questions some of the traditional assumptions that implicitly underlie the orientation of most price–perceived-quality research. A new orientation is suggested that focuses on factors mediating the relationship. Finally, an empirical illustration of selected factors that should be given greater attention in future research is provided.

Although diverse topics have been investigated under the rubric of price–perceived quality, an implicit research goal has often been to determine how pervasive the tendency is in consumers to judge higher-priced products to be superior to lower-priced products in the same class, even under conditions where objective differences between the products are negligible or nonexistent (McConnell 1968; Shapiro 1973; Wheatley and Chiu 1977). Based on the straightforward cue properties of price and its availability and visibility in purchase situations, the argument has frequently been made that the use of price as a cue for predicting product quality is rather widespread (Etgar and Malhotra 1981).

Even a cursory review of empirical findings, however, suggests that the price–perceived-quality relationship is neither particularly general nor robust. For example, the relationship appears to be nonlinear (Peterson

This research was supported in part by the Institute for Constructive Capitalism, the University of Texas at Austin. The opinions expressed in this chapter are those of the authors and do not necessarily reflect the view of the institute.

1970; Peterson and Jolibert 1976) and highly variable across individuals (Shapiro 1973) and products being judged (Gardner 1971). Additionally, the cue value of price for drawing inferences about quality diminishes or does not behave in an additive fashion when other product-quality cues, such as brand name (Gardner 1971; Jacoby, Olson, and Haddock 1971) or store image (Stafford and Enis 1969) are present. Moreover, there is little evidence to suggest that the knowledge obtained in this area has been or can be applied directly to the actions of consumers in real-life buying situations.

The fact that the nature of the price–perceived-quality relationship is complex and varied has undoubtedly hampered researchers' efforts to reach a general understanding of the implications of this relationship for consumer behavior. Furthermore, substantial progress toward reaching that goal may not be possible until a basic change has occurred in the orientation that most researchers have taken when investigating this relationship.

The need to reexamine the traditional approach to the relationship has perhaps been stated most emphatically by Bowbrick (1982). He derided investigations of the price–perceived-quality relationship as "pseudoresearch" and recommended that the entire research effort be abandoned. In Bowbrick's opinion, such research was doomed to failure from the beginning because the price–perceived-quality hypothesis was too general and untestable to produce anything other than trivial results.

For reasons discussed below, Bowbrick's contention is considered premature and oversimplified, if not substantially in error. At the same time, though, his basic proposition—that too much emphasis has been placed on documenting the "university" of the effects of price information on perceptions of product quality—merits serious attention. Indeed, it is argued here that this emphasis, not the research program, is what should be abandoned.

Sometimes price has diagnostic value and sometimes it does not when consumers are attempting to judge the quality of a product. Therefore, a productive focus for research would be to investigate under what conditions price information is likely to lead to an inference about product quality. The value of this orientation is that it highlights the need for researchers to formulate hypotheses about the variable(s) that *mediate* the relationship between price cue and quality inference. One way to better understand the conditions that lead to a price–quality inference is to examine the reasons why a universal price–perceived-quality relationship is not found (and should not be expected) for all people across all products.

The failure to find support for a universal relationship should not be surprising if it is assumed that the tendency of an individual to employ price as a cue for quality is a function of that individual's consumption experience. Indeed, support for such a universal relationship should be highly suspect. The reason is simple. If consumers' inferences of quality based on price mirror reality perfectly, the upper limit of any price–perceived-quality effect will be bounded by the objective relationship between price and product quality. In other words, the price–perceived-quality relationship should not be expected to be any stronger or any more general than the actual (objective) price–quality relationship.

Although it is impossible to assess the "true" relationship between price and product quality, certain evidence suggests it is far from perfect. For example, Gabor (1980) reported simultaneous price differences of 17 percent to 40 percent for a variety of identical products in one geographically constrained shopping area. It seems unlikely that consumers would fail to detect such price variance in the clear absence of quality differences.

Studies that have attempted to examine directly the objective relationship between price and product quality (Friedman 1967; Morris and Bronson 1969; Swan 1974; Riesz 1978) suggest that the overall association is quite low. For a sizable number (21 percent) of primarily nondurable products, the relationship was actually observed to be negative (Riesz 1978). This finding may partially account for the fact that price–perceived-quality experiments employing nondurable products consistently demonstrate weaker effects than those employing durable products. Thus, if subjects in an experiment respond as a function of their experience as consumers, a strong price–perceived-quality relationship should not be expected, even when price is the only cue for judging quality.

A related reason why this relationship is far from universal has to do with product-quality variation within a class of products. Obviously, a condition that is indispensable for obtaining the price–perceived-quality effect in an experiment is that subjects perceive the products within the class being investigated to vary in quality. To the extent product-quality variation is low or absent and subjects are aware of this lack of variation a price–perceived-quality effect would not be expected. In other words, it does not make sense to ask an individual how much of the variation in Y is due to factor X in situations where the individual does not perceive variation in Y.

The above point seems obvious. Yet, when one examines the literature it appears to have been ignored consistently by researchers in the selection of products for study. Often, products seem to have been selected for investigation without consideration given to whether or not they meet minimum requirements for internal validity (that is, do subjects believe that products in the class being studied vary in quality?).

The importance of this problem in determining whether or not consumers make inferences about quality based on price cues is illustrated in table 15–1 (see the Overall Means). One hundred and thirty-one undergraduate students in various business classes at the University of Texas

Table 15–1
Preliminary Survey Results

Item			Cluster Means			
		Sample Mean	1	2	3	4
Rank	Name	(N = 131)	(n = 25)	(n = 43)	(n = 41)	(n = 22)
1	Stereo	4.95	**5.40**	**5.28**	**5.05**	3.59
2	Camera	4.87	**5.20**	**5.14**	4.68	**4.32**
3	Diamond ring	4.85	**5.25**	**5.28**	4.46	**4.23**
4	Carpet	4.70	**5.04**	4.58	**5.00**	**4.00**
5	Dress shoes	4.53	**5.00**	**5.05**	4.34	3.32
6	Wine	4.48	**4.80**	**5.12**	4.05	3.68
7	Skis	4.42	**4.92**	**4.74**	4.34	3.36
8	Man's dress shirt	4.31	**4.76**	**4.51**	**4.42**	3.18
9	Woman's blouse	4.21	**4.58**	**4.63**	4.13	3.14
10	Perfume	4.15	**4.54**	**5.02**	3.56	3.14
11	Panty hose	3.78	**4.33**	**4.07**	**3.87**	2.46
12	Ice cream	3.76	**4.32**	**4.00**	**3.78**	2.64
13	Electric shaver	3.61	**4.00**	**3.79**	3.46	3.09
14	Beer	3.37	**4.20**	3.12	**3.61**	2.46
15	Ball-point pen	3.28	**4.08**	2.35	**4.05**	2.73
16	Coffee	3.30	**4.04**	**3.40**	3.15	2.55
17	Bread	3.00	**3.64**	**3.07**	2.93	2.27
18	Suntan lotion	2.83	**3.40**	**3.19**	2.54	2.05
19	Paper towels	2.70	**3.80**	2.23	**2.95**	1.86
20	Gas	2.47	**3.40**	2.46	2.07	2.14
21	Toothpaste	2.41	**3.12**	2.16	**2.61**	1.73
22	Aspirin	2.15	**3.12**	2.09	1.88	1.66
	Overall Mean	3.73	4.32	3.88	3.68	2.89

Note: Means are based on a scale that ranged from 1 (Strongly Disagree) to 6 (Strongly Agree) such that "the higher the price of the item, the higher the quality." Cluster means in **boldface** are higher than overall mean.

were asked to indicate the extent to which they agreed with the statement "the higher the price, the higher the quality" for each of twenty-two products or services commonly employed in price–perceived-quality investigations. As can be seen in the table, their price–perceived-quality effect vary markedly as a function of the product or service being investigated. This general finding—that the effect appears to be present for durable products and absent for nondurables or consumable products—has been reported previously by other researchers (Gardner 1970; Lambert 1972). Interesting exceptions to the general finding are wine and perfume—two products that are commonly thought to have substantial variations in quality and whose quality is difficult to evaluate objectively.

The failure to find a universal price–perceived-quality effect is understandable considering the reality that consumers experience. Nevertheless, there are instances when price cues do appear to play a major role in an individual's perception of the quality of a given product. Consequently, researchers could make a significant contribution to better understanding the behavior of consumers if the conditions under which price becomes a prominent cue for making inferences about product quality could be identified. In this regard, our study examined two hypothesized mediators of the price–perceived-quality relationship—quality risk and price-reliance schema.

Empirical Study

An experiment was conducted to examine the role of both *situational* and *individual* difference factors in enhancing or attenuating the price–perceived-quality effect. In particular, the situational factor dealt with products in the same class. Several researchers have suggested that the perceived risk associated with making an unsatisfactory choice is a source of motivation for consumers to select higher-priced products (Lambert 1972; Shapiro 1968, 1973). To date, however, no experimental study has sought to examine that assumption explicitly, by varying the level of risk (probability of product failure) as well as the level of gains or losses associated with each level of risk.

The individual difference factor was labeled "price-reliance schema." Specifically, subjects were classified as schematic (do make price-to-quality inferences) or aschematic (do not make such inferences) with regard to the price–perceived-quality effect. Based on this classification scheme, comparisons of preferences for high- or low-priced products between schematics and aschematics were made. The rationale for introducing such a classification scheme is discussed later.

Finally, it should be noted that the primary dependent measure employed in this study was product preference rather than product quality judgment. Thus, subjects' perceptions of quality can only be inferred from their product choices. This approach was not viewed as a serious limitation because the ultimate reason for investigating the price–perceived-quality effect is to better understand the process by which consumers arrive at their product preferences. Nevertheless, it is recognized that a complete understanding of this effect will only be achieved when perceived quality is directly and adequately measured and then related explicitly to product selection.

Risk Factors

When consumers make a choice between two products or brands in the same class, they must evaluate two types of risk. A Type 1 risk is that the product they select will not meet the minimum standard of quality that is expected of it. In such situations, price is thought to have diagnostic value with regard to quality, and risk can be minimized by selecting the higher-priced product (Lambert 1972). A Type 2 risk is that products only differ in price and not in quality. In such cases, selection of the higher-priced product would incur a monetary loss equal to the price difference between the high- and low-priced product. It was assumed that consumers consider and balance both types of risk when making purchase decisions.

Both types of risk were experimentally manipulated by varying price differential and quality risk (that is, the probability that the product would not meet minimum quality standards) between comparison products. It was predicted that subjects would demonstrate a weaker price–perceived-quality effect as price differential increased when holding quality risk constant. Conversely, a stronger effect was predicted as quality risk increased when price differential was held constant. In general, the strongest effect was predicted when price differential was low and quality risk high, while the weakest effect was predicted when a high price differential and a low quality risk were present.

Furthermore, it was assumed that the weights consumers assign to the above risks may fluctuate as a function of the absolute price of the products. Past research (French, Williams, and Chance 1972) suggests that income limitations may moderate the strength of the price–perceived-quality effect for certain (expensive or durable) products. A consumer may have to purchase a lower-priced product, independently of his or her belief that the higher-priced product is of better quality, because of income constraints. To investigate this hypothesis, product combinations that varied in absolute magnitude of price were presented to subjects with the assumption that as absolute price increased, subjects would be more likely to express a preference for the lower-priced comparison product, independent of quality risk.

Price-Reliance Schema

The experiment also examined the role of individual differences in producing the price–perceived-quality effect. The approach employed in this study to investigate the influence of individual differences differed substantially from past research which has attempted to document that certain "personality types" are more likely than others to demonstrate the effect. Typically, such research (Lambert 1972) has measured global or general personality characteristics (for example, ascendancy, emotional stability, and sociability) and related these attributes to price–perceived-quality behavior. In keeping with current theory that suggests attitudes and personality traits should be measured within a limited domain when the goal is to use them as predictors of specific behavior (Schuman and

Johnson 1976), an attempt was made to predict the presence or absence of the price–perceived-quality effect based on classifications of individuals on a specific personality-trait measure—price-reliance schema.

It has long been established in studies of cognitive processes that individuals actively organize, select, filter, augment, and attenuate incoming information from their environment. Some of the mechanisms employed to organize and control the massive amounts of information that are encountered each day are assumed to be innate, while others are learned or emerge through experience. The latter are referred to by various labels such as schemata (Markus 1977) or judgmental heuristics (Nisbett and Wilson 1977; Tversky and Kahneman 1974). Over time it is assumed that each individual develops and consistently employs a limited number of cognitive schemata or heuristics to process a wide variety of information in an efficient and meaningful manner. Since people have different, as well as shared experiences, it is assumed that the nature (degree of elaboration, complexity, and so forth) of the schemata they employ (or their readiness to invoke the same schema to process the same information) will sometimes be identical and sometimes not. Furthermore, since experience may be limited and all processing involves some degree of error, schemata not only can lead to efficient shortcuts in processing information but to errors (for example, faulty categorizations and incorrect inferences) as well.

For the present purpose, the work by Markus (1977) on Self-Schema theory is of particular interest. Traditionally, an implicit assumption in personality theory has been that all individuals share the same schemata for processing information of a given type. In contrast, Markus argues that for any given trait (for example, independence–dependence) certain individuals will have a schema for processing information related to that trait while other individuals will not. To the extent incoming information is consistent with the orientation of the schema, the information will be processed quickly, efficiently, and accurately. To the extent incoming information is not consistent with the orientation of the schema or if the individual is aschematic (does not have a schema for processing information along that dimension), that information will be processed slowly, inefficiently, and with more errors, or not even processed at all.

The importance of distinguishing schematics from aschematics in trait-related research can be seen at two levels. At a theoretical level, the validity of the basic research operation is promoted. That is, the distinction permits a researcher to investigate how a particular cognitive rule or heuristic is applied to processing information in a given category for only those subjects (schematics) who have the rule to begin with. In turn, at an empirical level, variance that was once attributed to error because of the performance of aschematics can now be accounted for. Although this approach is relatively new, the support for it is quite compelling (Markus 1977; Markus and Smith 1981).

The logic underlying Markus's Self-Schema theory may have implications for studying the price–perceived-quality effect. Clearly, an implicit assumption in past research is that all consumers have a price-reliance schema and the focus of the research has been to see for what products that schema will be invoked. However, one of the reasons the price–perceived-quality effect is sometimes observed to be much weaker than anticipated may be a reflection of the fact that a number of the subjects in a study did not have a price-reliance schema. Thus, regardless of the product, and even if only given price cues to judge quality, certain subjects (those who are aschematic) will not make an inference about quality because they lack a rule for doing so.

The possibility that some consumers may have a strong schema for making price–quality inferences while others may be aschematic is suggested in data reported by Shapiro (1973). He found that the mean quality ratings of five different product pairs (which did not differ in quality) were consistently higher for the higher-priced products. When the percentages of subjects actually demonstrating the effect were examined, however, a much different picture emerged. Depending upon which of the five products was being rated, there were almost as many subjects who rated the lower-priced product to be of *higher* quality than its higher-priced counterpart as there were subjects who demonstrated the "traditional" price–perceived-quality effect.

Results similar to those observed by Shapiro were obtained from cluster analysis of the price–perceived-quality responses to the twenty-two products or services reported in table 15–1. As can be seen in that table, the cluster analysis produced four groups of subjects. There are subjects (Group 1) who appear to have a strong price-reliance schema in that for every product they are the most likely to report the existence of a price–quality relationship. In contrast, there also appears to be a group of aschematic subjects (Group 4). These subjects do not perceive the existence of a price–quality relationship for most of the products investigated. Finally, there are a number of subjects (Groups 2 and 3, collectively about two-thirds of the sample) who appear to possess a price-reliance schema that is only invoked for certain product types.

As a consequence of these findings, the price-reliance schematicity of a second group of subjects was also examined in our study. Specifically, their responses to the items (excluding stereo and camera) in table 15–1 were used to classify them as either being schematics, mixed schematics (product dependent), or aschematics. It was predicted that schematics would indicate the strongest preference for the high-priced products while aschematics would indicate the weakest preference, with mixed schematics falling at an intermediate level. Specific details of the measures and instruments are provided in the next section.

Method

Subjects

Subjects in the experiment were ninety upper-division undergraduate or first-year graduate business students in one of three classes at The University of Texas. Study materials were completed by subjects during a regular class period.

Study Materials and Design

Subjects were administered a packet of materials containing a cover story for the research, product information that varied according to the experimental condition, scales that measured product preference and strength of preference, and the price-reliance schema survey.

Cover Story and Product Information. The cover story indicated that a New York-based salvage company was considering selling products in Texas via catalog offerings. The purpose of the study was to pretest the catalog and a sample of its products. Subjects were informed that the salvage company offered merchandise from large shipments that was found, on the basis of sampling by the original purchaser, to have an unacceptable proportion of product failures (all products were originally destined for major department stores, such as Macy's and Sears). Once merchandise was rejected, it was turned over to the salvage company to be disposed of at the best possible price. In so doing, the salvage company removed the brand name and sold the merchandise at a price below current market level. No warranties were offered and products were not returnable after purchase.

Table 15–2
Constant Values for Group A Products

Product Type	Minimum and Maximum Sample Failure Rate (percentages)	Selling Price (dollars)
Television	2—5	450
Stereo receiver	3—6	300
Camera	4—7	188

Product Information. Following the cover story, subjects were asked to read "typical" product information that the salvage company would provide in its catalog and decide which of two products they would prefer to buy. Specifically, each subject was given general information about three different product types—a color television, a stereo receiver, and a camera. For each product type the subject was asked to select for purchase a product from one of two groups (A and B). In all cases, Group A products were higher priced and had lower expected failure rates (based on initial sampling that had led to the original rejection of the shipment) than Group B products. The groups were respectively comprised of multiple shipments with various sample failure rates (SFRs); thus ranges of SFRs were provided. Table 15–2 gives the values that were constant in all experimental conditions for Group A products.

For Group B products, three factors were varied to reflect different levels and types of risk. The first factor, risk ratio, defined the maximum level of failure for the Group B products relative to the maximum level for Group A products. Three values were employed—2:1, 3:1, and 4:1. For example, the lowest maximum risk (2:1) for a Group B camera was 14 percent (2 times the 7 percent maximum SFR for Group A cameras) and the highest (4:1) was 28 percent. All the levels of risk ratio are shown in table 15–3.

The second factor, risk overlap, defined the minimum level of failure for the Group B products relative to the range of failure for Group A products. Three levels were employed—0 percent, 50 percent, and 100 percent overlap. For example, the minimum risk for a Group B camera would be 8 percent in a zero-percent overlap condition compared to a minimum risk of 4 percent in a 100 percent overlap condition. All levels of risk overlap are shown in table 15–4.

The third factor, price differential, was manipulated by varying the prices of Group B products relative to Group A prices. Two levels of price differential were employed—a 10 percent and 30 percent difference. For example, the Group B television was either offered at a price of $405 (10

Table 15–3
Risk Ratio Levels
(percentages)

Product Type	Group A Maximum Failure Rate	Group B Minimum Failure Rate		
		2:1	3:1	4:1
Television	5	10	15	20
Stereo receiver	6	12	18	24
Camera	7	14	21	28

Table 15–4
Risk Overlap Levels
(percentages)

Product Type	Group A Minimum Failure Rate	Group B Minimum Failure Rate		
		0 percent	*50 percent*	*100 percent*
Television	2	6	4	2
Stereo receiver	3	7	5	3
Camera	4	8	6	4

percent less than the Group A $450 television), or $315 (30 percent less than $450). All price values are shown in table 15–5.

After reading the product information for each product type, subjects were asked to indicate whether they would choose a product from Group A (high price) or Group B (low price). In addition, subjects were asked to indicate the strength of their preference—Strong, Somewhat Strong, or Not Strong at All. After all three product types were evaluated, subjects completed the price-reliance schema survey which was comprised of the items in table 15–1 with exception of the stereo and camera. These items were eliminated from the survey to avoid confounding survey responses with responses to the product types in the experiment.

In brief, the experimental design contained four factors that were completely crossed—product type (three-levels), price differential (two levels), risk ratio (three levels), and risk overlap (three levels)—resulting in fifty-four cells. Each subject was required to evaluate product information for each of the three product types. Product materials were arranged, however, so that no subject received duplicate product-information configurations (risk and price differential) for the three product types. There were five replications of each of the fifty-four cells.

Results

Based on findings reported in table 15–1, a very strong overall price–perceived-quality effect was expected for products used in this experiment. The results confirm that expectation. Of the 270 choice responses that were made, 79 percent were in favor of the high-priced (Group A) products. In addition, subjects expressed strong feelings about their choices; a majority of the 270 responses received either a "very strong" (34 percent) or "somewhat strong" (48 percent) rating. Of more interest, however, is the association between product choice and strength of feelings about that choice [$X^2(2) = 25.54$; $p < .001$]. Subjects

Table 15–5
Price Values
(dollars)

Product Type	Group A Prices	Group B Prices 10 percent	30 percent
Television	450	405	315
Stereo receiver	300	270	210
Camera	188	170	132

felt "very strongly" about their choices in 40 percent of the instances when the higher-priced product was selected, versus 10 percent when the lower-priced product was selected. Such findings are consistent with the notion that selection of higher-priced products attenuates unpleasant feelings of uncertainty regarding the correctness of the choice. The contribution of uncertainty to the price–perceived-quality effect, particularly with regard to risk aversion, is examined in greater detail in the next section.

Experimental Factors

Product Type. As was noted in table 15–1 and in past research, a stronger price–perceived-quality relationship is usually observed for relatively expensive durables compared to relatively inexpensive nondurables. No past research, however, has examined the relationship of absolute product price to the price–perceived-quality effect among durables only. It was suggested earlier that income limitations may cause consumers to select a lower-priced product, independently of their perceptions of quality, when the absolute level of product price approaches the upper limit of the income constraint. The results in table 15–6 suggest support for such an effect in that absolute price (product-type factor) is inversely related to selection of the higher-priced product. For example, only about 69 percent of the subjects selected the higher-

Table 15–6
Percentage of Choice Responses: Product Price by Product Type

Product Type	Product Price High	Low
Television	68.8	31.2
Stereo receiver	81.1	18.9
Camera	86.7	13.3

Note: $X^2(2) = 8.60; p < .05$

priced ($450) television, while about 87 percent selected the higher-priced ($188) camera.

These results, however, must be interpreted with caution. In this experiment, absolute price level is confounded with product type. Subjects may have been more willing to take greater risks in selecting a television as compared to a stereo receiver or camera because they have more knowledge, experience, and/or interest in the latter than the former. A "social image" influence may also have been present (Lambert 1972). To the extent selection of a higher-priced product to fulfill status motives is product specific, the status value of higher-priced stereos and cameras may be much greater, among college students, than it is for a television set. A final consideration is that the absolute level of risk associated with purchase of the low-priced product was confounded with level of absolute price. For example, the maximum risk of failure attached to the selection of the lower-priced television was much greater than the level attached to the lower-priced camera at each risk ratio (the greatest risk was 20 percent and 28 percent, respectively). Nevertheless, the results suggest that the strength of the price–perceived-quality effect may begin to decline within a class of products when the absolute level of price of products in that class is high. This hypothesis merits further investigation.

Risk Factors. As expected, subjects were very sensitive to the risk of product failure when selecting between higher- and lower-priced products. Table 15–7 reveals that preference for Group B products declines substantially as the level of risk increases from a ratio of 2:1 to a ratio of 4:1. In addition, the subjects' overall tolerance for risk is relatively low. That is, even when there was only a few percentage points difference in risk (as in the 2:1 condition), the majority of subjects' choices favored the higher-priced product. This result lends support to the notion that subjects will select higher-priced products in order to reduce product-

Table 15–7
Percentage of Choice Responses as a Function of Product Price (High and Low) and Risk Ratio for Each Product Type

| | | Risk Ratio | | | | | | |
| | Low (2:1) | | Moderate (3:1) | | High (4:1) | | | |
Product Type	High	Low	High	Low	High	Low	X^2	p
Television	50.0	50.0	80.0	20.0	76.7	23.3	7.20	.05
Stereo receiver	73.3	26.7	76.7	23.3	93.3	6.7	3.90	ns
Camera	70.0	30.0	96.7	3.3	93.3	6.7	8.47	.05

Note: Degrees of freedom for each analysis equals 2.

quality risk. As is indicated in later results, however, the tendency toward risk aversion is moderated by increasing the price differential between higher- and lower-priced products.

The minimum risk of Group B products (that is, risk overlap), was not found to be significantly related to product selection [$X^2(2) < 1.00$]. Thus, even in those cases where the minimum risk for the lower-priced product was below the highest risk for the higher-priced product, subjects were not more likely to choose the lower-priced product than when the minimum risk for the lower-priced product exceeded the maximum risk of the higher-priced product. Since maximum risk (risk ratio) for Group B products was associated with product selection and minimum risk was not, this suggests that subjects were more concerned with how "bad" rather than how "good" things can turn out when selecting the lower-priced product.

Price Differential. The findings in table 15–8 clearly indicate that subjects were sensitive to the magnitude of the price difference between higher-and lower-priced products, or what was labeled Type 2 risk. Overall, about one-third of the subjects selected Group B products when there was a large (30 percent) price differential between Group A and B products. This percentage was substantially less when the price differential was small (10 percent). This result is consistent with the notion that the risk of product failure and the monetary gain potentially associated with purchase of a lower-priced product are treated in a compensatory fashion.

Analysis of Variance of Preference Scores

The analyses above consisted of basic pairwise comparisons with a dichotomous dependent variable (product choice). A second set of analyses employed a more sensitive measure of product choice and attempted to uncover interactions between the factors of interest. Specifi-

Table 15–8
Percentage of Responses as a Function of Product Price (High and Low) and Size of Product Price Differential for Each Product Type

| | Price Differential | | | | | |
| | Small | | Large | | | |
Product Type	High	Low	High	Low	X^2	p
Television	75.6	24.4	62.2	37.8	1.84	NS
Stereo	97.8	2.2	64.4	35.6	9.09	.003
Camera	95.5	4.5	77.8	22.2	5.06	.05

Note: Degrees of freedom for each analysis equals 1.

cally, product choice and strength of choice were combined to produce a single measure of product preference (a common technique employed in experimental studies of preference, for example, Wilson 1979). This procedure resulted in the construction of a six-point scale that measured a subject's preference for the higher-priced product. If a subject selected the higher-priced product in a pair and indicated that he or she felt very strong about the choice, a score of "6" was assigned to the preference for the higher-priced product. In contrast, selection of the lower-priced product with a very strong rating would be assigned a "1" since this score represents the lowest preference for the higher-priced product. Preference scores were subjected to a 3 x 2 x 3 x 3 (product type, price differential, risk ratio, and risk overlap, respectively) analysis of variance with the results being reported in table 15–9.

As can be seen in table 15–9, the analysis of preference scores produced findings that are consistent with the prior analyses of choice. Prod-

Table 15–9
ANOVA on Preference Scores as a Function of Product Type, Price Differential, Risk Ratio, and Risk Overlap

Source	df	Sum of Squares	Mean Square	F	p
Model	53	179.974	3.396	2.13	.0001
A: Product Type[a]	2	18.363	9.182	5.77	.0005
B: Price Differential[b]	1	42.404	42.404	26.66	.0001
A × B	2	5.119	2.560	1.61	ns
C: Risk Ratio[c]	2	36.229	18.115	11.39	.0001
A × C	4	4.881	1.220	< 1.00	ns
B × C	2	17.341	8.671	5.45	.005
A × B × C	4	13.904	3.476	2.19	ns
D: Risk Overlap[d]	2	0.674	0.337	< 1.00	ns
A × D	4	9.970	2.493	1.47	ns
B × D	2	0.319	0.160	< 1.00	ns
A × B × D	4	6.193	1.548	< 1.00	ns
C × D	4	4.637	1.159	< 1.00	ns
A × C × D	8	8.519	1.065	< 1.00	ns
B × C × D	4	3.970	0.993	< 1.00	ns
A × B × C × D	8	7.452	0.932	< 1.00	ns
Error	216	343.600	1.591		
Corrected Total	269	523.574			

[a]Product types are television, stereo receiver, and camera.
[b]Price differentials are low (10 percent), and high (30 percent).
[c]Risk ratios are low (2:1), moderate (3:1), and high (4:1).
[d]Risk overlaps are none (0 percent), moderate (50 percent), and complete (100 percent).

uct type, price differential, and risk ratio all produce significant preference effects while risk overlap does not. In addition, a significant interaction between price differential and risk ratio is obtained (see figure 15–1). Consistent with a risk–gain trade-off model, subjects expressed the strongest preference for the higher-priced product when the difference in price between the higher- and lower-priced product was low and the risk of failure for the lower-priced product was high. Conversely, the higher-priced product received the lowest preference rating when the price differential was large and its associated risk of failure was small.

In summary, the results reveal clear and consistent stimulus-related effects when subjects are asked to select between higher- and lower-priced products. The higher-priced alternative is clearly the most attrac-

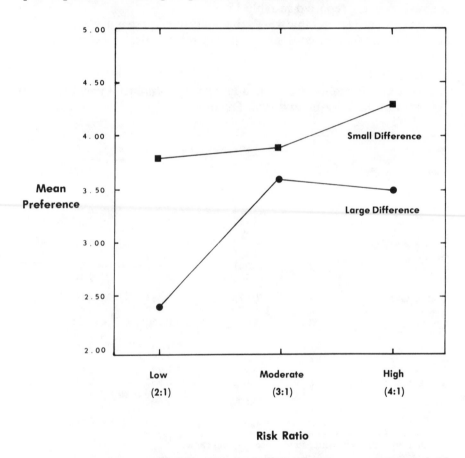

Figure 15–1. Mean Preference for the High Product as a Function of Price Differential and Risk Ratio (6 = Strongest)

tive under conditions where low gain and high risk is associated with the lower-priced alternative. In contrast, the attractiveness of the higher-priced alternative is diminished substantially when the lower-priced alternative allows the substantial gains with minimal risk.

Price-Reliance Schema

The last analysis attempted to examine the role of individual rather than stimulus factors in predicting the selection of product alternatives that vary in price. Responses on the price-reliance schema survey were combined to produce an index representing the "price-reliance schema" of each subject. The overall average score was 3.52, where 6.00 was the most-positive and 1.00 was the least-positive endorsement of a price–quality relationship. Individual mean scores ranged from 2.16 to 4.77 and possessed a relatively symmetrical distribution.

Based on their individual index score, subjects were rank ordered and then assigned to one of the three groups. Subjects with the highest twenty-four scores were labeled "Schematic," which means they were hypothesized to have a strong schema for judging quality from price cues. Subjects with the lowest twenty-four scores were classified as "Aschematic" in that they were hypothesized to have, at best, a weak price–perceived-quality schema. All other subjects ($n = 39$) were labeled as "Mixed" and were hypothesized as having a price–perceived-quality schema that varied in strength from moderately weak to moderately strong. (Three subjects were dropped from the analysis due to missing data on the schema survey). Obviously, the numerical cutoff points for these classifications were somewhat arbitrary. Nevertheless, this method resulted in the formation of groups of sufficient size to provide reliable estimates of group average preference for the higher-priced product.

Based on this classification scheme, average preference scores (to counteract problems of independence, preference scores for each product choice were averaged within a subject) were subjected to analysis of variance. As can be seen in figure 15–2, subjects with strong price–quality schema—Schematics—provided the highest mean preference ratings for the higher-priced products, while Aschematics had the lowest mean ratings. As expected, subjects with a mixed schema provided intermediate mean preference ratings. The overall effect due to the individual difference factor was reliable [$F(2/84) = 3.58$; $p < .04$], and can be attributed primarily to the large difference between the preference ratings of the Schematics and the Aschematics. Thus, the data provide support for the role of both individual differences and situational properties in mediating the price–perceived-quality relationship.

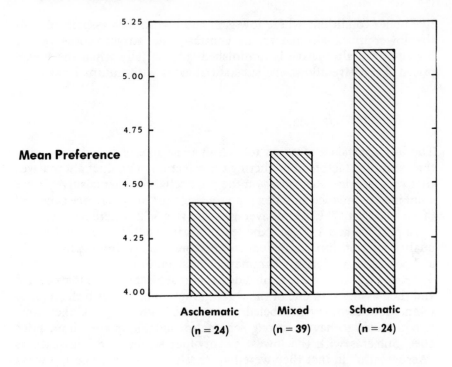

Mean Preference

Figure 15–2. Mean Preference for High Priced Products as a Function of the Subject's Price-Reliance Schema (6 = Strongest)

Summary and Conclusions

Past research on the price–perceived-quality relationship has clearly established one "fact"—*some consumers* use price as a cue to quality for *some products*. Surprisingly little research has been conducted, though, to identify *which* consumers are likely to be price reliant when judging product quality, or under *what* conditions price is used as a cue of product quality. Stated more generally, little attention has been focused on factors that are likely to mediate the price–perceived-quality relationship. By explicitly investigating these factors, a more comprehensive understanding of consumer behavior should ensue. Two possible mediating factors are quality risk and price-reliance schema. The conceptual underpinnings of each of these factors have been examined and an empirical investigation of them presented.

The investigation demonstrated that when the individuals perceived risk of product failure to be high for selected lower-priced products, and little could be gained from that risk, they preferred higher-priced (comparative) products. Conversely, when risk was low and potential gain high for the lower-priced products, they were less likely to prefer the higher-priced (comparative) products. In addition, individuals who were relatively more price reliant, were more likely to prefer the higher-priced (comparative) products than were individuals who were not as price reliant, where degree of price reliance was determined from a cluster analysis of questionnaire responses.

The managerial implications of the concepts and findings are intriguing. For example, a marketing strategy emphasizing a price–quality relationship is not likely to be uniformly effective for all products or services for reasons previously ignored by researchers. In particular, not all consumers are likely to possess a schema for linking the price of a product to its quality. Second, even if they possess such a schema, it is only likely to be activated under certain (for example, risky) conditions for selected products.

Before generalizing from any of the empirical findings, however, it is important to take into account inherent study limitations. These exist because the empirical investigation was designed to provide illustrative rather than substantive results. Consequently, the nature of the individuals studied (business students from one university), and the experimental data (responses to a paper-and-pencil task involving verbal descriptions of hypothetical products) require that these findings be termed tentative. Even so, the findings are intuitively logical and add credence to the major concepts and arguments set forth. Hopefully they will stimulate further research on a topic that, in spite of possessing a voluminous literature, is greatly underinvestigated.

References

Bowbrick, P. (1982), "Pseudoresearch in Marketing: The Case of the Price–Perceived-Quality Relationship," *European Journal of Marketing* 14 (8):466–70.

Etgar, M. and N. Malhotra (1981), "Determinants of Price Dependency: Personal and Perceptual Factors," *Journal of Consumer Research* 8 (September):217–22.

French, N.J. Williams, and W. Chance (1972), "A Shopping Experiment on Price–Quality Relationships," *Journal of Retailing* 48 (3):16, 126.

Friedman, L. (1967), "Psychological Pricing in the Food Industry," in *Prices: Issues in Theory, Practice, and Public Policy*, A. Phillips and O. Williamson, eds., Philadelphia: University of Pennsylvania Press.

Gabor, A. (1980), "Price and Consumer Protection," in *Economics of Consumer Protection*, D. Morris, ed., London: Heinemann Educational Books.

Gardner, D. (1970), "An Experimental Investigation of the Price–Quality Relationship," *Journal of Retailing* 46 (3):25–41.

——— (1971), "Is There a Generalized Price–Quality Relationship?" *Journal of Marketing Research* 13 (May):241–43.

Jacoby, J., J. Olson, and R. Haddock (1971), "Price, Brand Name, and Product Composition Characteristics as Determinants of Perceived Quality," *Journal of Applied Psychology* 55 (6):570–79.

Lambert, Z. (1972), "Price and Choice Behavior," *Journal of Marketing Research* 9 (February):35–40.

Markus, H. (1977), "Self-Schemata and Processing Information about the Self," *Journal of Personality and Social Psychology* 35 (January):63–78.

——— and J. Smith (1981), "The Influence of Self-Schemas on the Perception of Others," in *Personality, Cognition and Social Interaction*, N. Cantor and J. Kihlstrom, eds., New York: Lawrence Erlbaum Associates.

McConnell, J. (1968), "The Price–Quality Relationship in an Experimental Setting," *Journal of Marketing Research* 5 (August):300–303.

Monroe, K. (1973), "Buyers' Subjective Perceptions of Price," *Journal of Marketing Research* 10 (February):70–80.

Morris, R. and C. Bronson (1969), "The Chaos of Competition Indicated by *Consumer Reports*," *Journal of Marketing* 33 (July):28–37.

Nisbett, R. and T. Wilson (1977), "Telling More Than We Can Know: Verbal Reports of Mental Processes," *Psychological Review* 84:231–59.

Olson, J. (1974), "Cue Properties of Price: Literature Review and Theoretical Considerations," *Working Series in Marketing Research*, no. 20, College of Business Administration, Pennsylvania State University.

Peterson, R. (1970), "The Price–Perceived-Quality Relationship: Experimental Evidence," *Journal of Marketing Research* 7 (November):525–28.

——— and A. Jolibert (1976), "A Cross-National Investigation of Price and Brand as Determinants of Perceived Product Quality," *Journal of Applied Psychology* 61 (4):533–36.

Riesz, P. (1978), "Price versus Quality in the Marketplace, 1961–1975," *Journal of Retailing* 54 (4):15–28.

Schuman, H. and M. Johnson (1976), "Attitudes and Behavior," *Annual Review of Sociology* 2:161–207.

Scitovsky, R. (1945), "Some Consequences of the Habit of Judging Quality by Price," *The Review of Economic Studies* 12:100–105.

Shapiro, B. (1968), "The Psychology of Pricing," *Harvard Business Review* 46 (July–August):14–25, 160.

——— (1973), "Price Reliance: Existence and Sources," *Journal of Marketing Research* 10 (August):286–94.

Stafford, J. and B. Enis (1969), "The Price–Quality Relationship: An Extension," *Journal of Marketing Research* 6 (November):456–58.

Swan, J. (1974), "Price-Product Performance Competition between Retailer and Manufacturer Brands," *Journal of Marketing* 38 (July):52–59.

Tversky, A. and D. Kahneman (1974), "Judgment under Uncertainty: Heuristics and Biases," *Science* (185:1124–31.

Wheatley, J. and J. Chiu (1977), "The Effects of Price, Store Image, and Product and Respondent Characteristics on Perceptions of Quality," *Journal of Marketing Research* 14 (May):181–86.

Wilson, W. (1979), "Feeling More Than We Can Know: Exposure Effects without Learning," *Journal of Personality and Social Psychology* 37 (June):811–21.

16
The Measurement of Quality Competition in Strategic Groups

David J. Curry and
David J. Faulds

S peaking before the 1983 national meeting of the American Marketing Association, Bradley Gale stated that the "strategy issue of the 1980s is going to focus more on product quality—how to measure, track, and improve product quality." Our approach to this issue departs from others because we do not rely on data from consumer surveys nor do we concentrate on single products, services, or stores. Instead we focus on manufacturers who compete with one another in several related product lines as members of a broad-line strategic group (Porter 1980). Our goal is to provide an appropriate procedure for including quality considerations into corporate strategic planning by conducting research on quality that cuts across product lines and avoids "a fixation with the brand as the unit of analysis" (Wind and Robertson 1983, page 13). This approach replaces a short-run orientation with a moderate- to long-term outlook.

To achieve this goal, at least two preliminary problems must be solved. The first is to develop a measurement procedure that translates loosely connected facts about quality into a quantitative scale that represents the quality levels for various manufacturers competing against one another. This scale should be stable for the time limits necessary for strategic planning (three to five years). Stability requires the aggregation of a large body of information to present a clear overview of quality competition. The information we use was collected by Consumer's Union and published in *Consumer Reports* magazine over a twenty-year period beginning in 1961. Ours is a modeling approach that compresses this data into a single scale that summarizes quality competition among broad-line firms across the product lines in which they compete. A macroview will probably sacrifice some clarity within individual lines and/or for shorter time periods.

Second, when this broad measurement is used, a better understanding of the role of quality competition as it affects both the demand side (consumer attitudes and behavior) and the supply side (production costs, inspection costs, warranty costs, and so forth) must be developed. Only through a comprehensive understanding of both sides can management realistically determine the role of quality in influencing sales, rate of return on investment, and other "bottom-line" measures.

Quality Considerations in Strategic Planning

Our research on the effects of quality on a firm's performance and its use as a planning variable uncovered a growing body of important, but often isolated, attempts to address the role of quality in corporate planning. We have tried to link previous efforts in a rudimentary framework designed to motivate a systematic study of quality as it affects both the firm's demand and supply sides and overall long-run performance.

Figure 16–1 shows these links as a "performance engine" fueled by product quality and quality competition. On the demand side, various gears drive consumer behavior. The primary constituents are consumer prepurchase deliberations, purchase behavior, and certain postpurchase effects. On the supply side, quality plays a vital role in determining a firm's production costs because management's policy bears on manufacturing methods, procedures, and materials. Quality also limits or expands a firm's ability to tout its products in marketing communications and often influences a firm's pricing policy and distribution channels. These two broad categories together influence a firm's profitability, return on investment, and other key performance measures.

Figure 16–1 is suggestive but inconclusive. Stronger conclusions regarding many of the cogs in this engine can be found in recently published articles. Day and Deutscher, in a study of consumer deliberations before purchasing major appliances, asked consumers about each brand's "value for money," a contrast of quality and price. This measure is marginally related to awareness of product value and to actual brand choice. "Both the order of recall and value for money questions show some capacity to influence choices" (Day and Deutscher 1982, p. 196). These results were strongest for manufacturers with full lines conducting national advertising campaigns, a finding that agrees in principle with those of Farris and Reibstein (1979) about a quality–advertising interaction.

In the purchase process itself, quality is often a determining factor (see Olshavsky, chapter 1 and Mehrotra and Palmer, chapter 5 in this book) and is frequently included in factorial experiments designed to predict consumer preferences (Green and Wind 1975). The role of price–qual-

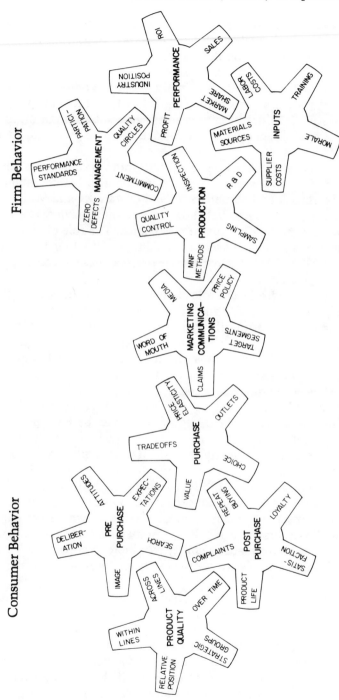

Figure 16–1. Product Quality Drives a Firm's Performance

ity trade-offs in purchase decisions has been studied more extensively than the role of quality alone. (This is discussed by Monroe and Krishnan, chapter 13; and Peterson and Wilson, chapter 15, both in this book; and by Friedman 1967; Hagerty 1978; and Wheatley, Chiu, and Goldman 1981, among others.) Finally, theoretical research by Schmalensee (1982) provides a quantified model of how product quality affects price elasticity. Schmalensee's results agree with our notion that higher quality levels, especially for higher-priced durable products, lowers price elasticity.

A discussion by Hawkins, Best, and Coney (1983) points out the role of quality in postpurchase satisfaction (see also Newman and Werbel 1973; Westbrook and Fornell 1979; and Olshavsky and Miller 1972), repeat buying (see also Kiechel 1981), complaint behavior, word-of-mouth communications, and cognitive dissonance. The role of quality in postpurchase processes would seem crucial to a firm's long-run profitability yet very few studies identify this role or trace these effects back through the sales system.

On the supply side, the role of quality control has been discussed extensively by Juran (1974) and others (Box, Hunter, and Hunter 1978), who are concerned primarily with statistical quality control in manufacturing processes. Philip Crosby, of the quality management institute in Winter Park, Florida, contends that manufacturing higher-quality products reduces, rather than increases, a firm's production costs. Crosby's premise has been empirically confirmed in case studies by International Telephone and Telegraph (ITT) and by a large-scale analysis using the Profit Impact of Market Share (PIMS) data base by Phillips, Chang, and Buzzell (1983), who found that a position of high relative quality and low relative cost is perfectly feasible. Their results "also question existing views that attainment of a high quality position is likely to come only at a cost premium" (Phillips, Chang, and Buzzell 1983, page 41). When a company makes a concerted effort to improve product quality, certain unexpected efficiencies occur, some of which are engineering based while others are a result of improved morale on the part of the labor force as well as labor's ability to adhere to consistently high standards, if such standards are stated clearly and reinforced by management (Crosby 1979).

Perhaps the most comprehensive study of quality and marketing communications is by Farris and Reibstein (1979), who found a significant interaction between a firm's advertising expenditures and its product quality. Higher expenditures in both quality and advertising affect profits positively. However, these two variables, acting together, increase profits beyond the level expected if their effects were only additive. Farris and Reibstein conclude: "Marketers who *tell* consumers about quality differences in their products command higher prices than marketers who depend on high quality to communicate *itself* to consumers" (1979, p. 177).

Finally, turning to a firm's overall performance, the research by Phillips, Chang, and Buzzell (1983) confirms that quality influences directly a firm's market position and indirectly its rate of return on investment. This result comes from a causal model estimated using data from more than six hundred firms competing in numerous categories. Phillips, Chang, and Buzzell found that product quality had a direct, positive effect on return on investment (ROI) in the case of consumer nondurables, capital goods, and component businesses, and an indirect effect across all six types of businesses studied (1983, p. 37).

For a synthesis of the role of quality in supply-side and demand-side corporate functions, the reader is referred to Leonard and Sasser (1982).

Measuring Quality and Quality Competition

Our major objective is to provide a solution for measuring quality competition among firms competing in several related product lines. Clearly the construct *quality* is difficult to define for most product categories (cf. Maynes 1976; and several of the chapters in this book). Managers submitting relative quality ranks to PIMS (1978) might disagree with results from consumer surveys and with laboratory testers at Consumer's Union because different aspects of quality are emphasized. Industry representatives tend to define quality in terms of materials, methods, and production techniques while consumers may judge it on the basis of benefits received and the image fulfilled. Consumer's Union uses an extended notion of consumer acceptability: a product's convenience, safety, and number of features.

Previous attempts to measure quality fall roughly into six categories: (1) PIMS, (2) conjoint methods, (3) revealed-choice methods, (4) multidimensional scaling methods, (5) consumer testing agencies, and (6) direct ratings from consumer surveys.

The PIMS technique (see PIMS 1978) uses management judgment to measure the relative quality of brands competing in a single product line. Comparisons using this approach may vary according to a particular manager's ability to consistently recall and assess competitors' quality. Different respondents within the same firm may base their judgments on different time periods and internalized facts (see Phillips 1981; John and Reve 1982). The PIMS approach differs from ours in that any one competitor is compared directly with only three others. This limitation does not permit a detailed assessment of all competitors in single or multiple lines.

Decompositional multiattribute models, including both multidimensional scaling (MDS) and conjoint analysis, sometimes include a quality dimension. MDS studies, unlike PIMS, normally involve consumer surveys about corporate image. Such studies (Clevenger, Lazier, and Clark 1965; Doyle and Fenwick 1975; Sims 1979; Singson 1975; Spector 1961) decompose overall corporate similarity measures to reveal the dimensions of image. A separate quality factor or a single, bipolar price–quality factor may emerge from the analysis.

Research involving conjoint analysis has, at times, included a quality factor or a quality surrogate, namely, the presence of the Good Housekeeping Seal (Green and Wind 1975). A few researchers, such as Hagerty (1978), have also suggested using conjoint analysis to model directly price–quality trade-offs. Other techniques, such as discrete-choice modeling (Currim 1982), use revealed-choice data to assess price–quality trade-offs, but these studies are conducted almost exclusively with individual brands and results are confounded by the differential availability of these brands to various populations.

Numerous studies have used individuals' direct ratings of quality for brands in a single line. These ratings may be on a five-point scale (Olshavsky and Miller 1972; Wheatley and Chiu 1977; Wheatley, Chiu, and Goldman 1981); on a seven-point scale (Park and Winter 1978); or variations like a binary scale (Park and Winter 1978). These methods have been used primarily in experiments investigating the relationship between perceptions of price and quality (see Monroe and Krishnam, chapter 13, this book). They have been concerned with issues of consumer information processing rather than with measurement of quality competition among manufacturers. Very few previous studies adopt a multiline view or attempt a long-run quality assessment, an important feature of our method. The entire body of literature can be criticized for a lack of emphasis on construct validity and a lack of rigorous tests for reliability. (For exceptions to this criticism see Phillips 1981; and John and Reve 1982).

The laboratory testing methods of Consumer's Union, the source of data for our study, are well documented in *Consumer Reports* and are critically analyzed by Morris (1971) and in a technical note available from the present authors.

Consumer Reports's quality rankings represent, at best, an ordinal scale of quality for the brands compared in a single study, and these data are treated as ordinal for our modeling approach. The problems of construct validity and reliability are addressed only indirectly in this research, because we assume that Consumer's Union attempts to apply consistent standards to the brands compared in any single study. Accepting these data at face value is not meant to suggest a total disregard for issues regarding external validity or reliability, but rather it represents a pragmatic view that *Consumer Reports* is the sole source of data of product quality generated over a long time period in the United States. Furthermore, *Consumer Reports* is the primary source of information about quality of major and minor appliances. (See *Appliance Manufacturer*, April 1980.)

Study Data Base and Methodology

The data base[1] contains information condensed from *Consumer Reports* magazine starting with January 1961, and data from a number of other published sources, for example, directories of U.S. subsidiaries of foreign firms, *Moody's*, and so forth. Over 900 studies are recorded involving nearly 14,000 brands in 600 distinct product classes, produced by more than 2,000 manufacturers. The data items relevant for the present research include the study identification, each study's product-class designation, and for each brand in a given study, its name, manufacturer, price, and quality rank.

Method

This study involves two different portfolios of products—major appliances and housewares—and two levels of analysis within each one of these broad-line categories. One level involves an analysis among only those broad-line manufacturers that have emerged during the twenty-year study period, through merger and acquisition. For both major appliances and housewares, five broad-line manufacturers were identified. These manufacturers compete in all, or nearly all, of the individual lines represented in an industry. General Electric (GE), Whirlpool, and White Consolidated Industries (WCI), compete in all eight major-appliance categories while Magic Chef and Raytheon compete in six of the eight. Major appliances were cited by Porter as an example of a broad-line strategic group:

> For example, in the major appliance industry, one strategic group (with GE as the prototype) is characterized by broad product lines, heavy national advertising, extensive integration, and captive distribution and service. Another group consists of specialist producers like Maytag focusing on the high-quality, high-price segment with selective distribution. Another group (like Roper and Design and Manufacturing) produces unadvertised products for private label [1980, p. 129].

Similar broad-line manufacturers can be identified for housewares: Dominion, GE, Hoover, Sunbeam, and Westinghouse. Details of the historical analyses that determined the broad-line manufacturers in each industry are discussed by Curry (1985) and by Faulds (1983).

A second set of analyses, performed on individual manufacturers regardless of their corporate affiliation, involved fifteen firms competing in the major-appliance categories and thirteen firms in housewares.

Scaling Model

To assemble our data, the data base was searched for studies in any of the eight major-appliance categories and any of the eleven housewares categories. Seventy-two and thirty-six studies were found in these two product groups, respectively. For each study a quality-dominance matrix was formed containing the following typical entry:

$$q(i,j) = \begin{cases} 0 \text{ if manufacturer } i\text{'s quality rank was} \\ \quad \text{better than manufacturer } j\text{'s,} \\ \\ 1 \text{ if } j\text{'s exceeds } i\text{'s,} \end{cases}$$

where $i \equiv$ the row manufacturer and $j \equiv$ the column manufacturer. (Ties were coded as .5.) Within the major-appliance categories (and separately for the housewares categories) these individual dominance matrices were aggregated using element-by-element addition. The composite matrix has a typical entry $Q(i,j)$ where:

$Q(i,j) \equiv$ the frequency of times a product from manufacturer j was judged as having superior quality to a product from manufacturer i.

[Note that $Q(i,j) + Q(j,i) = FREQ(i,j)$: the frequency of times i and j met when they were not tied in quality.]

Finally, within each industry these absolute frequencies were converted into proportions:

$$PROP(i,j) = \frac{Q(i,j)}{FREQ(i,j)}$$

$PROP(i,j)$ is the number of times that an appliance produced by firm j was judged to be of better quality than one produced by firm i. A similar interpretation is valid for competition in the housewares categories. In either case $PROP(i,j) + PROP(j,i) = 1.0$.

The proportions matrices represent the data for contructing quality scales that were derived from the Law of Comparative Judgment (LCJ) proposed by Thurstone (1927) and subsequently modified by Gulliksen (1956), Torgerson (1958), and others. The LCJ postulates that each manufacturer has some true scale value on a quality continuum, and that the manufacturer's quality rank in any one *Consumer Reports* study is a function of this true score plus some error. The effects contributing to error include sampling (*Consumer Reports*'s judgments are based on a sample of the manufacturer's output), fallibility in the *Consumer Reports* test procedures, and so on.[2]

Although ordinal comparisons from a single *Consumer Reports* study do not contain sufficient information to scale the strength of one manufacturer's dominance over another, such information is contained in the aggregate-level data from all studies. For example, if manufacturers *i* and *j* produce products nearly equal in quality, then each should rank above the other about 50 percent of the time. Furthermore, at the aggregate level, errors from individual studies tend to cancel out.

There are several versions of the LCJ and for our research the condition *C* (equal error variance) case was estimated. (A detailed explanation of the issues involved in choosing this version is given in the technical report.)

Results

Major Appliances

Table 16–1 shows the quality values for the five broad-line manufacturers and data on observed and reproduced proportions regarding quality dominance. These proportions serve as a basis for testing the fit of the quality scales. In all cases the raw scale values were linearly transformed to range between 0 and 100 for ease of interpretation.[3] The LCJ results in an interval scale so that this sort of transformation does not change the inherent relationships between the quality values for the various firms. However, the zero point on the scale is arbitrary and should not be interpreted as an absence of quality nor should 100 be interpreted as perfect quality. The scale does, however, carry information about differences between quality values and about ratios of these differences.

Table 16-1
Quality Scales for Major Appliances: Broad-line Analysis

Quality Value[a]	Manufacturer	Quality Dominance[a,b,c]			
		GE	WCI	Raytheon	Magic Chef
100	Whirlpool	.41/.42	.33/.38	.33/.34	.31/.24
71	General Electric		.47/.54	.40/.42	.25/.31
55	WCI			.50/.46	.33/.35
41	Raytheon				.39/.39
0	Magic Chef				

[a]Entries are *OBS./PRED.* proportion of times the column manufacturer's quality exceeded the row manufacturer's.

[b]The frequency of direct competition varied between pairs of manufacturers from a low of 38 (Magic Chef versus Raytheon) to a high of 66 (GE versus White Consolidated). The mean frequency was 51.

[c]A weighted version of Mosteller's (1951c) chi-square test for the quality scale resulted in an observed $\chi^2 = 4.61$ $(df = 6)$ which would not reject the model even at $\alpha = .40$.

According to data for the broad-line manufacturers, Whirlpool ranks first by a substantial margin over GE and the other competitors. The largest difference among adjacent competitors is between Raytheon and Magic Chef; this suggests that Magic Chef has fared particularly poorly in direct competition. The observed proportions in the quality-dominance matrix verify the scale's implications. For example, Whirlpool products were judged superior to GE products in 59 percent of the studies. Whirlpool products dominated White Consolidated products in 67 percent of the studies, Raytheon products in 67 percent, and Magic Chef products in 69 percent. A review of all triples in this proportions matrix reveals no violations of weak or moderate stochastic transitivity.[4] Mosteler's test for lack of fit cannot reject the model for alpha levels as high as .40 $(\chi^2 = 4.61, df = 6, p < .40)$. Therefore, all indications are that the quality data from the seventy-two studies are quite succinctly represented by the quality scales shown in table 16-1.

The scale values for all fifteen manufacturers are shown in table 16-2, along with the conglomerate each company belongs to, if any. The fit of the model to these data was not as good as for broad-line manufacturers. However, the fit was judged to be adequate when missing data in the observed proportions matrix is considered.

These results indicate that the quality of products from two subsidiaries of the same broad-line manufacturer is often quite varied. For example, Raytheon owns the Amana Corporation, which is second for individual companies, and McGraw-Edison, which is near the bottom. White Consolidated also suffers in the broad-line analysis due to highly

Table 16–2
Quality Scales for Major Appliances: Individual Manufacturers

Manufacturer	Corporate Owner	Quality[a]
Maytag	—	100
Amana	Raytheon	75
Frigidaire	WCI	70
Whirlpool	—	68
General Electric	—	58
Gibson	WCI	54
Westinghouse	WCI	46
Norge	Magic Chef	31
Tappan	AB Electrolux	27
Kelvinator	WCI	24
White	WCI	20
Magic Chef	—	7
McGraw–Edison	Raytheon	7
Admiral	Magic Chef	2
Philco–Ford	WCI	0

[a]Entries are *OBS./PRED.* proportion of times the column manufacturer's quality exceeded the row manufacturer's.

varied quality from its subsidiaries. It appears that both Whirlpool and General Electric have an advantage because they refrained from merging while White Consolidated, Raytheon, and Magic Chef were heavily involved in corporate acquisitions. In essence, neither Whirlpool nor GE "contaminated" the quality of its products by merging with other stand-alone manufacturers.

Consumer Value, Market Shares, and Buying Intentions

To aid an interpretation of quality scaling, we attempted to find additional published information about consumer perceptions and sales of major appliances. We also used the price information available for these products from *Consumer Reports* to create a rough index of value (a quality and price contrast) for each manufacturer. For consumer perceptions, we used a study commissioned by *Appliance Manufacturer* published in 1980. In this research, National Family Opinion Inc. (NFO) drew a representative sample of 2,000 households from their file of 100,000. NFO inquired about patterns of current ownership and asked each respondent which brand they considered the best quality (ignoring price) in seven major-appliance categories. They also asked which brand the respondent would buy today considering quality, price, and all other relevant factors. To supplement this we found current (September 1981) market-share information, which is contained in table 16–3.

Table 16-3
Market Shares, Consumer Perceptions, and Buying Intentions for Major Appliances

Product Category	Market-Share Leader 1981[a] (percentages)		Consumer Survey Results[b]	
			Best Quality	Would Buy Today
Compactors	Whirlpool	45	—	—
Dishwashers	Design & Mnf.	45	Kitchen Aid	Kitchen Aid
Disposers	GE & Mnf.	35	—	—
Dryers (gas and electric)	Whirlpool	40	Maytag	Sears Kenmore[c]
Freezers	Whirlpool	30	Amana/GE	Sears Kenmore
Washers	Whirlpool	40	Maytag	Sears Kenmore
Electric ranges	GE	35	GE	GE
Gas ranges	Magic Chef	20	Tappan	Sears Kenmore
Refrigerators	Whirlpool	31	GE	Sears Kenmore

[a]*Appliance* (September 1981), p. 42.
[b]*Appliance Manufacturer* (April 1980), p. 83.
[c]Whirlpool is a major supplier for Sears Kenmore for dryers, freezers, washers, and refrigerators.

For table 16-3 the price data from *Consumer Reports* for the same period covered by the quality data were compressed into a price scale by treating the data as both ordinal and as ratio scaled. These two scales correlated exceedingly high for the broad-line manufacturers ($r = .99$; $p < .01$) and for all fifteen major-appliance manufacturers ($r = .98$; $p < .01$). The two methods converged to the same scale for price to reassure the scales' summary of price positions. The price values were subsequently transformed to a 0-to-100 range, as with quality. On this scale, lower values represent lower average prices and higher values represent prices consistently above average.

When the quality and price scales are used together, a rough indication of value is the difference $q_m - p_m$ for each manufacturer.[5] For the broad-line manufacturers the value indices calculated in this manner are as follows: for Whirlpool, the index is 85; for General Electric, 67; for White Consolidated, 21; for Magic Chef, 0; and for Raytheon, -59. The most important feature of this index is that Whirlpool and GE provide major appliances with above-average quality at reasonable prices and, hence, offer consumers considerably more value than the other manufacturers. At the other extreme, Raytheon, though offering reasonable and even high quality in some cases (particularly from Amana), charges high prices resulting in much lower value. Raytheon's prices were 1.2 standard deviations above the other four broad-line manufacturers when averaged over all major-appliance categories.

With respect to quality alone, the consumer survey shows several cases that corroborate our scaling results. Maytag was judged best in quality in two lines—washers and dryers—and Amana was judged first in freezers. Table 16–2 shows Maytag and Amana ranked one and two in quality over the twenty-year period. GE is positioned fifth using the *Consumer Reports* data, aggregating all product lines, while consumers judged it best specifically for electric ranges and refrigerators. The survey and our quality-scaling results are mutually supportive even though the consumer survey measures attitudes at one point in time and separates the product lines. The only surprise might be the failure of Whirlpool to be judged best by consumers in any lines.

When our attention is turned to consumer behavior as documented by sales (market share) and the "would buy today" results from the survey, the picture changes. For example, even though consumers judge Maytag best in washers, their buying sentiments lean toward Sears Kenmore because of the price difference and other possible considerations. To quote the staff writers of *Appliance Manufacturer:* "[These results] may suggest that consumers understand the extra cost attached to 'high quality' brands; they become more practical at purchase time" (*Appliance Manufacturer*, April 1980, p. 82). Porter made a similar statement about the strategic pitfalls firms often encounter when they near maturity:[6]

> High quality can be a crucial company strength, but quality differentials have a tendency to erode as an industry matures. Even if they remain, more knowledgeable buyers may be willing to trade quality for lower prices in a mature business where they have purchased the product before [1980, p. 249].

The most telling indicator of consumers' willingness to trade some quality for a lower price is the market-share data in which Whirlpool leads in five categories and GE in two. These results represent a near clean sweep for the two companies with the highest value indices from our study. The consumer-survey data corroborates the share data as well because Whirlpool manufactures for Sears Kenmore in every category where Whirlpool leads.

To summarize, the quality scale constructed using the LCJ fits the data for the broad-line manufacturers extremely well and fits adequately for the fifteen individual firms. Even though the recent consumer survey asked consumers to judge quality on a line-by-line basis, the results tended to agree with ours. Finally, we took price levels into consideration to gauge the relative value of the offering from each broad-line manufacturer. Both market-share and consumer-intention data seemed to agree very closely with the value positions reported for Whirlpool and GE.

Housewares

The quality-scale values for the five broad-line manufacturers in the housewares category are shown in table 16–4, for the thirteen individual firms in this product category, in table 16–5. Sunbeam clearly ranks first in quality among the broad-line manufacturers, followed by GE, Hoover, Westinghouse, and Dominion. The relative positions suggest that Sunbeam and GE offer superior-quality appliances, while those offered by Hoover, Westinghouse, and Dominion are poorer in quality. The largest gap—thirty-eight points—among adjacent competitors is between GE and Hoover.

The observed and predicted proportions of the quality-dominance matrix indicate that the model accurately represents the data (x^2 = 9.44; df = 6; p < .15), because the model cannot be rejected at normal levels of significance.

Table 16–5 presents the quality scale for the thirteen individual firms but does not represent the data as well as the scale developed for the broad-line manufacturers: the goodness-of-fit test was high enough to reject the model at an α = .01. The test, however, is very conservative because of its treatment of missing data and the method it uses to transform proportions (an arcsin transformation). In the present case, the nine cells that contained missing values contributed forty-two points to the observed x^2 of 90.8 (df = 66).

The results of the analysis indicate that Sunbeam's appliances rank at the top in quality, followed by Oster, GE, and so on through Regal–Ware and Knapp–Monarch. The thirty-six-point gap between Sunbeam and its subsidiary Oster is considerably larger than the difference between any other adjacent firms on the scale. This further supports the contention that affiliated firms do not always maintain similar quality standards.

The price-position and standard-price scales for the broad-line manufacturers correspond very well (r = .91; p < .03). However, the product

Table 16–4
Quality Scales for Kitchen Appliances: Broad-line Analysis

| Quality Value | Manufacturer | Quality Dominance | | | |
		GE	Hoover	Westinghouse	Dominion
100	Sunbeam	.41/.37	.07/.21	.15/.16	.25/.10
73	General Electric		.21/.32	.28/.26	.29/.19
35	Hoover			.33/.43	.13/.33
21	Westinghouse				.31/.39
0	Dominion				

Table 16–5
Quality Scales for Kitchen Appliances: Individual Manufacturers

Manufacturer	Corporate Owner	Quality
Sunbeam	Allegany	100
Oster	Sunbeam	64
General Electric	—	59
Proctor–Silex	—	52
Hoover	—	43
Corning	—	40
Waring	—	39
West Bend	—	32
Westinghouse	—	26
Iona	—	22
Dominion	—	16
Regal–Ware	—	8
Knapp–Monarch	—	0

moment correlation between the two price scales for the thirteen individual manufacturers was $r = .74$ and $p < .004$. This discrepancy could be attributed to the fact that several firms compete in only a few product lines. Corning competes in only two categories whereas Sunbeam competes in all except broilers. Overall, the two price scales converge reasonably well to the price positions for firms competing in this product category.

Market-Share Information

Unfortunately there are no related studies to interpret or corroborate the quality scales; therefore, we were restricted to using only market-share data.

A check of the available market-share information (see table 16–6) indicates that Sunbeam is the market leader in blenders and mixers and is second in electric frying pans. General Electric is the market leader in steam-irons (55 percent) and is second in mixers, electric can openers, and electric knives. Dominion leads in electric slicing knives and is third in blenders and mixers, while West Bend leads in electric frying pans. Both Dominion and West Bend, however, have low quality. This suggests that despite quality differentials, more knowledgeable buyers may be willing to trade quality for considerably lower prices in a mature industry in which they have purchased products before (Porter 1980). Overall, the market-share results are consistent with the suggestion that consumers recognize differences in value.

To summarize the results for kitchen appliances, the quality scale fits the data extremely well for the five broad-line manufacturers and adequately for the thirteen individual firms. The kitchen-appliance manufacturers, unfortunately, have not published any related studies to corroborate the quality scale; therefore, we used only the available market-share information to determine whether consumers respond to differences in product quality. The information suggests that they do.

Discussion and Strategic Implications

Our research is part of a more extensive effort to integrate product quality into the strategic planning process. To do this, it is important to fit the present methodology into the philosophy and paradigms being published in competitive strategy and marketing planning literature. Our discussion, therefore, centers around the role of quality in planning and the advantages we feel our method offers. Our method is not designed to replace others but may be a useful complement in many situations where a broad perspective is needed.

Many strengths and weaknesses of this method revolve around data that cuts across several product lines and is collected over long periods. The problem is that such data provides little opportunity to study single lines in depth and may be misleading in cases where quality levels change rapidly over time. The conventional microview of single-brand or single-line analysis is seemingly impossible with this methodology.

Two aspects of this conclusion require further analysis. The method's inability to deal with single-line problems and short time periods is not a flaw of the modeling procedure per se, but a function of the

Table 16–6
Market-Share Information (1981 Data)

Product	GE	Sunbeam	Waring	Dominion	Proctor–Silex	West Bend
Blenders[a]	—	1	2	3	—	—
Mixers[a]	2	1	4	3	—	—
Electric frying pans[a]	3	2	—	—	—	1
Electric can openers[a]	2	3	5	6	—	—
Electric slicing knives[a]	2	3	—	1	—	—
Steam irons[b]	55	15	—	—	20	—
Toasters[b]	17	6	—	—	56	—

Source: *Appliance Manufacturers Magazine* (January 1982), p. 87, and other issues.
[a]Manufacturers' order of rank in market share.
[b]Manufacturers' percentage of market share.

lack of sufficient ordinal data (at least from *Consumer Reports*) about quality for single lines. This problem has several solutions. However, a number of recent articles about marketing strategy have criticized studies for giving undue attention to a single brand and/or single line. Wind and Robertson express these sentiments:

> Research by marketing scholars is seldom conducted at the product category, strategic business unit (SBU) or corporate level. A review of pricing research by Rao (1982), for example, indicates that it is conducted almost exclusively at the brand level. As we move from brand strategy to product category, SBU and corporate level strategies, the marketing literature has less and less to contribute. The role of "corporate marketing" is particularly unclear and many diversified firms focus their marketing activities at the operating division (SBU) level, with only a limited corporate marketing function. This focus reflects the weakness of the marketing literature in dealing with corporate level issues—whether new business decisions, mergers and acquisitions, the allocation of resources among various businesses, or harvesting existing businesses [1983, p. 13].

A strength of our method, based on the comments of Wind and Robertson, is its ability to aggregate comparative quality data from several related product lines. Other issues concerning quality (and price) measurement are that a method should not mix disparate sizes or models or differing time horizons (Farris and Reibstein 1979). Our method avoids these problems because *Consumer Reports* normally defines each product category very narrowly: Upright and cabinet freezers are judged separately, side-by-side and top-bottom refrigerators are separated, and so forth. Furthermore, even though the *Consumer Reports* studies, on which a quality scale is based, are conducted at different times, comparisons are made at one fixed point in time for any given study. Comparable products from competing firms are pitted against one another in an ordinal comparison. These individual data points are then pooled consistently to create the final scale. Each individual data point is time dependent, and model or product-type specific.

We do not view our methodology as a replacement for consumer surveys or management assessment techniques. These three approaches normally address different aspects of the issue of quality and adopt different time horizons. For many product groups, including major appliances and housewares, *Consumer Reports* is the primary source of information about product-quality ranking, ahead of *Good Housekeeping*, friends and relatives, salespeople, and endorsements (see *Appliance Manufacturer*, April 1980). Therefore, where a spot consumer survey might indirectly reveal *Consumer Reports*'s results, our method provide:

a direct summary of these assessments. Of course, many consumers do not subscribe to *Consumer Reports* or fail to refer to it for certain product classes. In situations where short-term rather than long-term considerations influence quality judgments, our method would not be as responsive as consumer surveys.

The strengths and weaknesses of our method, consumer surveys, and management assessment techniques must, therefore, be judged relative to specific corporate objectives and marketing environments. For product groups in which there is considerable stability in manufacturing methods, such as major appliances, one can make a fairly strong case that quality is a stable attribute of a product portfolio over time from a single manufacturer. Because of the long interpurchase times of major appliances, consumers have little experience with competing brands and are expected to develop attitudes based on published sources, family tradition, and experience across product lines (see Day and Deutscher 1982). Similar arguments apply, perhaps not quite as well, to products in the housewares group because most people buy relatively few toasters or blenders in their lifetimes.

Under stable conditions and when management is interested in adopting a portfolio view, our methodology offers distinct advantages over consumer surveys. The method is less expensive because *Consumer Reports* absorbs the basic testing costs. In industries where substantial data is not available from *Consumer Reports*, it may be possible to use data from other testing agencies. There are seventeen major consumer-product testing organizations throughout the world. Some of these publish data about quality in even more precise terms than *Consumer Reports*. Stiftung Warentest in West Germany publishes attribute-by-attribute judgments for each brand using a five-point scale, and explicitly lists the weights with which these scales are combined into an overall quality rating. By searching these other sources of "objective" quality ratings, the number of observations for many brands can be increased.

Regarding the role of quality in strategic planning, Phillips, Chang, and Buzzell state, "In view of the potential importance of product quality, it is surprising so little attention has been paid to it by marketing scholars. Marketing management texts generally ignore the topic and only a handful of empirical studies exist" (1983, p. 42). In our search of marketing literature we found strategic paradigms that incorporate quality considerations in one way or another, but most lack any strong suggestions about how quality competition should be measured.

With regard to the importance of product quality, Schmalensee argues that a pioneering brand with acceptable quality has a considerable edge over subsequent entrants. He contends that this is "a product differentiation advantage of early entry that has nothing to do with advertising or consumer irrationality" (Schmalensee 1982). Rather the advantage is a function of the pioneer having acceptable quality and consumers having time to find out about this quality through (longer) experience with the brand. When the first brand performs satisfactorily it "becomes the standard against which subsequent entrants are rationally judged. It thus becomes harder for later entrants to persuade consumers to invest in learning about their qualities than it was for the first brand" (Schmalensee 1982).

Schmalensee's finding that the advantage to later entrants is an increasing function of consumer risk and interpurchase times, is of particular relevance to the appliance industry. This suggests that the conditions of high price and infrequent purchases increase the height of the entry barrier to subsequent competitors.

Our study offers empirical evidence that corroborates Schmalensee's theoretical findings. For example, GE was the pioneer in the categories of electric ranges and disposers, where it leads in market share; while Whirlpool, the pioneer in compactors, leads in that share. Schmalensee's theory helps explain the premium prices charged by Maytag and Amana in washers and freezers, respectively, lines in which they pioneered. In housewares, pioneering firms such as Sunbeam (mixers and blenders), GE (steam irons), and Proctor–Silex (toasters) maintain a dominant marketing position. However, pioneers such as Regal–Ware (electric frying pans) and Dominion (electric can openers) have not been able to maintain a market leadership. Overall the results from both product categories are generally consistent with Schmalensee's theoretical findings.

The following strategic paradigms incorporate quality in one way or another, although operational procedures for measuring quality are not mentioned. Kotler (1980) emphasizes quality considerations in his fortification strategy where a market leader offers above-average quality at reasonable prices (cf. Whirlpool and GE in major appliances and GE and Westbend in housewares). Kotler also emphasizes a role for product quality in three of the nine strategies he suggests for a challenger. A prestige-goods strategy involves a challenger launching a higher-quality product than the market leader and charging a higher price. This strategy has been followed recently by Maytag with its high-quality Jenn Air ranges. In rebuttal, Amana challenged Maytag in the clothes washer category by acquiring Speed Queen and retooling the manufacturing equipment to ensure higher quality. A prestige-goods strategy has been followed by Sunbeam in houseware lines including blenders and mixers.

Reddy provides an overview of the specific steps needed to integrate quality considerations into a firm's ongoing competitive strategy. He documents the importance of these steps by reviewing four cases where improved quality provided significant long-term returns to the companies involved. However, Reddy indicates:

Based upon my experience, a decision to feature quality may take several years to implement at the production level, several more years for the buyer to become aware of the difference, and from five to ten years in all before the full benefits of the strategy can be realized. We are, in brief, discussing strategies that will effect and shape the company's operations for a decade or more and necessarily require long-term belief and commitment [1980, p. 55].

Directions for Future Research

For future projects, we are considering changes in modeling product quality using these data and exploring additional substantive research areas.

Methodological Changes

Because the LCJ may be used in a number of cases, we hope to make contributions to the theory and methods of pair comparisons. For example, in the two cases presented in this chapter, all observations were treated as having equal weight; old observations and new ones had equal impact on an overall quality scale. This approach is reasonable in fairly mature industries like major appliances and housewares but may be quite misleading for volatile industries in their growth stages. Therefore, several schemes for weighting individual observations are under consideration:

1. weight more-recent observations more heavily;
2. weight observations from different product lines proportionally to sales in those lines; and
3. weight observations from different pairs of manufacturers proportionally to the frequency of times those manufacturers met.[7]

The development of these schema is problematic and ultimately we will be interested in whether the scaling results are sensitive to changes in weights. Because of the possibility of several weighting factors and many weighting schemes for a single factor, we believe that a dedicated research effort involving sound theory with accompanying simulation studies will be necessary prior to accepting any one scheme for routine application.

A second methodological issue under consideration is using other scaling models besides the Law of Comparative Judgment for data available from consumer testing agencies. The LCJ is a unidimensional PROBIT model. Other models that would be applicable are the unidimensional LOGIT and ORDERED LOGIT models, which differ from ours in the way they use ordinal quality data and in their respective parametric assumptions. LOGIT modeling uses only the "first choice" from each *Consumer Reports* study: the brand(s) rated best in quality in a study. ORDERED LOGIT uses all of the place data from a study, as does the LCJ. Both types of LOGIT models assume that error is distributed accordng to a Type I extreme-value distribution rather than the normal density assumed by the LCJ. An interesting methodological issue is whether the application of slightly different models would substantially change the quality position results for a particular broad-line group. We believe any differences in results would be minor, and we are more interested in supplementing the present methodology with quite different modeling techniques and data to answer more-pressing questions in the field of corporate marketing strategy.

Substantive Issues

A search through the data base suggests that sufficient observations exist for a number of other industries where our approach could be applied. For example, strategic groups exist in consumer electronics (televisions, radios, stereos, and so forth), cameras and accessories (film, lenses, and projectors), and household tools (drills, saws, routers, and the like). A natural follow-up to the study in this chapter is to model quality and price competition in those industries.

A pragmatic and more exciting direction for future research is to begin to investigate questions relating to national and international corporate marketing strategy. To do this we must explore the connections between product quality and other strategic marketing variables and the levels of key performance measures that we are accumulating on a firm-by-firm basis. These performance measures include sales, profit, and ROI figures for the various companies on the data base. The other marketing-strategy variables include price and advertising expenditures by product line and a firm's total research and development costs. Eventually, causal modeling approaches patterned after the work with PIMS by Phillips, Chang, and Buzzell (1983) might be applied to the data we collect.

With regard to international marketing strategy, the data base will allow quality comparisons between products manufactured by firms from different countries and a description of the influx of foreign competition in each product category. With sales and profit data, the effects on performance of this influx can be ascertained.

The role of product quality from foreign manufacturers as it affects domestic competition and consumer behavior is not well understood.

During the last twenty years, many U.S. firms have had to shift to a defensive posture on their "home turf" in products such as appliances, electronics, and automobiles. This shift, though driven by several factors, has been tied fundamentally to a concern for product quality. Whether high quality is a result of improved manufacturing processes, enlightened management, or improved labor attitudes is only of secondary concern to most consumers because nationalistic motives have been replaced by the need for function and value.

On the data base, we are coding the parent company of each manufacturer and that company's national affiliation in order to improve our understanding of the role of quality in international competition. We hope to supplement the evaluations of Consumer's Union with data from consumer testing agencies in several other nations in order to trace the effects of these ratings within each country as well as throughout the trade network in which these countries participate. For example, do West Germans use published quality information more than the Japanese, French, or Australians before purchase decisions are made? Which nationalities are more likely to use published sources of quality information and how important is this information in relation to other sources? As Wind and Robertson have stated:

> The marketing literature is almost exclusively domestic and most marketing texts simply add on an international marketing chapter. The sheer size and growth rate of the U.S. market may have encouraged such ethnocentrism, but conditions have changed. Given unfavorable balance of payments, higher market growth rates in a number of other regions, equivalent standards of living in much of Western Europe and Japan, greater foreign competition in the domestic market, and the increased importance of multinational operations for most international firms, we can no longer ignore the multinational dimensions of marketing thought and research [1983, p. 15].

Notes

1. In constructing the data base, we acknowledge the assistance of the following individuals: Peter Riesz (technical assistance); Debra Castle, Barb Wilfred, and David Born (data entry); Sue Helfers and Kim Van Eck (data entry and SAS programming); and Chris Jantz (SAS programming). We also acknowledge the continuing financial support of the Department of Marketing, the College of Business Administration, The University of Iowa.

2. The technical report available from us discusses these and other issues regarding the use of *Consumer Reports* data.

3. Conclusions from interval scales are invariant with respect to positive, linear, transformations, that is, new scale = α (old scale) + β for > 0. The transformation applied in the present case is the following:

$$q_j^* = [q_j - MIN(q_j)] + MAX\,[q_i - MIN(q_j)]$$

where:
q_j^* ≡ the transformed quality score for manufacturer j;
q_j ≡ the original (untransformed) quality score for manufacturer j; and
MIN, MAX = are the minimum and maximum values of the argument in parentheses in each case.

4. The three versions of stochastic transitivity are defined in the technical note available from us, and further information is provided concerning violations.

5. Several different approaches to creating a value index are feasible, including the "number of quality units per dollar" (Q/P) and the difference between quality and price (Q – P). In the present case, the order of value is not sensitive to differences in these two approaches.

6. Both the major-appliance and housewares industries are mature. For example, Qualls, Olshavsky, and Michaels (1981) stated that the various major-appliance lines averaged more than eight years in the introductory stage of their product life cycles and more than twenty-four years in the growth stage(s). The market for products in the eight traditional lines of major appliances is primarily a replacement market. Similar statements can be made for many of the houseware lines, although some of these are still in the growth stage.

7. The x^2 test used in the research reported in this chapter does weight by this factor.

References

Appliance Manufacturer (1980), April.

Box, George E.P., William G. Hunter, and J. Stuart Hunter (1978), *Statistics for Experimentors*, New York: John Wiley and Sons, Inc.

Clevenger, Theodore, Gilbert A. Lazier, and Margaret Clark (1965), "Measurement of Corporate Images by Semantic Differential," *Journal of Marketing Research* 2:80–82.

Crosby, Philip B. (1979), *Quality Is Free*, New York and Scarborough, Ont.: Mentor Books.

Currim, I.S. (1982), "Predictive Testing of Consumer Choice Models not Subject to Independence of Irrelevent Alternatives," *Journal of Marketing Research* 19:208–22.

Curry, David J. (1985), "Measuring Price and Quality Competition among Conglomerates: Methodology and an Application to the Major Appliance Industry," forthcoming *Journal of Marketing*.

Day, George S. and Terry Deutscher (1982), "Attitudinal Predictions of Choices of Major Appliance Brands," *Journal of Marketing Research* 19 (May):192–98.

Doyle, Peter and Ian Fenwick (1974–75), "How Store Image Affects Shopping Habits in Grocery Chains," *Journal of Retailing* 50 (Winter):39–52.

Farris, Paul W. and David J. Reibstein (1979), "Low Prices, Ad Expenditures and Profits Are Linked," *Harvard Business Review* (November–December): 173–84.

Faulds, David J. (1983), "Measuring Price and Quality Competition in the Kitchen Applicance Product Category: Preliminary Results," working paper, University of Iowa (May).

Friedman, Peter Monroe (1967), "Quality and Price Considerations in Rational Consumer Decision Making," *The Journal of Consumer Affairs* 1 (Summer): 13–23.

Gale, Bradley T. (1983), "Study Product Quality–Profit Relationship So Firms Can Leapfrog over Foreign Competitors," *Marketing News (*21 January), 4–5.

Green, Paul E. and Yoram Wind (1975), "New Way to Measure Consumer Judgments," *Harvard Business Review* 53 (July–August):107–117.

Gulliksen, Harold (1956), "A Least-Squares Solution for Paired Comparisons with Incomplete Data," *Psychometrika* 21 (June):125–34.

Guttman, Louis (1946), "An Approach for Quantifying Paired Comparisons and Rank Order," *Annals of Mathematical Statistics* 17 (June):144–63.

Hagerty, Michael R. (1978), "Model Testing Techniques and Price–Quality Tradeoffs," *Journal of Consumer Research* 5 (December):194–205.

Hall, William K. (1980), "Survival Strategies in a Hostile Environment," *Harvard Business Review* 58 (September–October):75–85.

Hawkins, Del. I., Roger J. Best, and Kenneth Coney (1983), *Consumer Behavior*, Plano, Tex.: Business Publications, Inc.

John, George and Torger Reve (1982), "The Reliability and Validity of Key Informant Data from Dyadic Relationships in Marketing Channels," *Journal of Marketing Research* 19 (November):517–24.

Juran, Joseph M., ed., (1974), *Quality Control Handbook*, 3rd ed. New York: McGraw-Hill.

Kiechel, Walter (1981), "Three (or Four, or More) Ways to Win," *Fortune* (19 October), 181, 184, 188.

Kotler, Philip (1980), *Marketing Management: Analysis, Planning and Control*, 4th ed., Englewood Cliffs, N.J.: Prentice-Hall, chap. 11.

Leonard, Frank S. and W. Earl Sasser (1982), "The Incline of Quality," *Harvard Business Review* (September–October):163–71.

Levin, Irwin P. and Richard D. Johnson (1983), "Estimating Price–Quality Tradeoffs Using Comparative Judgments," working paper (June), Department of Psychology, University of Iowa, Iowa City.

Maynes, E. Scott (1976), "The Concept and Measurement of Product Quality," in Nestor E. Terleckyj, ed., *Household Production and Consumption*, New York: National Bureau of Economic Research.

Morris, Ruby T. (1971), *Consumer's Union: Methods Implications, Weaknesses and Strengths*, New London, Conn.: Litfield Publications.

Mosteller, Frederick (1951c), "Remarks on the Method of Paired Comparisons: III. A Test of Significance for Paired Comparisons When Equal Standard

Deviations and Equal Correlations Are Assumed," *Psychometrika* 16 (June): 207–18.

Newman, Joseph W. and Richard A. Werbel (1973), "Multivariate Analysis of Brand Loyalty for Major Household Appliances," *Journal of Marketing Research* 10 (November):404–9.

Olshavsky, Richard W. and John A. Miller (1972), "Consumer Expectations, Product Performance and Perceived Product Quality," *Journal of Marketing Research* 9 (February):19–21.

Park, C. Whan and Frederick W. Winter (1979), "Product Quality Judgment: Information Processing Approach," *Journal of the Market Research Society* 21 (July):211–17.

Phillips, Lynn W., Dae R. Chang, and Robert D. Buzzell (1983), "Product Quality, Cost Position and Business Performance: A Test of Some Key Hypotheses," *Journal of Marketing* 47 (Spring):26–43.

Phillips, Lynn W. (1981), "Assessing Measurement Error in Key Informant Reports: A Methodological Note on Organizational Analysis in Marketing," *Journal of Marketing Research* 18 (November):395–415.

PIMS (1978), *The PIMS Data Manual*, Cambridge, Mass.: Strategic Planning Institute.

Porter, Michael E. (1980), *Competitive Strategy*, New York: The Free Press.

Qualls, William, Richard W. Olshavsky, and Ronald E. Michaels (1981), "Shortening of the PLC—An Empirical Test," *Journal of Marketing* 45 (Fall):76–80.

Reddy, Jack (1980), "Incorporating Quality in Competitive Strategies," *Sloan Management Review* 21 (Spring):53–60.

Schmalensee, Richard (1982), "Product Differentiation Advantages of Pioneering Brands," *American Economic Review* 54 (June):349–65.

Sims, J. Taylor (1979), "Measuring the Industrial Firm's Image," *Industrial Marketing Management* 8 (November):341–47.

Singson, Ricardo L. (1975), "Multidimensional Scaling Analysis of Store Image and Shopping Behavior," *Journal of Retailing* 51 (Summer):38–52 + .

Spector, A.J. (1961), "Basic Dimensions of Corporate Image," *Journal of Marketing* 23:47–51.

Thurstone, L.L. (1927), "A Law of Comparative Judgment," *Psychological Review* 34:273–86.

Torgerson, Warren (1958), *Theory and Methods of Scaling*, New York: John Wiley and Sons, Inc.

Wheatley, John J., John S.Y. Chiu, and Arich Goldman (1981), "Physical Quality, Price and Perceptions of Product Quality: Implications for Retailers," *Journal of Retailing* 57 (Summer):110–16.

Wheatley, John J. and John S.Y. Chiu (1977), "The Effects of Price, Store Image, and Product and Respondent Characteristics on Perceptions of Quality," *Journal of Marketing Research* 14 (May):181–86.

Wind, Yoram and Thomas S. Robertson (1983), "Marketing Strategy: New Directions for Theory and Research," *Journal of Marketing* 47 (Spring):12–25.

Westbrook, Robert A. and Claes Fornell (1979), "Patterns of Information Source Usage among Durable Goods Buyers," *Journal of Marketing Research* 16 (August):303–12.

Index

About the Contributors

Scott D. Alden is currently a doctoral student in marketing at the Graduate School of Business, University of Southern California. His interests include store-location analysis and retail consumer behavior, particularly store patronage and fashion adoption and consumption.

P. Greg Bonner is an assistant professor on the faculty of the Department of Marketing, Rider College. Dr. Bonner received the B.A. in economics from Boston College in 1968, the M.A. in economics from Temple University in 1974, and the Ph.D. in business administration (marketing) from Temple University in 1984. He has completed numerous empirical research projects for Campbell Soup Company, the most recent of which dealt with the relationship between a consumer's salt perception and salt behavior. In addition to food consumer behavior, his other research interests include situational theory and health-care marketing. Dr. Bonner has published in the *Association for Consumer Research Proceedings*.

John E. Calfee is special assistant to the director of the Bureau of Economics at the Federal Trade Commission. He received the B.A. from Rice University, the M.A. from The University of Chicago, and the Ph.D. in economics from The University of California, Berkeley in 1980. Mr. Calfee's research has been published in *Advances in Consumer Research, Proceedings of the American Psychological Association, University of Virginia Law Review*, and other professional publications.

Kim P. Corfman is a doctoral student in marketing at the Graduate School of Business at Columbia University, New York, New York. Ms. Corfman completed the B.A. at Princeton University in Romance languages in 1976. She earned the M.B.A. at Columbia University in 1982. Her research interests include preference and decision models. She recently presented a paper on group-choice behavior at the ORSA/TIMS fall meetings in Orlando, Florida.

David J. Curry is a professor of marketing at The University of Iowa, Iowa City. He received B.S. and M.B.A. degrees from the University of Colorado, Boulder and the Ph.D. in business administration in 1973 from the University of California, Berkeley. Dr. Curry's research has focused on measurement and methodology, consumer information processing, and marketing strategy. His articles have appeared in *Multivariate Behavioral Research, Applied Psychological Measurement, Educational and Psychological Measurement, The American Philosophical Quarterly, Decision Sciences, Organizational Behavior and Human Performance,* and the *Journal of Consumer Research* among others. He and coauthor David Faulds are currently constructing an extensive international data base for researching consumer-product quality.

William R. Darden is presently the Robert A. and Vivian Young Distinguished Professor of business administration at The University of Arkansas. He received the B.S. and M.S. in industrial management from The Georgia Institute of Technology. He received the Ph.D. in business administration from The University of North Carolina. He has published over one hundred papers and articles in journals such as *Management Science, Journal of Marketing Research, Journal of Marketing, Journal of Consumer Research, Journal of Advertising Research, Journal of Business Research,* and others.

David J. Faulds is a doctoral candidate in the Department of Marketing at The University of Iowa where he is also completing the M.S. in applied statistics. He received the B.A. from The University of Wisconsin, Green Bay and the M.B.A. from The University of Wisconsin, Oshkosh. Mr. Fauld's research has been published in the *American Marketing Association's Annual Proceedings* (1983) and in the *Retail Patronage Theory Workshop Proceedings.* His research interests are in the areas of international marketing, pricing, and strategic planning.

Gary T. Ford is associate professor and chairman of the faculty of marketing in the College of Business and Management at The University of Maryland. He received the B.B.A. from Clarkson College, and the M.B.A. and Ph.D. in marketing from State University of New York at Buffalo in 1973. The results of Dr. Ford's research have been published in the *Journal of Marketing Research, Journal of Marketing, Journal of Consumer Research, Journal of Business,* and other journals and conference proceedings.

Jonathan Gutman is an associate professor on the faculty of marketing in the Graduate School of Business, University of Southern California, where he has served as departmental chairman. He completed his education at Pomona College, receiving the B.A. in 1960, the M.S. from Purdue University in 1962, and the Ph.D. in psychology from The University of Southern California in 1967. Before joining the faculty at USC, Dr. Gutman held positions at Marplan and Hunt–Wesson Foods. His main research interest is in the development of the means-end chain model about which he has published many articles including those appearing in the *Journal of Marketing* and the *Journal of Advertising Research*. His other areas of research interest are in entertainment and retailing. His publications in these areas have appeared in journals such as the *Journal of Retailing, The Public Opinion Quarterly,* and the *Journal of Personality and Social Psychology.* His consulting experience includes conducting many advertising strategy development studies based on the means-end chain methodology.

Morris B. Holbrook is an associate professor on the faculty at the Graduate School of Business, Columbia University. Dr. Holbrook completed the B.A. at Harvard College in English in 1965. He earned the M.B.A. and the Ph.D. in business administration at Columbia University, in 1967 and 1975, respectively. He has conducted research in a number of areas related to marketing in general and consumer behavior in particular. Recently, his work has focused on the consumption experience with emphasis on its esthetic and playful components. This research has been presented at numerous conferences and has appeared in journals such as the *Journal of Consumer Research, Journal of Marketing Research, Journal of Marketing, Journal of Advertising Research, Journal of Retailing, Communication Research,* and *Empirical Studies of the Arts.*

Linda F. Jamieson is currently enrolled in the Ph.D. program at the School of Management, The University of Texas at Dallas. She earned the B.A. in Latin at The University of Vermont in 1969 and the M.S. in management in 1982 at The University of Texas at Dallas. From 1969 to 1982, Ms. Jamieson held various retailing management positions with Target, Bradlees, and Sears, Roebuck & Co.

R. Krishnan is an assistant professor on the faculty of the Department of Marketing at Brauch College–Cuny, New York, New York. Mr. Krishnan holds the B.A. in mechanical engineering. He received the M.A. in industrial engineering and operations research from The Indian Institute of Technology, Delhi, India. Later, he worked in Voltas Ltd., India for two years as an executive in the management services division. Mr. Krishnan will receive the Ph.D. in marketing in 1984 from Virginia Polytechnic Institute and State University. His publications have appeared in *Advances in Consumer Research* and *Causal Modeling Conference Proceedings* of the American Marketing Association. His research interests lie in the area of behavioral pricing. His present research is an examination into the factors that affect the price–perceived-quality relationship.

E. Scott Maynes is professor in the Department of Consumer Economics and Housing at Cornell University. Maynes was educated at Springfield College (B.S.), Wesleyan University (M.A.), and The University of Michigan (Ph.D. in economics). Before moving to Cornell, Maynes served as study director in the Survey Research Center, University of Michigan and then was a member of the economics faculty at The University of Minnesota. Maynes had foreign research assignments in New Delhi, Washington, D.C., Buenos Aires, and London. While his earlier research focused on consumer behavior and survey research methods, his recent research has dealt with the concept and measurement of product quality, informationally imperfect markets, consumer policy, and videotex and the new information technologies. His major work is *Decision Making for Consumers* (Macmillan, 1976). Maynes's research has appeared in the *Journal of the American Statistical Association, Review of Economics and Statistics, Journal of Consumer Affairs,* and *Journal of Consumer Policy.* Maynes served for nine years on the Board and Executive Committee of Consumer's Union and in 1981–1982 he was consultant to the National Consumer Council, London.

David Mazursky is currently a lecturer in the School of Business Administration at The Hebrew University in Jerusalem. He earned the Ph.D. in marketing in 1983 from New York University.

Sunil Mehrotra is manager of research and competitive analysis with the Major Appliance Business Group of the General Electric Company. He received the M.B.A. from The University of Chicago and the M.S. in engineering from Purdue University. He has published in the *Journal of Advertising Research* and has spoken at various marketing conferences.

Kent B. Monroe (D.B.A., Illinois), is professor of marketing at Virginia Polytechnic Institute and State University. He has pioneered research on the information value of price and has contributed chapters on pricing in *Modern Marketing Management* (Random House, 1980). He is also the author of *Pricing: Making Profitable Decisions* (McGraw–Hill, 1979) and editor of *Advances in Consumer Research,* vol. 8. Dr. Monroe has presented papers before various national associations and has authored articles in the *Journal of Marketing, Journal of Marketing Research, Management Science, Journal of Business Research,* and *Journal of Consumer Research.* He is a member of the editorial boards of the *Journal of Marketing Research* and the *Journal of Retailing,* is associate editor for buyer behavior for the *Journal of Business Research,* and was 1980 program chairman for the Association for Consumer Research. He has served as a consultant on pricing, market research, marketing strategy, and retail location, and has also served as a market research analyst for the Postal Rate Commission. He has testified before the Postal Rate Commission and the Federal Trade Commission. Currently, his research and writing include pricing perceptions, retail patronage behavior, and methodology for synthesizing knowledge.

Leonard A. Morgan graduated from Auburn University with the B.S.E.E. and joined General Electric on the Test Program in 1954. He had assignments in Baltimore, Cleveland, and Pittsfield before joining the Medium Transformer Department in Rome, Georgia, where he served in various engineering and marketing positions. In 1968, he was named manager of engineering, Distribution Transformer Department, Hickory, North Carolina; and in 1971, manager of engineering, Power Transformer Department, Pittsfield, Massachusetts. In 1978, he was named manager—engineering consulting, Bridgeport, Connecticut.

Richard Nelson is a group research manager at Campbell Soup Company. Mr. Nelson received the B.B.A. from The University of Wisconsin in 1965.

Richard W. Olshavsky is a professor on the faculty of the Marketing Department, Indiana University, Bloomington, Indiana. Previously, he was an assistant professor on the faculty of the Psychology Department, Georgia Institute of Technology, Atlanta, Georgia. He completed his education at Carnegie–Mellon University, where he received the B.S. in mechanical engineering in 1963, the M.S. in experimental psychology in 1965, and the Ph.D. in experimental psychology in 1967. Dr. Olshavsky's research and teaching interests lie in the area of consumer behavior with an emphasis on choice behaviors. His articles have appeared in journals such as the *Journal of Consumer Research, Journal of Marketing Research, Journal of Marketing, Decision Sciences, Journal of Experimental Psychology, Review of Economics and Statistics, Cognitive Psychology,* and *Organizational Performance and Human Behavior.*

John Palmer is a partner of Moran & Tucker Inc., a market research firm with headquarters in Greenwich, Connecticut, where he is in charge of product-development research. Mr. Palmer completed his education at Massachusetts Institute of Technology and received the M.S. from The Sloan School in 1965. He spent ten years in Europe as a marketing research consultant, and while there, was involved in the development of several advances in consumer research, most notable in connection with information-processing theory, conjoint analysis, and microbehavioral simulation. Much of this work has been published in

European professional journals. Since returning to the United States six years ago, Mr. Palmer has been involved in several major projects, with companies in different industries, on researching product quality and designing appropriate quality-improvement strategies.

Robert A. Peterson is the Sam Barshop Professor of marketing administration and the Charles Hurwitz Centennial Fellow at the Institute for Constructive Capitalism, The University of Texas at Austin. Currently he is the chairman of the Department of Marketing Administration. Dr. Peterson received the Ph.D. in business administration from The University of Minnesota in 1970. He is an active researcher, having published more than one hundred books, articles, and scholarly papers. Included among his books are *Strategic Marketing Management: Cases and Comments, Perspectives on Strategic Marketing Management* (with Roger A. Kerin), and *Marketing Research*. His articles have appeared in such journals as *Management Science, Journal of Applied Psychology, Journal of Marketing, Journal of Marketing Research*, and *Journal of Business*. He is on the editorial review boards of the *Journal of Marketing, Journal of Marketing Research, Journal of the Academy of Marketing Science, Social Science Quarterly*, and the *International Marketing Review*.

Thomas J. Reynolds is an associate professor in the School of Management at The University of Texas at Dallas. He earned the A.B. in philosophy at Notre Dame and the M.A. and Ph.D. in mathematical psychology at The University of Southern California. His publications span several academic areas and are included in such journals as *Educational and Psychological Measurement, Multivariate Behavioral Research, Psychometrika*, and the *Journal of Marketing Research*. In addition to his academic position, Dr. Reynolds currently serves as president of the Institute for Consumer Research, a research and consulting company specializing in the assessment of strategic positionings and the development of strategic options.

JoAnn Schwinghammer was associated with the Minnesota educational system for seven years. She is presently a researcher with the Center for Marketing Research and Modeling, College of Business Administration, University of Arkansas. She is also completing her dissertation in the area of human values and patronage socialization.

Raymond C. Stokes is the director of the Division of Consumer Studies in the Bureau of Foods, Food and Drug Administration, where he has been for the past eight years. Previously he was director of the Consumer

Research Institute, which was food-industry funded to study public-policy issues relating to the marketing of food. He has much experience in the food industry having been vice-president of research and development at Uncle Ben's Foods, senior vice-president at Comet Rice Mills, Inc., and director of consumer research at M&M's Candies. In 1950 he received the B.S. in electrical engineering, and in 1953 the M.S. in industrial engineering and the M.S. in psychology from Oklahoma State University. His Ph.D. in consumer psychology was granted by Purdue University in 1974. His recent publications are in the area of public policy and regulatory aspects of food marketing.

William R. Wilson is an M.B.A. student and an assistant instructor on the faculty of the Department of Marketing Administration at The University of Texas at Austin. Previously, Dr. Wilson was an associate professor on the health science faculty and a researcher at the Institute for Social Research, The University of Michigan, Ann Arbor, where in 1975 he received the Ph.D. in social psychology. His teaching and research interests lie in the area of attitude formation and the role of affect in information processing. His articles have appeared in journals such as *Personality and Social Psychology, Science,* and the *Journal of Experimental Social Psychology.*

About the Editors

Jacob Jacoby, a psychologist by training, is Merchants Council Professor of marketing and director of New York University's Institute of Retail Management. He is a past president of both the Association for Consumer Research and the Division of Consumer Psychology (Division 23) of the American Psychological Association. Among other honors, he received the American Marketing Association's 1978 Maynard Award for the article in the *Journal of Marketing* that made the most significant contribution to marketing thought during that year. Dr. Jacoby has served on the editorial boards of the *Journal of Marketing Research* and *Journal of Consumer Research* and has reviewed for numerous other journals and government agencies. He has also served as a consultant or conducted research for various clients in government (for example, the U.S. Senate, Department of Justice, Food and Drug Administration, Federal Trade Commission) and industry (for example, American Home Products Corp.; the American Association of Advertising Agencies; Bristol Myers; E.I. DuPont; Firestone Tire and Rubber; GAF; General Electric; the Grocery Manufacturers of America; McCormick & Co.; The Million Dollar Round Table; The National Football League; Pillsbury; Procter & Gamble; The Proprietary Association; and Standard Oil of California).

Jerry Olson is professor of marketing and Binder Faculty Fellow at The Pennsylvania State University. He received the M.S. and Ph.D. in psychology from Purdue University where, in his dissertation research, he tested a model of the cue-utilization processes involved in quality perception. Currently, Dr. Olson is interested in the cognitive processes involved in consumer behavior, and how cognitive structures of knowledge stored in memory are used in those processes. In addition to this work, he is pursuing active research programs in advertising effectiveness, attitude theory and belief formation, and philosophy of science. He has published a number of papers on these topics in academic journals, conference proceedings, and books. Dr. Olson has served on the editorial review boards of several journals; presently, he is an advisory editor for the *Journal of Consumer Research*. He has been active in several professional organizations, including recently serving as president of the Association of Consumer Research.